# A WAR LIKE NO OTHER

# A WAR LIKE NO OTHER

## *The Constitution in a Time of Terror*

OWEN FISS

Edited and with a Foreword by Trevor Sutton

**THE NEW PRESS**

NEW YORK
LONDON

Requests for permission to reproduce selections from this book should be mailed to:
Permissions Department, The New Press, 120 Wall Street, 31st floor, New York, NY
10005.

Published in the United States by The New Press, New York, 2015
Distributed by Perseus Distribution

LIBRARY OF CONGRESS CATALOGING-IN-PUBLICATION DATA

Fiss, Owen M., author.
    A war like no other : the constitution in a time of terror / Owen Fiss, Trevor
Sutton.
        pages    cm
    Includes bibliographical references and index.
    ISBN 978-1-62097-097-3 (hardback) —ISBN 978-1-62097-098-0
(e-book)    1.  Terrorism—Prevention—Law and legislation—United
States.    2.  United States. Constitution.    3.  Civil rights—United
States.    4.  War on Terror, 2001–2009.    I. Sutton, Trevor, editor.    II. Title.
    KF9430.F57  2015
    344.7305'32517—dc23                                            2014050102

The New Press publishes books that promote and enrich public discussion and
understanding of the issues vital to our democracy and to a more equitable world.
These books are made possible by the enthusiasm of our readers; the support of a
committed group of donors, large and small; the collaboration of our many partners
in the independent media and the not-for-profit sector; booksellers, who often
hand-sell New Press books; librarians; and above all by our authors.

www.thenewpress.com

*Composition by dix!*
*This book was set in Fournier MT*

Printed in the United States of America

10   9   8   7   6   5   4   3   2   1

To
Aharon Barak
*Always an Inspiration*

# CONTENTS

Foreword by Trevor Sutton    ix

*Part I: An Unfolding Perspective*    1

Chapter 1: In the Shadow of War    6
Chapter 2: The War on Terror and the Rule of Law    37
Chapter 3: The Perils of Minimalism    72
Chapter 4: Aberrations No More    103
Chapter 5: Law Is Everywhere    128

*Part II: The New Normal*    141

Chapter 6: Imprisonment Without Trial    146
Chapter 7: Torture and Extraordinary Rendition    172
Chapter 8: Criminalizing Political Advocacy    200
Chapter 9: Warrantless Wiretapping    225
Chapter 10: The Targeted Killing of Alleged Terrorists    262

Notes    287
Index    313

# FOREWORD

## Trevor Sutton

September 11, 2001: a day that changed everything. This has been a common mantra of government agencies and the media in assessing the effects of the terrorist attacks on the World Trade Center and the Pentagon. Some have described the attacks as changing the way the United States assesses and responds to threats to its national security. Others have gone further to suggest that the attacks changed the relationship between the United States and the world in a more general sense.

More than a decade after September 11, such views may seem overblown. The past two presidential elections—to say nothing of congressional midterm and state races—were perceived to have turned more on differences in the candidates' domestic policy agendas than matters of national security or foreign policy. Moreover, the winding down of the wars in Iraq and Afghanistan, the death of Osama bin Laden, the Obama administration's declaration of a "pivot" or "rebalance" toward Asia, and the challenge posed by an expansionist Russia all suggest a return to a more traditional national security strategy, one in which the threats posed by international terrorist organizations such as al-Qaeda—and more recently ISIS—are no longer the primary drivers of American foreign policy.

There is one area, however, where the legacy of September 11 has proven unusually enduring: the law. While the threat of terrorism may no longer dominate debate in Congress or command daily headlines as regulary as it once did, the legislative enactments and judicial decisions passed in response to the counterterrorism policies of the Bush and Obama administrations continue to cast a long shadow over many areas of the law, including constitutional jurisprudence. Freedom of speech and association; due process; habeas corpus; the Fourth Amendment warrant requirement; even the prohibitions on torture and extrajudicial killings—the law governing these constitutional principles looks vastly different in 2015 than it did in the summer of 2001.

The essays in this volume chronicle the reactions of one scholar, Professor Owen Fiss of the Yale Law School, to the counterterrorism practices of the Bush and Obama years. The volume begins in 2003—in the early days of the Iraq War, before the Supreme Court's decisions in *Hamdi v. Rumsfeld*, and before Barack Obama or John Roberts had risen to national prominence. From this point of embarkation, Fiss surveys and assesses the major legal controversies of the following decade, from Guantánamo to drones, with a particular focus on the constitutional dimensions of the disputes. Linking all the essays is Fiss's sustained concern for the offense done to the Constitution by the political branches in the name of public safety, and the refusal of the judiciary to hold those branches accountable. As Fiss observes, practices that at first seemed like temporary excesses of the Bush administration have become entrenched legal doctrines perpetuated by President Obama and enshrined in judicial opinions. How these constitutional aberrations outlasted the political climate that created them constitutes the central narrative of this volume.

In some respects, this is an unlikely book. Before 2003, Fiss, a scholar of equal protection, civil procedure, and free speech, had not published on topics relating to national security or the laws of war. That he would write ten essays relating to the fight against international terrorism over the next decade was not to be expected.

Fiss was not alone in embarking on a new project of legal analysis after September 11. The legal questions raised by the Bush administration's response to the attacks were terra incognita for nearly all legal academics and jurists. Cases that were obscure for all but law-of-war specialists—*Ex Parte Milligan, Ex Parte Quirin, In Re Yamashita, Johnson v. Eisentrager*—suddenly assumed burning importance, and questions that seemed like academic speculation—the reach of due process on the battlefield; the limits on executive detention outside the formal territory of the United States—were now being litigated in federal courts.

For Fiss, it was natural that the judiciary's duty to embody and apply public reason in the domestic context, a responsibility Fiss has argued for over the past forty years, could extend to the national security sphere. In vital respects, the legal issues raised by the War on Terror are about process—process not only in the conventional sense of rules that govern legal and administrative proceedings but also in the more profound sense of the bulwarks that stand between the individual and the awesome power of the state. Behind the major national security cases of the post–September 11 era—*Hamdi v. Rumsfeld, Hamdan v. Rumsfeld,* and *Boumediene v. Bush*—was the question of what role, if any, the judiciary should have in mediating the relationship between the Bush administration and those suspected of plotting or facilitating terrorism. Nested within this question was another inquiry, one that would continue to trouble courts into the Obama presidency: When does the judiciary's responsibility to defend fundamental rights take precedence over the executive's expertise in national security and foreign relations?

In Fiss's view, the major victories in the legal battle over the fight against terrorism were pyrrhic. The Supreme Court's decisions in *Hamdi*, *Hamdan*, and *Boumediene*, along with the Detainee Treatment Act of 2005, gave as much to the executive branch as they took away, and left many vital questions unanswered—for example, whether the use of military commissions to try detainees off the battlefield violated constitutional due process. These deficiencies have been compounded by the actions of the lower courts, which have handed the government victory after victory in suits alleging torture, warrantless surveillance, and extrajudicial killings. To an even greater degree than in the era of the Burger and Rehnquist Courts, the actions of the judiciary in the post–September 11 era have fallen short of "the law as it could be," to borrow the title of Fiss's 2003 book.

Each of the chapters in this book is preceded by a short comment in which I identify the political and historical context of the essay that is the source of the chapter. The essays in Part I are meant to be read in sequence. They reflect Fiss's evolving appraisal of the legal implications of the United States' fight against terrorism and his dismay that the figure who seemed best poised to repudiate the policies of the Bush era, Barack Obama, ultimately acted to perpetuate them.

"In the Shadow of War," the first essay of the volume, is an adaptation of a speech delivered at the University of Miami on the eve of the Iraq War. It captures the anxiety and uncertainty felt by many in the legal community during the early years of the Bush administration, when it seemed as if the judiciary might grant the government virtually limitless power to prosecute its War on Terror. But the essay also documents an unusual moment in time, when it seemed possible to imagine a vindication of fundamental rights more sweeping than that which the Supreme Court ultimately delivered.

"The War on Terror and the Rule of Law" and "The Perils of Minimalism" both take as their subject the adequacy of the Supreme Court's response to the Bush administration's counterterrorism policies. Instead of heralding these decisions as vindications of constitutional rights, as many did, Fiss assesses them with a more critical eye. He examines how these decisions fell well short of their potential by failing to address or reach a consensus over crucial constitutional questions and by putting undue focus on technical issues at the expense of constitutional rights. As "The Perils of Minimalism" in particular argues, the consequences of these modest rulings can be inadvertently momentous, as with Justice Stevens's opinion for the Court in *Hamdan*, which, by failing to condemn the use of military tribunals as running afoul of due process, implicitly endorsed them as constitutionally sound.

"Aberrations No More" reflects a turning point in Fiss's thinking and expresses a profound disappointment. The essay evaluates the ways in which President Obama has failed to live up to the promise of his campaign to make a clean break with the national security policies of his predecessor. In his refusal to prosecute those who facilitated torture during the Bush administration, his endorsement of military commissions, and his perpetuation of the practice of imprisonment without trial, Obama transformed what could have been a lamentable but isolated chapter in American history into an enduring debasement of the Constitution.

"Law Is Everywhere" completes the sequence by proffering a counterexample to those who claim that there is no satisfying way to balance fundamental rights against public safety. The essay celebrates the career of Aharon Barak, Israel's most famous legal mind and a former president of its Supreme Court.

Fiss examines several of Barak's most powerful opinions—in particular a decision affirming the legality of the targeted killing of suspected terrorists but placing limits on its use—to illustrate how basic principles of fairness and humanity can flourish in even the most dire security environments.

In Part II, Fiss deepens his inquiry by addressing specific practices and policies implemented during the war against terrorism. "Imprisonment Without Trial" discusses one of the most hotly debated issues of the post–9/11 era: prolonged detention of alleged terrorists without charging them with a crime or placing them on trial. The essay continues many of the themes explored in the first half of the book, in particular the failure of the Obama administration to firmly repudiate the practices of the Bush administration that threatened what Fiss calls "the principle of freedom."

"Torture and Extraordinary Rendition" looks at the practice of extraordinary rendition, under which individuals suspected of terrorist affiliations are kidnapped and handed over to foreign governments for torture-based interrogation. Although many believe this practice has stopped under Obama, his administration has nonetheless chosen to defend the practice in federal court, to great success. In Fiss's view, the lower courts' assent to the government's position—effected through various doctrines of abstention—represents an abdication of the essential duty of the judiciary to hold the political branches accountable to the Constitution.

"Criminalizing Political Advocacy" focuses on a single case, *Humanitarian Law Project v. Holder*, in which the justices decided by a 6–3 vote to uphold a statute criminalizing political advocacy for foreign organizations that the secretary of state had designated as supporters of terrorism. For Fiss, the decision represents a break with the strong tradition rooted in the landmark 1969 case *Brandenburg v. Ohio* that seeks to protect political advocacy. The decision illustrates the corrosive effect of the specter of terrorism on constitutional liberties, even those that are relatively remote from the day-to-day prosecution of the War on Terror.

"Warrantless Wiretapping" was published before Edward Snowden's revelations of widespread NSA surveillance, yet the essay remains relevant for those seeking to understand how the current scandal came to pass. The essay traces how Bush's and Obama's counterterrorism policies led to the enlargement of the surveillance state in a way that made the more recent NSA scandal all but inevitable. In particular, Fiss notes that two components of the 2008 amendments to the Foreign Intelligence Surveillance Act—the enabling of blanket authorizations for electronic surveillance and the elimination of the FISA judge's authority to scrutinize the factual basis for a warrant application—permitted a pattern of conduct that violated the Fourth Amendment rights of millions of people.

The final piece, "The Targeted Killing of Alleged Terrorists," is the only essay in this volume that has not been previously published in some form. It examines the judiciary's refusal to judge a controversial counterterrorism policy, one that the Obama administration has expanded far beyond anything contemplated by President Bush: the use of drones to kill alleged extremists. In Fiss's view, this policy puts in jeopardy values even greater than those vindicated in *Hamdi* and *Boumediene*: the constitutional guarantee against execution without trial. In this sense, the essay is a coda to the disappointment expressed in "Aberrations No More."

These ten essays take up disparate topics, but they share a number of key themes. The most important of these is the centrality of constitutional norms to all of Fiss's arguments. While many of the legal controversies discussed in the book involve the meaning of statutes and international conventions (particularly those that seek to regulate the conduct of the executive during wartime), for Fiss these instruments embody and are backstopped by the rights and privileges found in the Constitution itself. No statute or treaty can abrogate the constitutional principles that Fiss identifies in the essays, such as the principle of freedom or the prohibition of torture.

The essays are also emphatic in their insistence that the judiciary hold the political branches accountable to the Constitution despite the extraordinary circumstances of the war against terrorism. The framework set out by Fiss recognizes the constitutional authority of the government to conduct war, but it also accepts that the Constitution places limits on the way that war may be waged. In Fiss's view, there is one Constitution in war as well as in peace.

Further, the constitutional limits placed on the government in prosecuting the War on Terror are not necessarily those applicable to more conventional wars. Fiss recognizes that the campaign to defeat al-Qaeda and its allies is a war, but he also cautions that it is an unusual war, one that has no clear temporal or geographic limitations. Thus, the prerogatives of belligerents in a traditional war, such as the right to hold enemy combatants until the termination of hostilities or place them on trial before military commissions, must be adjusted to fit the circumstances of a war that may continue indefinitely.

The constitutional norms propounded in these essays are understood by Fiss to be binding on United States officials wherever they act and against whomever they act—even if those acts occur outside the United States and affect only noncitizens. Although these norms may have different meanings in different settings, they are applicable everywhere. This vision of the Constitution shares much with that expressed by Justice Brennan in his dissent in the 1990 case *United States v. Verdugo-Urquidez*, which is examined in several of the essays.

The essays are also unified by a rejection of the tenets of a school of jurisprudence known as "minimalism," which has become increasingly popular in legal circles. Fiss makes his case against minimalism most strongly in "The Perils of Minimalism," where he objects to the limited nature of the Supreme Court's ruling on the use of military commissions to try suspected terrorists. Yet the essence of his critique—namely, that a preoccupation with technical distinctions at the expense of fundamental values can prolong and legitimate unconstitutional practices—is of more general application. For example, it guides Fiss's opposition to the judicial response to claims of targeted killings and extraordinary rendition filed against U.S. officials.

Finally, although the legal dimensions of the War on Terror are often perceived as affecting only those accused or suspected of terrorist activities, in Fiss's view the character of American society itself is also at stake. As Fiss observes repeatedly in "Criminalizing Political Advocacy" and "Warrantless Wiretapping," an analysis of the war's effects on freedom of speech and the right to privacy, when the Constitution is degraded in the name of public safety, the rights of all those subject to the authority of the United States government are at risk.

Despite their concerned tone, the message of all these essays is fundamentally one of hope. Through the example of Aharon Barak, Fiss remains committed to the belief that a well-functioning democracy can defeat even the most dangerous of foreign threats without compromising its most cherished values. Fiss, like Barak, is steadfast in his belief that the challenges intrinsic to the fight against terrorism should never cause us to lose sight of the principles that make us great.

# A WAR LIKE NO OTHER

# PART I

# AN UNFOLDING
# PERSPECTIVE

## Prologue to Chapter 1

Trevor Sutton

The federal judiciary's response to the Bush administration's prosecution of the War on Terror was one of the most closely watched and hotly debated topics in American public life of the previous decade. Today, after extensive litigation in federal courts, including several major Supreme Court decisions concerning the president's power to conduct war and defend the nation, a consensus of sorts has developed around a few basic—albeit vague—principles: the executive cannot act with unfettered discretion in seeking to eliminate terrorist threats; some constitutional rights operate outside the territorial United States; citizens and noncitizens alike should be afforded some measure of due process in determining their legal status under the laws of war.

It is tempting to view this hard-won consensus as self-evident and inevitable—that is, to conclude in hindsight that under no circumstances was the Supreme Court going to allow the executive to do whatever it wanted in the name of national security. But when the initial essay in this book, "In the Shadow of War," first appeared in 2003, less than two years after the September 11 attacks, the major legal battles of the Bush years had barely begun, and their outcome was far from obvious. Although the nation later soured on the Bush administration's handling of the Iraq War, in 2003 political opposition to the president's policies was feckless, where it existed at all. The Senate, with a Republican majority, had authorized the Iraq War with a vote of 98–2. It had passed the USA PATRIOT Act by similar margins a year and a half earlier. The war in Afghanistan remained popular, and the president himself enjoyed approval ratings north of 70 percent in some polls.

"In the Shadow of War" reflects the anxiety and uncertainty felt by many in the legal community during the early years of the Bush administration. The essay was originally delivered at a symposium at the University of Miami, shortly after the start of the Iraq War, at a time when the federal judiciary was only beginning to grapple with the basic dilemmas posed by the administration's treatment of enemy combatants. On fundamental questions—for example, what sort of due process is required in order to classify someone as an unlawful enemy combatant? what is the legal status of Guantánamo? what is the extraterritorial reach of the writ of habeas?—judges appeared prepared to defer to the Bush administration's sweeping claims that the exigencies of war trumped the judiciary's historical responsibility to police executive action.

Yet if it was not obvious in 2003 that the pendulum would swing back toward judicial oversight of the president's wartime powers, nor was it obvious that the pendulum would stop where it did—further in the direction of civil liberties than the Fourth Circuit's decision in *Hamdi v. Rumsfeld*, discussed in the essay, but short of where many, including Owen Fiss, would have hoped. In *Hamdi* and *Boumediene v. Bush*, the Supreme Court made clear that it was not giving President Bush a "blank check," to borrow Justice O'Connor's famous phrase, but it did leave a very high balance in the executive's account. By contrast, even in the heated months leading up to the invasion of Iraq, some American jurists were prepared to give a more full-throated defense of the Bill of Rights than that offered by the *Hamdi* and *Boumediene* Courts. Of particular note, in the 2003 case *Detroit Free Press v. Ashcroft*, the Sixth Circuit rejected as unconstitutional a directive ordering the closure of all immigration proceedings deemed of "special interest" to the fight against terrorism. With unusually sweeping language, the Sixth Circuit sternly admonished the Bush administration for seeking "to uproot people's lives, outside the public eye, behind closed doors," adding, "Democracies die behind closed doors."

As bombs dropped on Baghdad, there was hope in some quarters that the Supreme Court would proceed from principles similar to those expressed in the *Detroit Free Press* decision in assessing the lawfulness of the administration's counterterrorism policies. As the remaining chapters in this book will illustrate, such optimism was not rewarded.

# Chapter 1

# IN THE SHADOW OF WAR

On March 21–22, 2003, a symposium was held in Florida on my work. The symposium was sponsored by the University of Miami and was organized by Professor Irwin Stotzky, a true friend and an organizational wizard. He decided to hold the meetings not in the law school itself but nearby at the Biltmore Hotel in Coral Gables. The Biltmore is a magnificent hotel built in the 1920s and partakes of the elegance of that era. It is a National Historic Landmark, set among grounds and courtyards lush with palm trees and crowned by a bell tower that is a replica of the famed Giralda of Seville.

The glamour of the setting added to the joyousness of the occasion. It also introduced an element of unreality to what we were doing. For two full days we were ensconced in the beauty of the Biltmore, talking about issues of great importance to me and, presumably, to the academics present—school desegregation, free speech, civil procedure, and the history of the Supreme Court. Reason reigned supreme, lightened by the camaraderie among the participants and the presence of my family. The world, however, was in a very different place. It was dark and tragic. On Wednesday, March 19, only two days before, the United States had invaded Iraq.

The war was on our minds. One of the panelists, Aharon Barak, was unable to travel to Coral Gables from Israel because of the outbreak of the war. His absence was a constant reminder of the events occurring in Iraq. Moreover, all of us carried within ourselves the tragic losses of September 11 and knew full well the significance of the ongoing War on Terror. We were also mindful of the war in Afghanistan. It had begun in October 2001, shortly after the terrorist attacks on the World Trade Center and the Pentagon, and though the Taliban had already been ousted and the Northern Alliance had assumed power, sporadic fighting continued, as did the search for the leadership of al-Qaeda.

Although everyone at the symposium was aware of these developments, they were not publicly discussed. Neither the war in Iraq nor that in Afghanistan, nor even the War on Terror, was the subject of any of the panels or formal presentations, perhaps because the issues they raised seemed far removed from my teaching or scholarship. Yet I felt the need to break this unwitting pact of silence and used—seized?—the opportunity given to me in closing remarks for that purpose. For me, the Iraq War was a gross violation of international law and put into bold relief the disregard for the law that has so marked the post–September 11 era.

International law is a fragile enterprise. Based part on custom, part on the consent given in treaties, and part on the actions and the processes of international organizations, the authoritative character of international law, as both a descriptive and a normative matter, is always in dispute. Yet the rules regarding the use of force seem clear. The Charter of the United Nations, adopted by the United States and thus binding on it as a treaty, prohibits the use of force with two exceptions, one for self-defense[1] and the other when the Security Council determines that the use of force is needed to secure world peace. The Afghanistan war may have been consistent with the Charter, but this could not be said of the war that had just begun in Iraq.

Although the Security Council adopted a resolution condemning the September 11 attacks and in general terms affirmed the right of self-defense, it did not in so many words authorize the United States to invade Afghanistan either to overthrow the Taliban or to suppress al-Qaeda.[2] The defense of the legality of the war had to be based on the right of self-defense. The United States determined that al-Qaeda was responsible for the attacks of September 11 and that the war against Afghanistan, then controlled by the Taliban, was justified because of the symbiotic relationship between the Taliban and al-Qaeda.

By permitting the use of force for self-defense, the Charter creates a measure of unilateralism. Power is vested in an individual nation-state to determine whether it has been attacked, who is responsible for the attack, and even whether the relation between a state and some terrorist organization, such as al-Qaeda, is such as to justify an armed attack against another state. Only the strong are truly able to enjoy the freedom to make these judgments and to decide whether to use armed force, instead of less violent and more targeted alternatives, in response to an aggressive attack.

Law requires impersonality in order that the applicability of norms not turn on the personal identity of the subject, but every system of law operates in a way that allows the rich and powerful greater enjoyment of protected rights than that experienced by the poor and weak. Consider, for example, the provisions of the Bill of Rights guaranteeing free speech or the assistance of counsel. We may seek to enhance the prerogatives of the poor or weak in order to minimize the difference in the experience of these rights, but such an endeavor is driven more by egalitarian concerns—everyone should enjoy the blessings of liberty—than by a belief that these reforms are required to turn the First or Sixth Amendment into law.

In the domestic sphere, independent tribunals, backed by the power of the state, have the authority to determine whether an act of violence that is justified in the name of self-defense fully respects the bounds of that right. Such an institutional arrangement is lacking in the international sphere. This distinguishes the law of the nation-state from that of the world community, but it does not mean that the United Nations Charter and international conventions are not law. In the international context, law consists of the norms and principles that a nation-state is duty bound to respect and obey, and in the case of the Charter this duty arises from the solemn consent given to it by a nation-state. Those aggrieved by an alleged violation of the Charter may not be able to turn to an independent tribunal to determine whether those norms have been fully respected; nor can they rely on some world police to enforce a judgment of such a tribunal. But they can address the world community and demand that it make a judgment for itself and, if appropriate, impose on the party violating those norms whatever sanctions lie within the community's lawful grasp. Sometimes the only sanction may be shame. The responsibility devolves on each of us, as members of the world community, to make a disinterested judgment as to whether the norms of the Charter have been honored.

Understanding law in these terms, I venture to say that a strong—and, in my view, a convincing—case could be made for the legality of the war in Afghanistan. No such case, however, could be made for the war in Iraq. The invasion of Iraq was not precipitous. It was the product of a long and sustained buildup, and in the course of that buildup various defenses were offered on behalf of the use of force. None was persuasive. On occasion, the legality of the war was defended on the basis of a series of Security Council resolutions. The first, adopted in 1990, authorized the use of force against Iraq to eject it from Kuwait.[3] The second, adopted in 1991, imposed a disarmament obligation on Iraq after it was in fact ejected from Kuwait and a cease-fire was instituted.[4] The third—Resolution 1441, adopted in the fall of 2002—declared that Iraq remained in material breach of its disarmament obligations.[5] It also gave Iraq a "final opportunity" to comply with those obligations and warned Iraq of "serious consequences" if it did not comply.

Warning of "serious consequences" is not, however, the same as authorizing the use of military force against Iraq, either by the United States or by any other nation. It also seems far-fetched to assume that the determination in Resolution 1441 that Iraq was in material breach of the disarmament obligations imposed by the second resolution revived the authorization of force contained in the first resolution, since that resolution authorized the use of force only to eject Iraq from Kuwait. Bent on war, the United States sought yet another resolution to authorize the invasion of Iraq. Once it became clear that it would not obtain this authorization, the United States proceeded without Security Council approval and invaded Iraq.

Unlike the Afghanistan war, the invasion of Iraq could not be justified as falling within the right of self-defense granted in the Charter. There were no ties between Iraq and al-Qaeda. The Bush administration claimed that Iraq possessed weapons of mass destruction and that one day they might be turned upon the United States or other nations we are duty-bound to protect. However, the evidence supporting the claim that Iraq possessed weapons of mass destruction was thin. Even after the invasion, no such weapons have been found. Even if the evidence were otherwise, the concept of self-defense would have to be broadened to include a preemptive war. At the very least, such preemptive action requires that the feared Iraqi attack, against which the United States was purportedly defending itself, be imminent in order to qualify as an act of self-defense. Because no such claim could be made in the case of Iraq, the concept of self-defense would have to be stretched still further, beyond the breaking point—to sanction a preventive, as opposed to a pre-emptive, war.[6]

The Bush administration also claimed—all the more so once no weapons of mass destruction were found—that it was intent on ending the tyranny of Saddam Hussein and thus bringing freedom and democracy to the Iraqi people. In support of this claim, reference has been made to the use of force by NATO in Kosovo in the spring of 1999, and the precedent that it set for what has been called humanitarian intervention. This use of force also lacked Security Council authorization. Because the Kosovo intervention violated the Charter and the system of law that it establishes, the status of that precedent as law remains un-certain. In any event, even if it were viewed as law, a crucial dis-tinction must be made between military intervention designed to stop large-scale ongoing carnage or a genocide in progress—as in the case of Kosovo—and the use of force intended to topple a tyrant such as Saddam Hussein. Granted, Hussein, like most ty-rants, came to power through brutal and violent means, but the death and destruction that war inevitably entails, followed by military occupation, can never be justified as a means of ending a tyranny such as Hussein's. Other less deadly and less destructive alternatives always exist. The war in Iraq may have been within the strategic or economic interests of the United States—that remains to be seen—but it signaled a contempt for the most ele-mentary precepts of international law.

At the time of our meeting in Coral Gables, the Iraq War was so fresh and so immediate that no judgment could be made as to how that war would be conducted and what strains, if any, it would place on principles of law in the domestic realm. But the record already established by the Afghanistan war and, more generally, by the War on Terror was disturbing. The USA PATRIOT Act, proposed by the administration shortly after September 11, and immediately enacted by Congress, vastly increased the surveillance powers of the government.[7] The administration also subjected many noncitizens, especially those of Middle Eastern origin, to relentless questioning. Some were arrested on the weakest of grounds and detained or deported.[8]

Most disturbing of all, the administration decided to treat prisoners of the war against al-Qaeda and Afghanistan in ways that challenge the authority—indeed, the responsibility—of the judiciary to safeguard the Constitution. These practices touch on themes central to my work and central to all the papers in the symposium, and, more significantly, threaten one of the most cherished and elementary tenets of our legal system. The administration adopted a detention policy that puts the rule of law into question, and, much to my astonishment, in a number of key cases, this policy has been endorsed by the judiciary.

Habeas corpus is the historic means by which prisoners contest the constitutionality of their imprisonment. When the prisoner is being held by the United States government, the habeas writ must be sought in a federal court. On March 11, only ten days before we convened in Coral Gables, a unanimous panel of the Court of Appeals for the District of Columbia Circuit declared in *Al Odah v. United States* that no federal court could entertain the writ on behalf of a group of prisoners from the war in Afghanistan who were held by the United States at Guantánamo Bay Naval Station.[9] The court denied them any opportunity whatsoever to contest the legality of their imprisonment by the United States.

All of these prisoners were captured by or turned over to the United States forces. Most were seized in Afghanistan, some in Pakistan. With the possible exception of one, who played no role in the court's reasoning, the prisoners all denied that they were soldiers of the Taliban or al-Qaeda, or that they committed any violent acts against the United States. They claimed that they were present in the region either for personal reasons (for example, to visit relatives or arrange a marriage) or to provide humanitarian aid. They insisted that they were improperly seized, sometimes in a sweep of a village, sometimes by bounty seekers, who then turned them over to the Northern Alliance or to the United States. The Court of Appeals assumed, as it must when considering objections to jurisdiction, that these factual claims were true. Thus, although all were aliens—the prisoners were nationals of either Australia, Britain, or Kuwait, all allies of the United States in the war in Afghanistan—the court assumed that none was a combatant or even an enemy alien (a citizen of a nation with which the United States is at war).

The Court of Appeals viewed litigation challenging the constitutional validity of detention as a privilege, and limited the exercise of the privilege by aliens to those imprisoned within the territorial limits of the United States. It also ruled that Guantánamo was not within those limits. I find it odd to view litigation of this sort as a privilege. More is at stake than the liberty of the individual seeking the habeas writ. The United States is a government constituted by law, and a habeas corpus proceeding is a way of making certain that the government is acting within the limits of the law. Habeas serves a public, not just a private, function. Accordingly, access to a court capable of granting the writ should not be viewed as a privilege belonging to some individual or class of individuals but rather as a means of enabling the judiciary to perform a solemn duty: ensuring that the government is acting within the terms of the Constitution.

The circuit court also erred when it ruled that Guantánamo was not within the territorial limits of the United States. The limits of the United States extend to the territories over which it exercises sovereignty, and surely the United States exercises practical, if not formal, sovereignty over the territory on the island of Cuba occupied by the Guantánamo Bay Naval Station. Sovereignty means supreme dominion, and that is precisely what the United States has in Guantánamo. As a purely formal matter, the United States was given possession of the territory in a 1903 lease (modified in 1934), but it is a lcase without a term.

In support of its decision, the Court of Appeals drew an analogy between aliens in Guantánamo and those held in some foreign country. It noted that habeas proceedings in a federal court could not be commenced on behalf of an alien who might be held by agents of the United States in a foreign country because the Bill of Rights affords no protection to such persons. It then concluded that the same rule should apply to aliens held at Guantánamo. Because I view the Constitution more as a constraint on the government than as a scheme that distributes benefits to certain privileged categories of persons, I question the premise upon which the analogy rests. But even accepting that premise, the Court of Appeals erred in overlooking a crucial distinction between the prisoners in Guantánamo and those held by United States agents in, for example, France or Mexico. The alien held by the United States in a foreign country may seek relief in the courts of that country and may invoke its laws or even those of the United States to contest the validity of his detention. To what courts might the prisoners in Guantánamo turn if not to those of the United States?

*Al Odah* denied aliens held in Guantánamo the right ever to make their case—that they were not soldiers but humanitarian workers or were in the region for purely personal reasons and thus were being held illegally—in the only court that might have jurisdiction to hear that claim. *Al Odah* created what an English jurist has called a "legal black hole." [10] The court's position, I suspect, was not derived from a proper regard for the notion of sovereignty but rather sprang from a fear of interfering with the executive in the conduct of the war in Afghanistan or, for that matter, any war. A similar dynamic led the Court of Appeals for the Fourth Circuit in *Hamdi v. Rumsfeld*, decided only two months before, on January 8, 2003, to shield the government from having to explain and justify its detention of another prisoner seized in the course of the war in Afghanistan.[11] This time, however, the prisoner—Yaser Esam Hamdi—was an American citizen who was held not in Guantánamo but in Norfolk, Virginia.

Hamdi was born in Baton Rouge, Louisiana, and was in his twenties at the time of his capture in Afghanistan. He was seized by the Northern Alliance and then turned over to the United States forces. He was initially held by the United States in Kandahar, then transferred to Guantánamo, and finally moved to the United States Naval Brig off the coast of Norfolk. Like the prisoners in Guantánamo, he was held incommunicado, but Hamdi's father learned of his detention and, acting on his behalf, brought a habeas proceeding to contest the legality of the detention. Hamdi had not been charged with a crime. Although the United States held him as an enemy combatant, the petition filed on his behalf denied that he had fought for the Taliban or al-Qaeda and maintained that it was a denial of due process of law to detain him. Not everyone in Afghanistan, not even every American in Afghanistan, is an enemy combatant. As the petitioners explained in *Al Odah*, some go for personal or humanitarian reasons and may be improperly seized by the United States or its allies.

According to the Bush administration, anyone who fights against the United States stands outside the protection of the Constitution. He can be held incommunicado, denied the assistance of counsel, and interrogated in ways manifestly coercive. He need never be charged with a crime. Some may question whether the United States can ever treat an American citizen or, for that matter, any human being in such a way. Before even reaching that question, however, some judgment needs to be made as to whether the person being held—citizen or not—is in fact an enemy combatant, for that is the fact upon which the right of the government to detain him hinges. Hamdi's status as a combatant—contested in the habeas petition—is akin to a jurisdictional fact, and must be decided by a federal court in its role as the ultimate guardian of the Constitution. A federal court must assume responsibility for Hamdi's status and hear facts sufficient for it to assume responsibility for that judgment.

Initially, the government refused to respond on the merits to Hamdi's petition. This was deemed unacceptable by both the District Court and the Court of Appeals.[12] On remand, the government filed a motion to dismiss the petition and attached an affidavit that addressed the question of Hamdi's status as a combatant. The affidavit was sworn to and signed by an official in the Department of Defense named Michael Mobbs, who was special advisor to the under secretary of defense for policy. Mobbs did not indicate the sources of his information. He nonetheless declared that the military determined that Hamdi had traveled to Afghanistan in July or August 2001 and that he thereafter affiliated with the Taliban and received weapons training. Mobbs also stated in his affidavit that Hamdi had been engaged in a battle with the Northern Alliance and that he was taken into custody, with an AK-47 in his possession, when his unit surrendered. The affidavit described the transfer of Hamdi from one prison to another, and concluded by saying that interviews with Hamdi confirmed the details of his capture.

A hearing was then held before District Judge Robert G. Doumar on the sufficiency of the Mobbs affidavit. In the course of that hearing, Judge Doumar expressed his view—the basis for that view is not at all clear to me—that Hamdi had a firearm at the time of his capture and that he had originally gone to Afghanistan in July or August 2001 to join the Taliban. Judge Doumar made no written findings on these issues and, even more significantly, expressed no view as to whether Hamdi had fought against the United States following the invasion in October 2001. Judge Doumar believed that the claim of the government that Hamdi had fought against the United States was still very much in dispute, and ruled that some kind of hearing on that issue was necessary. He also ruled that in preparation for that hearing, the government had to turn over copies of Hamdi's statements and notes taken from interviews, the names and location of all those who questioned Hamdi, and any statements made by members of the Northern Alliance concerning the capture of Hamdi.

The Court of Appeals would have none of this. In an opinion by Chief Judge J. Harvie Wilkinson, the court held that the Mobbs affidavit was in and of itself sufficient to establish that Hamdi was an enemy combatant and that no further inquiry was necessary. Accordingly, the Court of Appeals refused to allow Hamdi to appear in court to contest Mobbs's affidavit. It relieved Mobbs of the obligation to take the witness stand, either to repeat his sworn statement in open court or to be questioned by Hamdi's lawyer or the trial judge. It did not allow Hamdi's lawyers to engage in any discovery whatsoever or to consult with Hamdi himself. Although the Fourth Circuit in *Hamdi* went a step beyond the D.C. Circuit in *Al Odah*—it at least took jurisdiction and required a response to the habeas petition by the government—it also repudiated the most elementary understanding of the judiciary's responsibility under the Constitution.

War is a perilous undertaking for all involved, and requires swift and decisive action by those in charge of field operations. Some deference must be given to the executive in the conduct of war, including its judgment as to whom to detain in the course of battle. This deference can be reflected in the kind of hearing

that is held, the scope of discovery, and, perhaps most significantly, the standard of review that is applied to judge the government's action. The executive might be required to show only,
as the government itself proposed, that there is some evidence
for detaining the individual as an enemy combatant. However,
the Fourth Circuit specifically rejected even this lax standard
of review because it presupposes some factual inquiry as to the
prisoner's status. Without such an inquiry, it is impossible to determine whether there is any evidence to detain the prisoner.

Although affidavits are often used in civil litigation, the
Mobbs affidavit could not be regarded as supplying the kind of
evidence that might justify imprisonment. Commonly, affidavits
are used in summary judgment practice, but only to show that
there is no genuine issue of material fact, never to resolve a contested issue of fact. Moreover, the party opposing the motion
for summary judgment always has an opportunity to respond to
whatever affidavit may be filed in support of the motion. The
affidavits used in support of a motion for summary judgment
are generally confined to statements that would be admissible as
testimony at trial—hardly a standard that the Mobbs affidavit, in
part based on unknown sources and multiple levels of hearsay,
could satisfy.

Similarly, although interlocutory injunctions are often based
on affidavits, such a practice is premised on the assumption that
there is no opportunity whatsoever to hold an evidentiary hearing. In addition, interlocutory injunctions are strictly limited as
to time—as a general matter, temporary restraining orders last
for ten days, plus one renewal, and preliminary injunctions are
in force only for the pendency of the trial for permanent relief.
The Mobbs affidavit—seeking to justify the continued imprisonment of Hamdi and sworn to by an official readily available
to testify—cannot reap the benefit of these rules, even by analogy. Oddly, the government proposed that its action be judged

by the "some evidence" rule, but because it stood entirely on the Mobbs affidavit it could not have met that standard.

Admittedly, the line between a highly deferential standard of review—some evidence—and the position of the Fourth Circuit—essentially no review at all—may seem slight. There may be little difference in outcome. Yet I believe that there is a fundamental principle at stake. Under the "some evidence" standard, the executive is held accountable for its action and the judiciary discharges its basic responsibility to hold the government to the Constitution. Ideally, a court should make the determination whether Hamdi is an enemy combatant, for that is the justification the government offers for holding him and denying him the protection of the Bill of Rights. At the very least, the government's claim should be tested in an evidentiary hearing. Requiring a finding that there is some evidence that Hamdi is an enemy combatant would be a step in the right direction. In contrast, under the no-review standard of the Fourth Circuit, which makes the unexamined affidavit of a government official in and of itself sufficient to deny the habeas writ, there is no basis within the law for responding to Hamdi's grievance and for justifying his continued detention.

Chief Judge Wilkinson stressed that Hamdi was seized in "a zone of active combat in a foreign theater of conflict."[13] This fact is undisputed, but it does not justify the refusal of the court to require a meaningful inquiry into Hamdi's status. Not everyone in Afghanistan, even those with guns, fought for the Taliban or al-Qaeda against the United States. Recognizing, however, that Hamdi was captured in an active war zone does require a more precise formulation of the limits of judicial responsibility and an acknowledgment that the jurisdiction of federal courts does not extend to the battlefield. Although a person captured and held in a combat zone can contest the legality of his or her detention before a competent tribunal, in the terms of the Third

Geneva Convention, the tribunal can be a military one governed by military rules. A combat zone is ruled by a military government. Federal judges need not hold court in Afghanistan or any other battlefield.

When, however, an individual is captured in an active combat zone but later brought and held within the United States—which I contend includes Guantánamo—then the determination of his status as a combatant can and must be made by a federal court. This may seem an arbitrary distinction, turning on the happenstance of where the prisoner is detained, but I do not think it is. Rather, it reflects the theory of our Constitution. Although the Bill of Rights does not in any strong sense rule the battlefield, the actions of the United States are governed by the whole of the Constitution, including the Bill of Rights, wherever the government has effective or absolute dominion over the prison. The task of the federal judiciary is to safeguard the Constitution, and to discharge this responsibility it must make judgments about the facts and hold the hearings necessary for this purpose.

The contested issue in *Hamdi* and *Al Odah* is whether the persons detained were soldiers of the Taliban. Put another way, the immediate issue in these cases is whether the prisoners were enemy combatants or, more simply, combatants. The war in Afghanistan also brought into play a distinction between two types of combatants—lawful and unlawful. The distinction between lawful and unlawful combatants has its roots in the early twentieth century and customary international law, and was later codified in two international conventions—the Third and Fourth Geneva Conventions, both adopted in 1949.[14]

A lawful combatant is the ordinary soldier engaged in an international armed conflict, who, once captured, is given prisoner-of-war status. The Third Geneva Convention provides that a lawful combatant has no obligation to give any information to his captors other than his name, rank, date of birth, and serial number. A lawful combatant can be prosecuted for any war crimes he may commit, but not for the ordinary acts of war—for example, killing soldiers of a hostile army. Lawful combatants can expect to be repatriated at the end of the war. In contrast, the protections for unlawful combatants—for example, members of an irregular militia or volunteer corps—are significantly less extensive. The Fourth Geneva Convention provides that they be treated humanely, that their religious practices be respected, and that they not be tortured or mutilated, but they lack the strict protections of the Third Convention for lawful combatants. Even the minimal protections of the Fourth Convention are not, by the terms of the convention itself, available to prisoners who are nationals of the party holding them.

At the time of the Coral Gables symposium, it was uncertain whether the "unlawful combatant" designation would be used by the administration in the conduct of the Iraq War. After all, the war was only two days old. This uncertainty lingered, especially in the case of Saddam Hussein, captured by United States forces in November 2003. However, the administration did not declare the prisoners of the Iraq War to be unlawful combatants. A different policy was pursued in the war in Afghanistan, where the president determined that all who fought for the Taliban or al-Qaeda were unlawful combatants.[15] This decision applied to the petitioners in *Al Odah* and *Hamdi*, and, more generally, to all the prisoners—some six hundred—who have been held in Guantánamo. Many have been interrogated relentlessly, some for sixteen hours a day, and plans have been set in motion to try them before military commissions. The judges in these tribunals will be chosen by military authorities; defense counsel will be members of the armed forces (those who can afford to do so may also retain civilian counsel who have the necessary security clearance); and conversations with counsel will be monitored, presumably just for purposes of getting information about terrorism that the interrogation has not yielded or to prevent communications between the prisoner and terrorist organizations.

The legal tests of the "unlawful combatant" designation have been fragmentary. One test involved the detention of an American citizen, Jose Padilla, who is accused of planning, on behalf of al-Qaeda, to engage in terrorist acts in the United States, including the detonation of a device that would disperse radioactive material (a so-called dirty bomb). Upon arriving in Chicago from Pakistan on May 8, 2002, Padilla was arrested under a warrant requiring him to appear as a material witness before a grand jury convened in the Southern District of New York. He was transferred from Chicago to New York, and counsel was appointed to represent him. Padilla consulted with counsel soon after, and the day before his court appearance the Department of Defense took custody of him without notifying his counsel and transferred him to a naval brig in Charleston, South Carolina, where he was held incommunicado on the theory that he is an unlawful combatant.

Acting as Padilla's next friend, the counsel who had previously been appointed to represent him sought a writ of habeas corpus in the Southern District of New York. The government responded with an affidavit once again signed by Michael Mobbs. This time, Mobbs's affidavit detailed the basis of the claim concerning Padilla's affiliation with al-Qaeda and his plans to engage in acts of terrorism. As a substantive matter, District Judge Michael B. Mukasey was willing to assume that all operatives of al-Qaeda, even those who are American citizens, are not entitled to the protection afforded to lawful combatants. According to Mukasey, neither the Third Geneva Convention nor general principles of international law confer prisoner-of-war status on members of terrorist organizations such as al-Qaeda. They could be treated as unlawful combatants and could be detained indefinitely without ever being charged with a crime. But he insisted on the need to hold a hearing to determine whether Padilla was in fact an operative of al-Qaeda. In contrast to the Fourth Circuit in *Hamdi*, Judge Mukasey was not prepared to make the Mobbs affidavit dispositive. The deference that the executive properly deserved was to be reflected in the standard of review—once again, some evidence. Judge Mukasey required that an evidentiary hearing be held on the habeas corpus petition and that counsel be given access to Padilla for purposes of preparing for that hearing.

This order was first entered on December 4, 2002.[16] By March 11, 2003, shortly before the symposium, Judge Mukasey found it necessary to reissue that order. The government had not yet allowed counsel to consult with Padilla. Defending its recalcitrance, the government submitted an affidavit by the director of the Defense Intelligence Agency, Vice Admiral Lowell E. Jacoby, claiming that the total isolation of Padilla for this extended period—he had already been held incommunicado for ten months—was necessary to cultivate in Padilla a complete sense of dependency upon his interrogators and to convince him of the utter hopelessness of his situation. The District Court was unwilling to acquiesce to this demand—certainly an affront to the basic American tradition against coerced confessions. Judge Mukasey once again explained why Padilla had a right to present facts at the habeas corpus hearing and why access to counsel was necessary for that purpose. He reissued his previous order.[17]

The government immediately appealed. On December 18, 2003, the Second Circuit went one step beyond Judge Mukasey.[18] It repudiated Judge Mukasey's substantive theory and held that even if the government's allegations concerning Padilla were true, he could not be detained as a prisoner without being formally charged with a violation of some federal criminal statute. The Second Circuit relied on 18 U.S.C. § 4001(a), which provides that no United States citizen can be detained without specific authorization by Congress. Disagreeing with Judge Mukasey, the Second Circuit held that the resolution permitting the use of force to fight the War on Terror—the resolution that had been treated as constituting the declaration of war against Afghanistan—did not provide the authorization required by Section 4001(a). Although this ruling denied the government the prerogatives it sought by classifying Padilla as an unlawful enemy combatant, it should be emphasized that Padilla is an American citizen captured not in the battlefield but at a Chicago airport and held in South Carolina. The Second Circuit's ruling did not apply to noncitizens, or even to Americans captured in Afghanistan or any other battlefield.

A second test of the government's position regarding unlawful combatants occurred in the case of another American citizen—John Walker Lindh—who was seized in Afghanistan.[19] Unlike Hamdi or the petitioners in *Al Odah*, Lindh acknowledged that he was a soldier of the Taliban. He denied that he had anything to do with al-Qaeda, and the government concluded that little was to be gained by interrogating him in the style of Padilla, Hamdi, or the detainees in Guantánamo. Instead, the government chose to try him for various federal crimes—most notably, conspiracy to kill American nationals—and selected as its venue the United States District Court for the Eastern District of Virginia. Eventually, he was allowed to consult with counsel.

In this case, the government deployed the "unlawful combatant" category to get out from under the principle that "it is no 'crime' to be a soldier"[20]—lawful combatants cannot be tried for ordinary acts of violence during military operations, but unlawful combatants can. Attorneys for Lindh denied that he was an unlawful combatant, and on that ground moved to dismiss the charge of conspiring to kill American nationals. The motion was denied. Lindh then pleaded guilty to lesser charges—providing services to the Taliban and carrying explosives during the commission of a felony—and was sentenced to twenty years in prison.[21]

Like Damocles' sword, the "unlawful enemy combatant" designation and the judicial endorsement of it will remain over Lindh's head until the day he dies. The predicate for the criminal charge was that Lindh is an unlawful combatant. So if the plea agreement is challenged and set aside, or if it is determined that Lindh breached his obligations under the agreement and the government is thus freed of its obligations under it, the government can pursue the options it originally had by virtue of Lindh's status as an unlawful combatant. It can go forward with the criminal prosecution for his combat activities in Afghanistan, try him for those activities before a military tribunal at risk of execution, or hold him incommunicado indefinitely.

Similar dangers are present even if the plea agreement remains in force. In paragraph 21 of the agreement, the government renounced any right it has to treat Lindh as an unlawful combatant, but that provision contains one notable—indeed astonishing—limitation. It permits the government to treat Lindh as an unlawful combatant for his combat activities in Afghanistan if, at any time during the rest of his life, Lindh violates either of two federal criminal statutes. One statute, the scope of which was enlarged by the USA PATRIOT Act, defines the federal crime of terrorism; the other prohibits trade and financial transactions with a nation against whom the president has declared a national emergency and imposed a boycott. The determination that Lindh has violated either of these statutes, and the resultant reinstitution of his unlawful combatant status, is, according to paragraph 21, to be made by the government, not a court. Even after the government makes this determination, presumably Lindh cannot be prosecuted in federal court for his combat activities in Afghanistan; under the plea agreement, all the charges other than the ones for which he was sentenced were dismissed. But the government can pursue the other strategies it had previously agreed to forgo—trying Lindh before a military tribunal at risk of execution for having fought for the Taliban or, perhaps more plausibly, holding him incommunicado indefinitely.

In denying Lindh's initial motion to dismiss, District Judge T. S. Ellis III invoked the definition of lawful combatants set forth in Article 4 of the Third Geneva Convention.[22] He operated on the premise that a combatant who does not meet this definition would be deprived of the protection of that Convention and treated as an unlawful combatant, thereby receiving only the minimal protection of the Fourth Convention.

Actually, Article 4 of the Third Convention establishes several categories of lawful combatants. According to Section 1 of Article 4, members of the armed forces of a party to a conflict are, without anything more, treated as lawful combatants. In Section 3, the same rule is applied even when the state detaining the prisoners does not formally recognize the government to which the prisoners give their allegiance. Four criteria are, however, set forth in Section 2 of Article 4 for determining whether members of a militia or volunteer corps not part of the armed forces of a party to a conflict are lawful combatants. That section provides that members of a militia or volunteer corps not part of the armed forces shall be treated as lawful combatants if the militia or volunteer corps (1) is commanded by a person responsible for his subordinates; (2) wears uniforms or an insignia recognizable at a distance; (3) carries arms openly; and (4) conducts its operations in accordance with the laws and customs of war.

Offhand, it would seem that Lindh was a lawful combatant simply by virtue of the fact that he was a member of the Taliban army. Under this approach, he would fall within Section 3, as opposed to Section 1, because the United States never recognized the Taliban. In any event, there would be no need to make the inquiry called for in Section 2. But Judge Ellis rejected this approach. He held that "all armed forces or militias, regular and irregular, must meet the four criteria" of Section 2 if their members are to be treated as lawful combatants, thereby obliterating the distinction between Sections 1 and 3, on the one hand, and Section 2 on the other.[23] Not only does this ruling violate the express terms of the Third Convention, it is also at odds with the humanitarian purposes of the convention. The Third Convention seeks to establish a general rule endowing the members of the armed forces of a party to a conflict or militias that are part of the armed forces of that party with lawful combatant status. Granted, a militia that otherwise would fall within Section 2 should not be entitled to the benefit of Sections 1 or 3 simply by calling itself an armed force. But the responsibility is on the court to determine whether, in fact, the combatants fall into those sections. It is precisely this inquiry that Judge Ellis failed to undertake.

When it came time to apply the four criteria of Section 2, Judge Ellis did not make his judgment on the basis of what Lindh or his unit or the militia of which he was a part did. Rather, he made a judgment about what the Taliban army did in its entirety, and then applied that judgment to everyone who fought for the Taliban, including Lindh. This blanket approach compounds Judge Ellis's initial error—subjecting regular armed forces to the four criteria of Section 2—for it does not permit any distinction among the various units that comprise the fighting force of a nation at war. Once again, such an approach contravenes the humanitarian purposes of the Geneva Convention.

The evidence that Judge Ellis marshaled in support of his conclusion about the Taliban also seems questionable. There was no contention that the Taliban carried concealed weapons.

Based on two secondary sources, one a book published in 1999, the other an article in the *Wall Street Journal* on October 26, 2001, Judge Ellis concluded that Taliban soldiers did not typically wear uniforms or insignia and, further, that the Taliban army had no internal system of military command and control. This last conclusion does not seem entirely plausible, but putting that concern to one side, the case for classifying the entire Taliban army as consisting of unlawful combatants because they lacked uniforms or a command structure still seems strained.

As a purely formal matter, the Section 2 criteria are stated in the conjunctive, which means that by proving that the Taliban failed to satisfy any single criterion—no uniform or no command structure—grounds would be established for classifying the Taliban as unlawful combatants. This wording, however, is derived from the fact that Section 2 seeks to determine whether a militia that is not part of the armed forces should be given the same status that the armed forces receive under either Section 1 or 3. But if, as Judge Ellis holds, the criteria are to be used more globally, to determine whether members of any armed forces are to be treated as lawful combatants, then it would be more appropriate to apply the criteria set forth in Section 2 in a way that reflects the underlying purposes of the Third Convention and a proper understanding of what turns on the classification. As used by the United States, the unlawful-combatant designation gives the nation holding the prisoner vast, almost boundless power over him, and it would seem odd that such power can derive simply from the fact that the Taliban lacked uniforms or an appropriate command and control system. It must also presuppose that the Taliban army failed to conduct their operations in accordance with the laws and customs of war or, put more simply, that they were guilty of war crimes.

Judge Ellis did in fact conclude that "the Taliban regularly targeted civilian populations." Yet he cited as his only evidence two books that were not about the conduct of the war or how the Taliban fought but about how the Taliban came to power. Such an approach has broad and sweeping implications—probably every tyrant targets civilians in his drive to seize and maintain power—and is alien to the very purposes of the Geneva Conventions, which were intended, after all, to temper the treatment of prisoners. At the heart of the Geneva Conventions is a concern with the way wars are fought, not how the governments at war obtained their power. Under Section 2, lawful-combatant status requires that the militia conduct its "operations" in accordance with the laws and customs of war, and the word "operations" should have been construed with this purpose in mind.

What moved Judge Ellis was not, I believe, his tortured and strikingly unpersuasive application of the Third Geneva Convention, but the determination of the president that all those who resisted the United States in Afghanistan were unlawful combatants. Judge Ellis acknowledged the president's decision and said that it was entitled to great deference, though he was meticulous in declaring a limit to this deference. As he put it, "Conclusive deference, which amounts to judicial abstention, is plainly inappropriate." [24] Yet I am left with the unmistakable impression that Judge Ellis did exactly what he said he should not do. He allowed the president's decision to serve as a substitute for his own independent judgment. He treated the president's decision, much as the Mobbs affidavit did in *Hamdi*, as sufficient in itself to determine the legality of the executive's action. In doing so, Judge Ellis in *Lindh*, much as the Fourth Circuit did in *Hamdi*, abdicated his responsibility under the Constitution.

Such abdication has not been confined to the disposition of claims by persons captured on the battlefield. In October 2002, the Court of Appeals for the Third Circuit acquiesced in a new deportation program of the attorney general that was justified in terms of war needs, though this time it was simply the ill-defined

War on Terror. The specific issue in this case—*North Jersey Media Group, Inc. v. Ashcroft*[25]—was whether newspapers or the public or even family or friends would be given access to deportation proceedings that had been designated by the attorney general as "special interest" cases. The attorney general feared that the access of the press or public might alert terrorists to the investigative tactics of the government or betray the precise knowledge that the government possessed.

The newspapers acknowledged that the right of access they claimed was only a qualified right that can be defeated by a special showing. In this context, acknowledging a right of access as a qualified right would allow the government to make a showing before the presiding judge in the deportation proceeding that special circumstances—including national security concerns—warranted closure. The presiding judge might, of course, agree with the government, but even if he or she did, the judge would be assuming responsibility for the closure. The Third Circuit, however, took that decision away from the individual judge by holding that the very designation by the executive of a national security interest in the proceeding defeated the right of access. The blanket judgment of the Third Circuit endowed the attorney general with the power to close deportation proceedings whenever he saw fit. There could be no particularized inquiry by a judge into the national security justification for closure in a specific case. Much like the Mobbs affidavit in *Hamdi* or the transfer of prisoners to Guantánamo, the attorney general's designation brought the reason of the law to an end.

The tide may yet turn—let's hope so. The Sixth Circuit has reached a different conclusion than the Third Circuit on the question of public access to "special interest" deportation proceedings.[26] In the months following the symposium in Coral Gables, the Supreme Court agreed to review the *Al Odah*, *Hamdi*, and *Padilla* decisions.[27] On December 2, 2003, the day before

filing its memorandum opposing the grant of the writ of certiorari in the *Hamdi* case, the government announced that it would,
as a matter of discretion, allow the prisoner access to counsel
subject to appropriate security restrictions.[28] It pursued a similar
strategy in the *Padilla* case, though in that instance it made the
announcement on February 11, 2004, when it filed its reply brief
in support of its application for the writ of certiorari.[29] After
the grant of the writ of certiorari in the *Al Odah* case, a panel
of the Ninth Circuit found that Guantánamo was, in fact, within
the sovereign jurisdiction of the United States.[30] Moreover, although it remained to be seen what the capture of Saddam Hussein and the occupation of Iraq would bring, it is noteworthy
that the administration had not yet moved the Iraqi prisoners
it had captured to Guantánamo or chosen to designate them en
masse as unlawful combatants.

Still, the challenge to law in the post–September 11 era is
unmistakable. The Iraq War stands as an affront to the international legal system, and as is evident in the lower court cases
I discussed, a number of good and able judges have renounced
their most basic responsibilities under the Constitution. War always poses a challenge to law. It involves a pursuit of interests
through violence rather than reason and often excites base fears
and passions. The wars in Afghanistan and Iraq, and the most
shapeless of all wars—the War on Terror—are not exceptions.
A practice of lawlessness has grown in the shadow of these wars,
and it poses a challenge for every law teacher.

The wars of the last two years have provoked protests and
petitions, and, like the war in Vietnam, the Iraq War is likely to
become the subject of national political contests. As citizens, we
need to attend to such contests and make our views known, but
never in a way that relieves us of our obligations as teachers of
the law. We must stand within the law and test the government's
actions by the law. Such an endeavor may lack the drama that

the events of the day call for—it is detailed, patient work, fully based on reason—yet it may be our most enduring contribution.

Upon retiring from the Supreme Court, Thurgood Marshall was asked by a reporter how he wished to be remembered. Marshall answered with a spontaneity and immediacy that attested to the truth of what he was about to say: "He did what he could with what he had." [31] He understood himself and the magnitude of his achievement, and in so doing provided a lesson for us all.

## Prologue to Chapter 2

Trevor Sutton

"It was as profound a day in the court as any in a long time." So wrote Anthony Lewis, a storied legal reporter and columnist for the *New York Times*, in a column published on June 29, 2004, the day after the Supreme Court handed down decisions in three cases arising out of the Bush administration's War on Terror. The most significant of the three cases—and the one to which Lewis devoted most of his column—was the Court's ruling in *Hamdi v. Rumsfeld*, which rejected the Bush administration's claim that it had legal authority to classify and detain an American citizen as an "unlawful enemy combatant" without an evidentiary hearing. Lewis's euphoric response to *Hamdi* captured the mood of much of the legal and media communities in the wake of the decision. The *Times* editorial page itself opined that the Court had "made it clear that even during the war on terror, the government must adhere to the rule of law." The *Washington Post*, meanwhile, called *Hamdi* a "Supreme Rebuke," and asserted that the case "sends a powerful message that Americans cannot just disappear at the hands of their government." Many other commenters seized on the language in Justice O'Connor's plurality opinion that "a state of war is not a blank check for the President when it comes to the rights of the Nation's citizens."

Not all were convinced that *Hamdi* was a watershed, however. Ronald Dworkin, writing in the *New York Review of Books*, cautioned that commentators who heralded *Hamdi* as "a significant victory for civil and human rights" may have "overstated the practical impact" of the decision. Dworkin observed that the procedure rules set out in the plurality opinion "omit important traditional protections for people accused of crimes," and added astutely: "The government may well be able to satisfy the Court's lenient procedural standards without actually altering its morally dubious detention policies." Yet even Dworkin could not help but optimistically declare that principles underlying the *Hamdi* decision could lead to "a much more powerful conclusion than the Court itself drew": that beyond a certain point the government must choose between subjecting a detainee to a criminal trial and holding him as an enemy combatant. In 2015, with Guantánamo prison still open, such a reading of *Hamdi* seems rose-colored at best.

This chapter, "The War on Terror and the Rule of Law," shares Dworkin's mixture of relief and reservation. More than even Dworkin, the essay—originally delivered in 2005 as the H.L.A. Hart Lecture at Oxford University—sees *Hamdi* for what it is: a step back from disaster but not a cause for celebration, especially when read in light of the other two decisions handed down the same day as *Hamdi*, specifically, *Rumsfeld v. Padilla* and *Rasul v. Bush*. As the essay demonstrates, what most obviously united these three cases was, in fact, disunity—that is, the inability of the justices to form a majority over fundamental questions about the scope and applicability of the Constitution to the president's wartime activities, both on and off the battlefield. With *Padilla* and *Rasul*, that disunity resulted in inconclusive rulings that disposed of the detainee plaintiffs' claims in a deeply unsatisfying and formalist manner. In *Hamdi*, the Court was bold enough to reach the merits of the case and to find that the president's position was untenable; but, as Owen Fiss's essay demonstrates, the justices could not agree on basic constitutional principles regarding the president's power to detain American citizens. In that sense, if *Hamdi* was a rebuke, it was a garbled one.

There is another theme that draws these three cases together, one that bears directly on Fiss's earlier work on the intersection of procedure and justice: the Court's preoccupation with procedural questions at the expense of—or as a refuge from—issues of fundamental rights. This tendency was most obvious in *Padilla*, where the Court simply dodged Jose Padilla's constitutional arguments by determining that the habeas petition was filed in the wrong district court. But it was also present in subtler ways in *Rasul* and *Hamdi*. In *Rasul*, the Court found that the foreign prisoners at Guantánamo had a statutory right to file a habeas writ without meaningfully addressing whether those prisoners had any constitutional rights to invoke in the first place. In *Hamdi*, the plurality's much-lauded refusal to grant the president a blank check concerned only the process by which the Bush administration classified American citizens as unlawful enemy combatants. The plurality did not contest the concept of "unlawful enemy combatant" itself, and found that the executive had statutory authority to detain Hamdi for as long as "active combat" continues in Afghanistan.

A postscript to this essay is in order. In chronicling the approach the Bush administration brought to its legal and political campaign to deprive the Guantánamo prisoners of access to civilian courts, Fiss notes the government's surprise decision to try Jose Padilla, a U.S. citizen, in federal court on a variety of charges, none of which was as grievous as the accusation that allegedly justified his imprisonment—namely, the intention of setting off a dirty bomb inside the United States. After the publication of the essay, a federal jury in Miami found Padilla guilty of conspiring to kill Americans overseas and to provide material support to terrorists. When the district court sentenced Padilla to seventeen years in prison, Padilla's mother expressed relief at the result. But this was not the end of Padilla's saga: the Eleventh Circuit subsequently reversed the sentence on the reasoning that it was too lenient and sent the case back for resentencing. In September 2014, the district court gave Padilla a new sentence of twenty-one years.

# Chapter 2

# THE WAR ON TERROR
# AND THE RULE OF LAW

A ll the world sighed. On June 28, 2004, the Supreme Court handed down its decisions arising from the so-called War on Terror. The decisions were greeted with a deep sense of relief. We had braced for the worst of all possible outcomes—an endorsement of the Bush administration's position. Such a result would have betrayed the most elementary principles of American constitutionalism. It would have also left vulnerable many of the constitutional courts around the world that had relied upon American principles to justify the restraints that they had imposed on their governments' counterterrorism policies. The Supreme Court must be credited with having avoided this outcome, and yet faulted for doing less than it should have.

The Court rendered three decisions. All three involved individuals who were imprisoned by the United States—in fact, held incommunicado for two years, with no access to family, friends, or counsel. All three cases put into question a fundamental tenet of the U.S. Constitution—what I will call the "principle of freedom." This principle denies the United States the authority to imprison anyone unless that person is charged with a crime and swiftly brought to trial. This principle is rooted in section 9 of Article I, guaranteeing the writ of habeas corpus—the historic means of testing the legality of detention—and, perhaps even more fundamentally, in the Fifth Amendment guarantee that no person shall be deprived of liberty without due process of law.

Over the years, the principle of freedom has been qualified to permit civil commitment proceedings, which allow the state to confine to a hospital or mental institution persons who are a threat to themselves or others. More recently, the principle has been adjusted to allow the United States to detain persons who might serve as material witnesses in a criminal prosecution or before a grand jury but who are likely to flee the jurisdiction. Presumably, such detention would be of limited duration. An even more fundamental qualification—and the one invoked by the government in these cases and recognized by international law—allows the armed forces to capture and imprison enemy combatants during ongoing hostilities.

All three cases before the Court were removed from an active theater of combat. One involved an American citizen—Jose Padilla—who was first arrested at O'Hare Airport in Chicago as he alighted from a plane.[1] He had arrived in Chicago from Pakistan via Switzerland. He was immediately taken to New York and then transferred to a naval brig in Charleston, South Carolina. The second case also involved an American citizen—Yaser Esam Hamdi.[2] He was first arrested in Afghanistan, taken to Guantánamo Naval Station, later transferred to a naval brig in Norfolk, Virginia, and finally, after the grant of certiorari by the Supreme Court, brought to the same naval brig in Charleston in which Padilla was being held. The third case involved a group of Australians and Kuwaitis who were first seized in Afghanistan and Pakistan and then imprisoned at Guantánamo.[3]

In all three cases, the prisoners, acting through various

representatives—some self-appointed, others appointed by the trial courts—sought writs of habeas corpus to challenge the legality of their detention, and in doing so invoked the principle of freedom. The government maintained that the prisoners were enemy combatants—one was allegedly affiliated with al-Qaeda and the others were said to be soldiers of the Taliban. All the prisoners denied the government's charges and demanded a meaningful opportunity to contest the factual basis of their detention. Admittedly, if the government failed to prove that they were enemy combatants, the government might still be able to detain them. The principle of freedom is not an absolute or unconditional protection of freedom but, rather, tightly identifies the circumstances under which an individual may be deprived of his or her freedom. If the prisoners were not enemy combatants, then the government would have the burden of charging them with a crime. Requiring the government to proceed in this way would bring into play the protections of the Sixth Amendment that specifically govern criminal prosecutions, including a speedy trial, trial by jury, the right to cross examination, proof beyond a reasonable doubt, and the right to counsel. A criminal prosecution would also fully reveal, beyond the numbing drumbeat of war, the gravity of what the government had in mind for these individuals—incarceration for a substantial period of time.

By the time these cases reached the Supreme Court, the government was prepared to recognize the right of the two prisoners who were American citizens—Padilla and Hamdi—to seek a writ of habeas corpus. The government sought to reduce this right, however, to a mere formality. The government insisted that there should be no evidentiary inquiry into the prisoners' claim that they were not enemy combatants; an affidavit from an official in the executive attesting to Padilla's and Hamdi's status as enemy combatants was, according to the government, in and of itself a sufficient basis for denying the writ. The demand for unlimited power on the part of the government was even more extreme in the case of the Australians and Kuwaitis. The government insisted that those prisoners had no right even to apply for a writ of habeas corpus, or, put differently, no federal court had jurisdiction to grant the writ. Although the Supreme Court did not embrace all these audacious and somewhat startling demands for executive power, it failed to vindicate the principle of freedom.

## A Technical Dodge

Padilla's habeas petition struck a note of urgency. The government held him as an enemy combatant, but the war that the government had in mind was not the kind that had been fought in Afghanistan and for which international law allows belligerents to detain enemy combatants. Rather, it was the vast, ill-defined, and never-ending War on Terror. Political rhetoric had been confused with a rule of law. Moreover, by the time the Supreme Court ruled on his petition in June 2004, Padilla had been imprisoned for more than two years. For most of that period he was held incommunicado, without access to family or counsel. Only after the grant of certiorari did the government allow Padilla access to counsel. The purpose of such extended isolation had long been manifest. In an affidavit filed in open court, Vice Admiral Lowell E. Jacoby, the director of the Defense Intelligence Agency, explained that the total isolation of Padilla for such an extended period was necessary to cultivate a complete sense of dependency in Padilla on his interrogators and to ensure that Padilla was convinced of the hopelessness of his situation.[4] At the time Jacoby swore to the affidavit, Padilla had already been held incommunicado for seven months.

According to the government, Padilla was associated with

al-Qaeda and was planning to engage in terrorist acts in the United States, including the detonation of a device—known as a dirty bomb—that would disperse radioactive material. The government's claim was supported by nothing more than an affidavit of an official in the Department of Defense, which contained multiple layers of hearsay. The federal district court in New York ruled that Padilla had a right to an evidentiary hearing to contest the veracity of the affidavit, and provided him with access to counsel for that purpose. The judge did not ground the right to counsel in the Bill of Rights, either the Due Process Clause of the Fifth Amendment or the Sixth Amendment's guarantee of the right to counsel in criminal prosecutions. Rather, he gave Padilla access to counsel simply as an exercise of his power to hold a hearing on Padilla's habeas petition.[5] The Court of Appeals went even further. Concluding that Padilla was being unlawfully detained, it ordered his release unless he was transferred to civilian authorities and either held as a material witness before a grand jury or charged with a crime.[6]

Refusing to address the lawfulness of Padilla's detention in any way, the Supreme Court simply ruled that Padilla's lawyer had filed the habeas petition in the wrong district court. Padilla had been brought from Chicago to New York on a material witness warrant requiring him to testify before a grand jury. The district judge in New York who had issued the material witness warrant appointed counsel to represent Padilla before the grand jury. Padilla in fact consulted with counsel, but two days before a scheduled hearing on a motion to contest his arrest on the warrant, the Department of Defense took custody of him and transferred him to the naval brig in South Carolina—all without prior notice to Padilla's counsel. Upon learning that Padilla was in the custody of the department, Padilla's lawyer immediately filed a habeas petition in New York in order to contest the legality of his detention, naming the secretary of defense as the respondent. In an opinion by Chief Justice William Rehnquist, the Supreme Court held that under the relevant statute the habeas application should have been filed in South Carolina, not New York, and that the proper defendant was not the secretary of defense but, rather, the commander of the Charleston brig. Padilla remained imprisoned, and his lawyer was required to begin the habeas proceeding once again.

The commander of the Charleston brig is a subordinate of the secretary of defense and fully subject to his control and discretion. The requirement that the commander be named as the respondent to the habeas petition is of no independent significance; it is derived from the more general rule requiring a prisoner to bring a habeas petition in the district in which he is confined. This rule allocating work among the federal district courts seeks to assign the habeas petition to the court where a hearing might be most conveniently held and also to prevent forum shopping by prisoners. On previous occasions, exceptions had been made to this rule, but Chief Justice Rehnquist insisted that those exceptions were not applicable in Padilla's case. Although this might indeed be true, Rehnquist did not explain why the Court could not create yet another exception. As the dissenters bitterly complained, the facts of Padilla's situation—the surreptitious transfer of custody from civilian to military authorities—were sufficiently unique to allow the Court to create another exception without enabling prisoners to shop for the most hospitable judge and without threatening the overall aims of Congress in distributing the responsibility for habeas writs among the district courts.

The responsibility of the Court to address the merits of Padilla's claim to freedom stands, however, independent of whether an exception should have been made to the rule for allocating habeas petitions among the district courts. The choice between the South Carolina and New York district courts did not raise any problem of subject-matter jurisdiction, and thus the government implicitly conceded that the petition was within the province of competence of the federal judiciary. As a result, the Supreme Court had full authority to rule on the merits of Padilla's claim for freedom, even if the habeas proceeding had been commenced in the wrong district court. Even more, Padilla's claim would remain the same no matter in which district court the case was commenced. It is therefore difficult to perceive how justice was served by requiring Padilla's lawyer—after Padilla had been confined incommunicado for two years—to start the proceedings afresh. Sometimes we accept the Court's forbearance as a matter of judicial statesmanship, but here my sentiments are of another sort. Given the stakes for the individual and the nation, the failure of the Court even to address the merits of Padilla's claim of freedom was, pure and simple, an act of judicial cowardice.

The institutional failure of the Court was manifest at the moment of decision. Subsequent developments only aggravated the offense. Following the Court's decision, Padilla's lawyers filed a new habeas petition in the South Carolina district court. The South Carolina district court granted Padilla's petition, but the Fourth Circuit reversed, affirming the summary power of the government to detain Padilla as an enemy combatant. With that victory in hand, and only days before it had to respond to Padilla's petition for a writ of certiorari, the government reversed its strategy. It filed a petition in the Fourth Circuit declaring its intention to transfer Padilla from military to civilian custody and to try him on criminal charges in a district court in Florida.

This stunning turn of events occurred on November 22, 2005. On that day—almost three and a half years after his initial arrest (May 8, 2002) and sixteen months after the Supreme Court declined to rule on the merits of Padilla's petition (June 28, 2004)—the principle of freedom was in effect vindicated. The government took upon itself the burden of charging Padilla with a crime, and by that act brought into play all the strictures of the Bill of Rights, including the provision guaranteeing Padilla access to counsel and a speedy trial. Of course, justice delayed is better than no justice at all, but the government never satisfactorily explained why it took this action so belatedly—only just before it would have been obligated, for a second time, to justify its position before the Supreme Court. Could it be, as the author of the Fourth Circuit opinion denying the government's petition later charged, that the government feared a reversal by the Supreme Court? [7]

The decision of the government to downgrade the charges against Padilla was also puzzling. The secretary of defense had initially charged Padilla with plans to detonate a radioactive device in the United States. The secretary maintained that stance and supported it with affidavits from subordinates throughout Padilla's protracted efforts to secure his freedom—which had lasted over three years and involved the Southern District of New York, the Second Circuit, the Supreme Court, the District Court for South Carolina, and the Fourth Circuit. The indictment against Padilla filed in November 2005 made no mention of his alleged plan to detonate a radioactive device in the United States. The charges now against him were "conspiracy to murder, kidnap, and maim persons in a foreign country," and providing "material support for terrorists." Before the press, the government defended its shift on the ground that pursuit of the original charge would have jeopardized vital intelligence sources, but many commentators questioned the truthfulness of that explanation.

In his habeas petition, Padilla maintained that his confinement violated a 1971 federal statute known as the Non-Detention Act. This statute can be viewed as a watered-down version of the principle of freedom. It is aimed at avoiding a repetition of the horrors arising from the detention during World War II of persons of Japanese origin then resident in the western United States. I say "watered-down" because the statute applies only to citizens (the Japanese interned in World War II included non-U.S. citizens as well as citizens) and because it required not that the prisoners be charged with a crime but only that the detention be authorized by Congress. As such, the law appears more concerned with unilateral action by the executive than vindicating the principle of freedom. It provides that "no citizen shall be imprisoned or otherwise detained by the United States except pursuant to an Act of Congress." [8]

In the original habeas proceeding, the Second Circuit held that Padilla's confinement violated the Non-Detention Act. This was a bold advance over the decision of the District Court for the Southern District of New York, which did not put the government to the burden of filing criminal charges against Padilla, but rather required only an evidentiary hearing on the question of whether he was an enemy combatant, and allowed indefinite detention if that charge were proved. The Second Circuit ruling was still limited, however, as it only governed situations like Padilla's that involved a citizen seized in the United States. The Second Circuit specifically declined to address whether the Non-Detention Act had any force for American citizens captured on the battlefield. [9]

## Watered-Down Due Process

Like Padilla, Yaser Hamdi—the prisoner in the second of the terrorism cases—also relied on the Non-Detention Act, but there was a crucial difference. Although Padilla, much like the Japanese who were interned, was taken prisoner in the United States, Hamdi was seized in Afghanistan, which, at the time of his capture (October 2001), was a zone of active combat. Yet

Justice Sandra Day O'Connor, writing for herself and three other Justices (William Rehnquist, Anthony Kennedy, and Stephen Breyer), held in *Hamdi* that even assuming that the 1971 act applied to American citizens captured on the battlefield, the specific requirement of the act—that the detention be authorized by statute—was satisfied. To that end, she relied upon a statute (Authorization for the Use of Military Force) that was passed by Congress one week after September 11, and used by the executive as the declaration of war against Afghanistan. It authorized the president to use all necessary and appropriate force against nations, organizations, or persons associated with the September 11 terrorist attacks.[10]

In a separate opinion in *Hamdi*, Justice David Souter, joined by Justice Ruth Bader Ginsburg, insisted that the terms of the Non-Detention Act were not satisfied—the statute authorizing the use of military force against terrorism was far too general to count as the requisite statutory authorization for Hamdi's detention. (Justice Souter also concluded that the 1971 Non-Detention Act governed prisoners taken on the battlefield and did not improperly interfere with the responsibilities of the president as commander in chief.) Yet in the interest of forming a majority, Justice Souter joined Justice O'Connor's opinion. Justice Souter said that by providing Hamdi with an opportunity to contest the factual predicate of the government's theory, the plurality's remand order was "on terms closest to those [he] would impose."[11] Justice Clarence Thomas embraced the government's position in its entirety, virtually denying any judicial review of the government's decision to detain Hamdi indefinitely. Justice Antonin Scalia and Justice John Paul Stevens took the opposite view—because Hamdi was an American citizen, the only options for the government were to prosecute Hamdi in federal court for treason or some other crime or to let him go.[12]

In the United States and abroad, Justice O'Connor's opinion

is best known for its statement that "a state of war is not a blank check for the President when it comes to the rights of the Nation's citizens."[13] In accordance with that aphorism, she did in fact place limits—procedural limits—on the president's capacity to detain citizens who had been captured on the battlefield and later detained in the United States.[14] She required that Hamdi be given the opportunity to contest the government's claim that he was a soldier of the Taliban and thus an enemy combatant. This charge had been supported by an affidavit from the same official in the Department of Defense (Michael Mobbs) who gave the affidavit in *Padilla*, although Hamdi's father, who had brought this habeas petition on his son's behalf, denied this allegation and said that his son went to Afghanistan in August 2001 to do relief work.

Justice O'Connor spoke to Hamdi's particular situation but in effect crafted a more general procedural scheme. With that purpose in mind, she explained that the procedural rights of prisoners held as enemy combatants must be carefully tailored "to alleviate their uncommon potential to burden the executive at a time of ongoing military conflict."[15] Accordingly, she allowed the government to support its charge that a prisoner is an enemy combatant by submitting an affidavit based on records maintained by the military of battlefield detainees. Such an affidavit would create a presumption, she said, that the prisoner is an enemy combatant and can be held on that basis. Then the prisoner would be given the opportunity to present evidence to rebut the presumption and to show that he is not an enemy combatant. The standard of proof Justice O'Connor contemplated remains unclear, but she did say that at this hearing Hamdi would have the assistance of counsel.

Justice O'Connor took up the counsel issue at the very end of her opinion. Her entire discussion of this issue amounted to one short paragraph, which followed a sentence that, because of its emotional tone, reads as though it was to be the conclusion of her opinion. In that sense, the counsel paragraph seems like a postscript—as though all the hard issues had already been resolved. Most of the paragraph is devoted to explaining why the right to counsel issue is moot: although Hamdi was denied access to counsel—or, for that matter, access to anyone at all—for a period of almost two years, following the grant of certiorari the government allowed Hamdi to meet with counsel without conceding any obligation to do so. Then this sentence appears, without any elaboration whatsoever: "He unquestionably has the right to access to counsel in connection with the proceedings on remand." [16]

A casual reader might think that the sentence was purely descriptive of Hamdi's situation and that the right to counsel to which Justice O'Connor referred might be the right the government already allowed him as a discretionary matter. On reflection, however, it may well be that this "right" to counsel applies more generally and has constitutional roots, not in the Sixth Amendment, which only applies to criminal prosecutions, but in the Due Process Clause of the Fifth Amendment. The remand required the concurrence of Justice Souter, and he spoke of the plurality's "affirmation" of Hamdi's right to counsel.[17] I therefore assume that Justice O'Connor and the three other justices who joined her opinion intended to avoid a ruling on the right to counsel issue but that they added the crucial sentence at the very last moment to secure Justice Souter's and Justice Ginsburg's votes.

Bargaining among the justices had a less felicitous outcome with respect to the nature of the tribunal that could determine whether Hamdi is an enemy combatant. Throughout her opinion, Justice O'Connor made it clear that the hearing must be held before "a neutral decision maker" [18] or "an impartial adjudicator." [19]

Clearly, that standard would be satisfied by a federal district court passing on an application for habeas corpus. Indeed, the case before the Supreme Court had begun in such a manner—Yaser Hamdi's father acting as next friend filed a habeas petition in the federal district court with jurisdiction over the Norfolk brig. But Justice O'Connor created another alternative: a hearing before a military tribunal that would not be a prelude but rather a substitute for the hearing on the habeas petition in the federal district court. She wrote: "There remains the possibility that the standards we have articulated could be met by an appropriately authorized and properly constituted military tribunal." [20] She could not, however, obtain a fifth vote for this proposition. Justice Souter was explicit that in joining Justice O'Connor's plurality opinion he did not mean to imply "that an opportunity to litigate before a military tribunal might obviate or truncate enquiry by a court on habeas." [21]

Doubts can, of course, be raised as to whether a military tribunal can ever, no matter how it is constituted, have the "neutrality" or "impartiality" that fair procedure requires. After all, it is an act of the military that must be judged, and a military tribunal is, as the name implies, staffed by members of the military. But Justice O'Connor's proposal—and that is all it is—can be faulted on more basic grounds. She did not fully grasp the significance of the issue to be resolved by the tribunal. The narrow technical issue is, as she said, whether the government made a mistake in classifying Hamdi as an enemy combatant. Yet the stakes are much greater than she allowed, because the classification of Hamdi as an enemy combatant was the basis for depriving him of the freedom that the Constitution guarantees. It was the basis for allowing the government to incarcerate him.

Accordingly, Hamdi's claim that he was not an enemy combatant should have been tried by a federal court, not simply because such a court can achieve a measure of neutrality unavailable to a military tribunal but also and more fundamentally because under our constitutional scheme it is the federal judiciary that has the responsibility of determining whether some individual has been deprived of a constitutionally guaranteed right, like the right to freedom. Federal judges are nominated by the president and confirmed by the Senate, and under our constitutional scheme are endowed with the authority to speak for the nation on the meaning of the Constitution.

The root of Justice O'Connor's error is clear. Much to the surprise of everyone, including the lawyers on both sides and some of her colleagues, she applied the *Matthews v. Eldridge*[22] formula to determine Hamdi's procedural rights. This formula was devised in the mid-1970s to determine whether an individual faced with the termination of welfare or disability benefits is, as a matter of due process, entitled to a hearing and what the character of that hearing must be. This formula requires a consideration of the benefits and costs of the proposed procedures and conceives of procedure as an instrument to arrive at correct decisions.[23] Although this formula has not been applied to require an evidentiary hearing for the termination of welfare benefits, it has always been assumed that if a hearing were required before benefits were terminated, that hearing need not be held before a federal judge. A supervisor in the welfare department would not suffice as a decision maker, because such an official would not possess the neutrality that fair procedure requires, but the hearing could be held before a member of the state civil service.[24] In the case of Yaser Hamdi, however, the issue is entirely different from that presented in *Matthews v. Eldridge*: not the fairness of a procedure to determine whether the state was correctly classifying the individual as it did but, rather, whether the prisoner is entitled to the substantive right to freedom guaranteed by the Constitution.

In saying this, I am not faulting Justice O'Connor, as some

have, for conflating property and liberty. She understood that what is at stake is not a welfare check, disability benefits, or some other form of property but Hamdi's liberty. Her error was to ignore the distinction between two types of liberties: those that are guaranteed by the Constitution itself—as, for example, by the First Amendment or by what I have called the principle of freedom—and those liberties that people enjoy in society but which are not constitutionally protected (one type of liberty can be called a constitutional liberty, the other a personal or social liberty).

A liberty of the latter type might be the liberty a parent has with respect to the control of his or her children. The Supreme Court had previously used the *Matthews v. Eldridge* formula to determine what procedures should be applied to deprive a person of such a personal liberty, as in *Lassiter v. Dept. of Soc. Servs. of Durham County*.[25] Although I disagree with the result in that case—appointed counsel need not be provided to an indigent person whose parental rights are to be terminated—I acknowledge the applicability of the formula. Similarly, I would say that if all that were involved in Hamdi's case were a personal liberty, the *Matthews v. Eldridge* formula would be applicable, and from that perspective a hearing before a military tribunal might suffice, once again assuming that the tribunal possessed the requisite impartiality. The formula requires only fair procedures.

But for liberties of the first type—liberties guaranteed by the Constitution itself—the individual is entitled to a hearing before a federal court on his or her claim. Imagine a tenured professor being fired by a state university for criticizing some public official. He can challenge that action as a violation of the First Amendment and is entitled to have that claim judged by a federal court and not simply by some administrative tribunal within the university structure.[26] He is entitled to something more than fair procedure. Likewise, I maintain that Hamdi was entitled to a hearing before a federal court, not a military tribunal, on his claim that he was being denied the liberty provided by the principle of freedom—a liberty that can be traced to the Due Process Clause of the Fifth Amendment, read in its substantive guise, and the provision of Article I limiting the suspension of the writ of habeas corpus.[27]

## The Uncertain Reach of the Constitution

The Supreme Court's failure in *Hamdi* is important but measured. Although the Court did not require a hearing before a federal court and thus did not honor the principle of freedom, it at least granted the prisoner some rights—an evidentiary hearing on the government's contention that he was an enemy combatant and access to counsel for such a hearing. The Court must also be credited for grounding these rights in the Due Process Clause, unfortunately misunderstood by the Court as a requirement of procedural fairness, not as a substantive guarantee of liberty. In the third decision handed down on June 28, 2004, *Rasul v. Bush*, the Supreme Court also granted procedural rights to prisoners captured in the theater of war and accused of having fought for the Taliban, but these rights were even more limited than those recognized in Hamdi.

Although the *Rasul* Court ruled that the prisoners had a right to file a habeas application in a federal district court and to require a response by the government, it did not specify what further rights—procedural or substantive—they had before that court. Even more significant, the Court grounded the limited right it did provide in the federal habeas statute, not the Constitution, and left uncertain whether the prisoners had any constitutional rights that might be vindicated in the habeas proceeding it allowed. The Court simply granted the prisoners the right to file a piece of paper.

The first and most crucial difference between *Hamdi* and *Rasul* is that, unlike Yaser Hamdi, the prisoners in *Rasul* were not American citizens. Two were Australians and twelve were Kuwaitis (at one point, two British citizens were involved in the litigation, but due to intense diplomatic pressure they were released after the grant of certiorari). All the prisoners denied that they took up arms against the United States and insisted that they were in the region for personal or humanitarian reasons. The second difference, which becomes of constitutional significance only because of the first difference, is that they were not held in Charleston or Norfolk but were moved from the battlefield to the Guantánamo Naval Station and imprisoned there.

The federal habeas statute (28 U.S.C. § 2241) provides that the district courts can grant habeas petitions only "within their respective jurisdictions." In *Rasul*, the government argued that this statutory language means that a district court can hear habeas petitions only from prisoners being held within its jurisdiction, and that because the prisoners were being held at Guantánamo they were not within the jurisdiction of the federal district court in which the habeas petition had been filed (the District of Columbia), nor, indeed, the jurisdiction of any district court. The Supreme Court, in an opinion by Justice Stevens, rejected this argument and established the following scheme for § 2241: prisoners being held within the jurisdiction of a district court must apply for the habeas writ within the jurisdiction of that court. However, prisoners held outside the jurisdiction of any district court, such as those held in Guantánamo, can apply for a writ from any district court that has jurisdiction over their custodian.

Justice Stevens was helped to his conclusion by the specter of having American citizens held at Guantánamo. As he put it, "[a]liens held at the base, no less than American citizens, are entitled to invoke the federal courts' authority under § 2241." [28] Drawing a linkage between American citizens and aliens seems entirely appropriate as a technique of statutory interpretation: given that § 2241 does not distinguish between the petitions of citizens and those of noncitizens, a construction of § 2241 that accommodates the petitions of American citizens at Guantánamo should accommodate the petitions of noncitizens being held there. What the linkage overlooks, however, is that the right to file a habeas petition is meaningless unless the prisoner has constitutional rights, and the constitutional rights of aliens and citizens are, under established doctrine, conceived of in quite different terms.

Citizens can claim the protection of the Constitution no matter where they are held by United States agents—South Carolina, Guantánamo, or even, for example, Yemen. The situation with aliens is quite different. Location is all-important. If the aliens live in South Carolina or any other state, they have the same constitutional rights as citizens. If they are being held in the South Carolina brig that contained Hamdi and Padilla, then presumably they too would be entitled to a due process right to a determination of their claim that they are not enemy combatants. Conversely, if they are being held by the United States government in a foreign country they have, under established doctrine, no constitutional rights, not even a right to a due process hearing before some neutral tribunal to ascertain whether they are in fact enemy combatants.

Where does Guantánamo fit in this scheme? The Court put Guantánamo closer to the South Carolina side, and was quite right in this judgment. The 45-square-mile area occupied by the Guantánamo Naval Base may, in some formal sense, belong to Cuba, but it is a territory over which the United States has exercised exclusive control for a century and has the right to do so forever. It is de facto part of the United States. If the Court did not conceive of Guantánamo in this way, it is not clear to whom the prisoners might turn to challenge their detention.

Their representatives might bring a legal proceeding in the country of their citizenship, but because they are being held in Guantánamo, not Kuwait or Australia, the courts of the countries of which they are citizens would not have the power or jurisdiction over the United States to order their release. As one English jurist, writing extrajudicially, put it, a legal black hole would have been created.[29]

To appreciate the risks of such a black hole, we need only consider the opinion of the lower court in *Rasul*. Although the Supreme Court overturned the Court of Appeal's holding, it did not directly contradict the lower court's view of the constitutional rights of Guantánamo detainees. That is because the Supreme Court discussed the status of Guantánamo in the context of interpreting the habeas statute. By contrast, the Court of Appeals, which had held that the district court did not have jurisdiction to hear the prisoners' petitions, approached the problem from another perspective. Instead of starting with the statutory question of jurisdiction, the Court first looked to whether the prisoners had any underlying constitutional rights. The Court of Appeals read the prevailing Supreme Court precedents to mean that if the prisoners were held by United States agents in another country—even one that was not a battlefield, say, Yemen—they would have no constitutional rights. The Court of Appeals was also of the view that Guantánamo was not part of the sovereign territory of the United States but rather like Yemen. Having reached this point in its analysis, the habeas proceedings made little sense to the Court of Appeals, even if the prisoners were, as a purely technical matter, deemed to be within the jurisdiction of the district court. As the Court of Appeals explained, "We cannot see why, or how, the writ may be made available to aliens abroad when basic constitutional protections are not."[30]

In contrast, the Supreme Court first examined the statutory

jurisdiction of the habeas court and in that context concluded that Guantánamo should be treated as part of the United States. It never reached the issue of what constitutional rights the prisoners enjoy and thus failed to engage the major premise of the Court of Appeals and the government. Seen in this way, Justice Stevens's opinion is not only a tribute to judicial minimalism but also a contrived effort to make the case seem easier than it is—as though all that is at stake is a technical dispute over the jurisdictional requirements of § 2241.

Justice Stevens was fully aware that in order to issue the writ under § 2241, the district court not only must have jurisdiction over the petition but must also determine that the detention violates the Constitution or laws of the United States. Of course, for the prisoners to have their constitutional rights violated, they must have constitutional rights in the first place. If the suit were filed by a United States citizen detained in Guantánamo, this would not be much of an issue because American citizens enjoy the protection of the Bill of Rights no matter where they are held, whether it be Guantánamo or Yemen or maybe even Afghanistan or Iraq (though in the latter cases adjustments should be made for the needs of the battlefield). But what about the constitutional rights of aliens, like the petitioners in *Rasul*, who never resided in the United States and had no other connection to it?

Justice Stevens addressed this question only in the most incidental way. In a footnote (note 15 of the opinion) he lists five allegations that, if true, would render the detention of the prisoners before him, as he put it, "unquestionably" unconstitutional or otherwise a violation of the laws or treaties of the United States: (1) the prisoners were not enemy combatants; (2) they were imprisoned for more than two years; (3) they were held in a territory subject to the long-term, exclusive jurisdiction of

THE WAR ON TERROR AND THE RULE OF LAW

the United States; (4) they had no access to counsel; and (5) they were not charged with a crime.

The meaning of this footnote is not at all clear. Not surprisingly, when the case returned to the trial level, two judges in the District Court for the District of Columbia, each presiding over different proceedings, read it differently. One judge granted the government's motion to dismiss the habeas petitions, concluding that the prisoners' reliance on footnote 15 was "misplaced and unpersuasive."[31] According to this judge, the Supreme Court "did not concern itself with whether the petitioners had any independent constitutional rights."[32] He further concluded that based on prior doctrine the prisoners had no underlying constitutional rights. This meant that although the prisoners had a statutory right to file a habeas petition—they had the right to file a piece of paper—the legal proceeding was of no practical import.

The other district judge denied the government's motion to dismiss.[33] On her reading, footnote 15 established that the prisoners had the same constitutional rights that they would have had if they were being held in Charleston—not a right to have a federal court ascertain their status as enemy combatants, for even Hamdi did not have that right, but presumably a right to a hearing before some impartial tribunal with the assistance of counsel. On this interpretation, the prisoners in Guantánamo—nationals of Australia and Kuwait—would be given the same rights as Hamdi.

This latter reading of footnote 15 would move the law in the right direction, but even with this gloss the footnote remains troubling. First, it does no more than give the nationals of foreign countries a right to fair procedure to ascertain whether they are in fact enemy combatants; it does not afford them any of the substantive protections of the Constitution, including the right to freedom or any other rights embraced within the Bill of Rights, most notably the protection against cruel and unusual punishment. Second, this reading of footnote 15 makes location crucial, specifically, the fact that the prisoners are being detained in Guantánamo, which has been under the exclusive control of the United States for more than a century. The *Rasul* prisoners are granted some protection, but those who are being held abroad—in Yemen, not to mention countries we are occupying by force of our military power—could not claim the protection of the Constitution.

Sadly, this limitation in the law would mean that the prisoners abused and tortured by the U.S. military authorities in Iraq at the Abu Ghraib facility—fully disclosed to the world only weeks before the Supreme Court's decision in *Rasul*—could make no constitutional claims against the United States. In the months following this disclosure, Congress and the president apologized to the victims of torture at Abu Ghraib. The line officers immediately responsible for the torture have been disciplined. Victims of such abuse might even advance claims under various federal statutes.[34] But they cannot, within the terms of settled doctrine, claim that officials of the United States violated the basic law of the nation—and that, in my view, is most unfortunate. Although it was no part of the business of the Supreme Court in *Rasul* to address the abuses in Abu Ghraib—the Court left the law where it found it—those events throw into bold relief the limitations of what the *Rasul* Court did in fact decide.

Footnote 15 ends with a reference to *United States v. Verdugo-Urquidez*[35]—one of the defining Supreme Court decisions of the modern period, and one of the cases upon which the Court of Appeals placed significant weight. *United States v. Verdugo-Urquidez* was decided in 1990—more than a decade before the Bush administration launched its War on Terror and invaded Afghanistan and then Iraq. The immediate context was a war of another type—the War on Drugs. But Chief Justice Rehnquist, the author of the Court's opinion, also expressed an interest in freeing the executive from the shackles of the Bill of Rights in foreign military operations.[36] To that end, he denied the protection of the Fourth Amendment, and, perhaps, the entire Bill of Rights, to aliens living abroad.

René Martín Verdugo-Urquidez was a citizen of Mexico, and the alleged violation of his rights occurred in Mexico. Federal drug enforcement agents, working with Mexican officials, searched his home in Mexico without a warrant and in the course of those searches seized certain documents. Prior to the search, Verdugo-Urquidez had been arrested by Mexican authorities, transported to the Border Patrol station in Southern California, and then turned over to United States marshals. He was accused of being one of the leaders of an organization in Mexico that smuggled narcotics into the United States and was placed on trial in the United States for violating federal criminal statutes. In the course of the trial, Verdugo-Urquidez moved, on the basis of the Fourth Amendment, to exclude the evidence seized in the raid on his Mexican residence. The Supreme Court held that the Fourth Amendment does not apply to a search by United States agents of a residence that is located in a foreign country and owned by an alien who did not reside in the United States and who did not otherwise voluntarily attach himself to the national community.

On a purely technical level, the Court's ruling was presented as a construction of the phrase "the people" as it appears in the Fourth Amendment. The Fourth Amendment provides: "The right of the people to be secure in their persons, houses, papers, and effects, against unreasonable searches and seizures, shall not be violated, and no Warrants shall issue, but upon probable cause, supported by Oath or affirmation, and particularly describing the place to be searched, and the persons or things to be seized." Although the term "the people" seems to be of universal scope, permitting no distinction between citizens and aliens, Chief Justice Rehnquist construed the phrase as a term of art that embraced only (a) citizens and (b) those aliens who have developed a sufficient voluntary connection with the United States to be considered part of the national community. Granted, Verdugo-Urquidez was being imprisoned in the United States, and tried in federal court for violating federal statutes, but this was not sufficient for Rehnquist to place him within the scope of "the people" protected by the Fourth Amendment.

Justice William Brennan dissented. In his dissent, he convincingly showed that no evidence, either in the debates or in the general history surrounding the adoption of the Bill of Rights, indicates that the phrase "the people" in the Fourth Amendment was meant to delineate a class of beneficiaries who would be protected by the amendment. The phrase "the people" was not a term of art but rather, he insisted, merely a rhetorical device to underscore the importance of the protection being granted. Justice Brennan also advanced a more cosmopolitan view of the Constitution, according to which the actions of the United States would be governed by the Constitution no matter where or against whom the United States acts. Brennan acknowledged that the meaning of the Constitution may vary from context to context; what the Fourth Amendment ban on unreasonable searches means in a suburban community in the United States differs from what it means on the battlefield or, for that matter, in a country that we occupy by virtue of our military power. But the actions of American officials would, according to Justice Brennan, always and everywhere be judged by the standards of the Constitution.

To defend his cosmopolitanism, Justice Brennan relied on the principle of mutuality: "If we expect aliens to obey our laws, aliens should expect that we will obey our Constitution when we investigate, prosecute, and punish them."[37] Such a principle seems unable to encompass all that Justice Brennan wanted—he was explicit that the Fourth Amendment applies to military activities abroad (though in such cases he would drop the warrant requirement and test the government's action only by the reasonableness requirement, which is necessarily sensitive to context). The principle of mutuality also suffers from circularity, for the question is whether the government's action constitutes a violation of the Constitution. Justice Brennan may well be right in proclaiming that "lawlessness breeds lawlessness,"[38] but we cannot invoke that axiom to determine whether the government has acted lawlessly.

A more plausible account of Justice Brennan's cosmopolitanism, of great sway in the Warren Court era, identifies the nation with the Constitution and underscores the constitutive nature of that all-important law: the Constitution creates the structure of government and defines the limits of its authority.[39] The constitutive view of the relationship between the nation and the Constitution not only reflects how the founders understood their project but also, and perhaps more important, accords with the practice of constitutional adjudication over the last two hundred years. The doctrine of enumerated powers, the keystone of constitutional adjudication in the nineteenth century, was premised on the view that Congress had no authority other than that granted to it by the Constitution. In the twentieth century, the first question of constitutional adjudication shifted from whether the Constitution had granted the power to Congress to whether Congress or some other officer of the United States violated a particular constitutional prohibition. Still, it was assumed that the prohibitions on the government defined the outer limits of its authority and that, as a juridical entity, the government of the United States has no existence outside of the Constitution.[40]

The limits on government authority can be derived from the

terms upon which power was conferred on the new government, from certain prohibitions on the government contained in the body of the Constitution—notably Article IV—and, above all, from the amendments to the Constitution adopted in 1791, the Bill of Rights. For the cosmopolitan, the Bill of Rights is conceived not as a testamentary document distributing a species of property to specific and limited classes of persons but rather as a broad charter setting forth the norms that are to govern the operation of government. "No person shall be deprived of life, liberty, or property without due process of law." "Congress shall make no law respecting the establishment of religion, or prohibiting the free exercise thereof; or abridging the freedom of speech." "Cruel and unusual punishment shall not be inflicted." For the cosmopolitan, rights are not property belonging to particular people but are the concretization of these sweeping prohibitions of the Constitution.

This view of rights does not necessarily give the protections of the Constitution the universal scope that Justice Brennan desired. It still remains for the Court to apply the norm in some specific case, and that necessarily entails a process of interpretation. The history or wording of the norm may delimit its scope, and the context will also determine the content of the right. All that can be said is that this way of viewing rights—as norms, not property—more easily accommodates cosmopolitanism and is more conducive to that orientation. It makes it more difficult for a justice to claim, as Chief Justice Rehnquist did in *Verdugo-Urquidez*, that the Fourth Amendment affords protection only to citizens or those who voluntarily associate themselves with the national community. It renders the effort to limit the Bill of Rights in this way more implausible, and suggests that those limits are not based on a strict interpretation of the text but on more extraneous or political considerations, such as giving the executive the flexibility Chief Justice Rehnquist believes is necessary to conduct foreign affairs effectively.

Chief Justice Rehnquist ended his opinion in *Verdugo-Urquidez* by proclaiming, "For better or for worse, we live in a world of nation-states."[41] The importance of the nation-state cannot be denied, even today, in the face of ever-increasing globalization. The cosmopolitan view of the Constitution does not, however, deny the importance of the nation-state but offers an alternative and, in my view, more appealing way of understanding the relation between the Constitution and the nation. Of course, noncitizens do not vote, and thus are not politically empowered to demand that the government justify its actions to them. But that does not mean that the government owes them no duties, as is indeed clear from the treatment of noncitizens who are residents of the country. They too cannot vote but are protected by the Constitution. Similarly, although the government does not act in the name of noncitizens, those in whose name it does act—"we the people"—may demand that it proceed in a certain way whenever it acts and regardless of against whom it acts.[42] The key provisions of the Bill of Rights—including but in no way limited to the Fourth, Fifth, and Eighth Amendments—present themselves as universal prohibitions and, as such, may be read as an expression of the demands by the founding generation as to the way the government they were creating must act.

Everyone who resides in the United States, aliens and citizens alike, are expected to obey the laws of the United States, and can be called upon to lend support to the government, through, say, the payment of taxes and perhaps even serving in the military. Yet, as is evident from the rules regarding the rights of those who flout the law, and who we can assume are justly convicted of doing so, the protection of the Constitution is not in any way limited to those who obey the laws or otherwise support the government. The obligations imposed on the government by the Bill of Rights are not a quid pro quo offered to its subjects but the expression of principles of right behavior.[43]

Chief Justice Rehnquist and Justice Brennan occupied polar positions in *Verdugo-Urquidez*. Justices Scalia, Thomas, and O'Connor joined Chief Justice Rehnquist's opinion without comment. Justice Thurgood Marshall joined Justice Brennan's opinion in a similar fashion. The remaining three justices—John Paul Stevens, Harry Blackmun, and Anthony Kennedy—were arrayed between the poles. None of these three believed that only those persons who voluntarily affiliated themselves with the national community were protected by the Fourth Amendment. Justices Blackmun and Stevens stressed the fact that Verdugo-Urquidez had been placed on trial in the United States for violating its criminal laws, and, as a result, the Fourth Amendment was applicable. Justice Blackmun dissented because, although he agreed with Chief Justice Rehnquist that there was no need for a warrant to search the residence of an alien outside the country, he insisted that to be valid under the Fourth Amendment the search must be reasonable. Blackmun thought that the case should be remanded to the lower court to make the reasonableness determination. Justice Stevens, like Justice Blackmun, applied the reasonableness standard but on the record before him thought there was sufficient basis to conclude that the search of Verdugo-Urquidez's house was reasonable. He concurred in the judgment.

The position of Justice Kennedy—then a very recent appointee to the Court—is harder to characterize. He was the crucial fifth vote that Chief Justice Rehnquist needed to endow his opinion with the status of law, and Justice Kennedy obliged him. Justice Kennedy began his separate concurrence by announcing that he joined the chief justice's opinion. He also said that his views did not depart in "fundamental respects" from those expressed by the chief justice,[44] but one is left to wonder whether this was in fact the case. Although he rejected the view that the Fourth Amendment's warrant requirement should be applied to the search of a foreign home of a non-resident alien, his reason was quite different from Rehnquist's. He did not read the phrase "the people" as a restriction on the universe of persons protected. As he put it, "explicit recognition of 'the right of the people' to Fourth Amendment protection may be interpreted to underscore the importance of the right, rather than to restrict the category of persons who may assert it."[45] In contrast to Chief Justice Rehnquist, Justice Kennedy simply posited that adherence to the Fourth Amendment warrant requirement abroad would be "impracticable and anomalous."[46]

Even more important, Justice Kennedy seemed to give a certain measure of extraterritorial force to the Constitution. He began from the proposition that "it is correct . . . that the government may act only as the Constitution authorizes, whether the actions in question are foreign or domestic."[47] Yet, building on a view articulated by the second Justice John Harlan, he maintained that this does not require that the government necessarily apply each and every provision of the Constitution abroad. Rather, the constitutionality of the government's actions abroad should be judged by a flexible standard based on some notion of fundamental fairness. In conducting searches of the homes of noncitizens abroad the Constitution does not require federal agents to obtain a warrant, as the Fourth Amendment might be read to require, but only that noncitizens be treated fairly. Justice Brennan's constitution would also allow adjustments to be made as to how the Bill of Rights is applied abroad but, as with the doctrine of selective incorporation, always within the disciplining force of the text of the amendments themselves. Justice Kennedy's constitution is more flexible, and thus less clear. My hunch is that Justice Brennan's approach would yield results

more approximating justice than Justice Kennedy's, but both describe a constitution without borders.

Such a view of the Constitution makes an appearance in
*Rasul*, though in the most oblique way. When Justice Stevens
cited *Verdugo-Urquidez* in footnote 15 in *Rasul*, he referred only
to Justice Kennedy's concurring opinion in that case, not Chief
Justice Rehnquist's opinion for the Court. The significance of
that selective reference is not clear to me. Perhaps Justice Stevens meant to embrace Justice Kennedy's constitutional cosmopolitanism. Or, conceivably, the reference was offered as an
inducement for Justice Kennedy to join the majority opinion. As
it turned out, however, Justice Kennedy did not join Justice Stevens's opinion, but wrote a short separate concurrence. In it, he
applied the same flexible approach outlined in his concurrence in
*Verdugo-Urquidez*, again expressing unease with creating "auto-
matic" rules.

Like Justice Stevens, Justice Kennedy acknowledged the
unique status of Guantánamo—that for all practical purposes
it was a territory of the United States. Yet he refused to treat the
case as though it were nothing more than an exercise in statutory
interpretation. Justice Kennedy understood that the petitioners
had to have some constitutional rights in order for there to be
any point in the habeas proceeding at all. Although he cautioned
against judicial interference with the rightful prerogatives of the
president acting as commander in chief, Justice Kennedy recognized that "there are circumstances in which the courts maintain
the power and the responsibility to protect persons from unlawful detention even where military affairs are implicated." [48] The
touchstone for Justice Kennedy was "military necessity" [49]—
only exigencies of war would prevent the exercise of the judicial
power implicit in the writ of habeas corpus. He also believed
that the government's insistence on military necessity in the case
at hand was contradicted by the fact that prisoners were being

held indefinitely (justified by the government on the theory that they were illegal enemy combatants, comparable to members of irregular militias, and thus not entitled to the usual protections of the Third Geneva Convention for prisoners of war, including repatriation at the end of the hostilities). Justice Kennedy wrote, "[p]erhaps, where detainees are taken from a zone of hostilities, detention without proceedings or trial would be justified by military necessity for a matter of weeks; but as the period of detention stretches from months to years, the case for continued detention to meet military exigencies becomes weaker."[50] Such a flexible or variable approach has its pitfalls because it vests enormous discretionary power in the judiciary, but at least one can see within it the possibility of confronting on a constitutional basis possible government abuse of alien prisoners who are not American citizens, such as occurred at Abu Ghraib, provided of course that Justice Kennedy's insistence upon fundamental fairness is not conditioned upon the anomalous territorial status of Guantánamo.

No one else joined Justice Kennedy's opinion. The timidity of the majority in *Rasul*, as well as that of the majorities responsible for *Padilla* and *Hamdi*, is no accident but, rather, a product of the situation in which the justices found themselves. Faced with the events of September 11, and then the invasions of Afghanistan and Iraq and the military occupations of these countries, the demands for power by the president and his administration must have pressed heavily on the justices. Although the justices are committed to the rule of law and the protection of the Constitution, they also see themselves as responsible for protecting the interests of the nation they serve. The justices are practical people, so they searched for ways to honor the Constitution without compromising vital national interests. As a result, they told Jose Padilla to start over in another court, they provided Yaser Hamdi with an opportunity to contest the legality of his classification but made it possible for that hearing to be conducted by a military tribunal, and they allowed the prisoners in Guantánamo to begin habeas proceedings without telling them in any clear way what rights they might assert in those proceedings. What is missing from this calculus—and, in my judgment, from all three of these much-discussed cases—is a full appreciation of the value of the Constitution as a statement of the ideals of the nation and as the basis of the principle of freedom and, even more, a full appreciation of the fact that the wholehearted pursuit of any ideal requires sacrifices, sometimes quite substantial ones. It is hard for the justices—or, for that matter, anyone—to accept that we may have to risk the material well-being of the nation in order to be faithful to the Constitution and the duties it imposes. Still, it must be remembered that the issue is not just the survival of the nation—of course the United States will survive—but the terms of survival.

# Prologue to Chapter 3

Trevor Sutton

Minimalism is a theory of—or, since proponents of minimalism eschew theories, an approach to—judicial decision making according to which judges should decide cases on the most limited grounds available. Minimalism's most famous advocate, Professor Cass Sunstein, described minimalist judges as those who "seek to avoid broad rules and abstract theories, and attempt to focus their attention only on what is necessary to resolve particular disputes." Sunstein contrasts minimalism with the judicial philosophy of "those who seek to decide cases in a way that sets broad rules for the future and that also gives theoretical justifications for outcomes." Minimalist jurists are modest, Sunstein argues. They recognize that the risk of judicial error is substantial and grave, and strain to avoid foreclosing other decisions in other cases through overbroad rulings. The paradigmatic minimalist jurist, in Sunstein's view, is Justice Sandra Day O'Connor, although Sunstein also claims Justices Ruth Bader Ginsburg, David Souter, Stephen Breyer, and Anthony Kennedy as minimalists. Justice John Paul Stevens, whose opinions in *Rasul* and

*Hamdan* serve as the central examples of minimalism's dangers in the following essay, depended on all four of these jurists to form a majority.

Sunstein sees many advantages in a minimalist approach to jurisprudence, but the virtue he is most eager to emphasize is minimalism's "close connection" with democracy. Minimalist judges promote democratic values, Sunstein argues, by confining their legal analysis to the unique features of the case before them, thereby reserving larger questions for the political branches. In Sunstein's view, broad rulings, even when they are correct, run the risk of short-circuiting "the kind of evolution, adaptation, and argumentative give-and-take that tend to accompany lasting social reform." Minimalism, by contrast, "requires the legislature to make crucial judgments" by "spurring processes of democratic deliberation." Many of the examples Sunstein gives in his minimalist opus, *One Case at a Time*, involve judges applying narrow constitutional principles to fact-specific inquiries. But sometimes the imperatives of minimalism can lead jurists to shun a constitutional resolution in any form and dispose of a case on purely statutory grounds. Although Owen Fiss's belief in the principle of freedom, examined in several essays in this volume, stands in opposition to both of these forms of minimalism, it is the second, statute-focused variety at which "The Perils of Minimalism" takes special aim.

This chapter, "The Perils of Minimalism," was first presented as a lecture at Tel Aviv University in 2008, and was later published in *Theoretical Inquiries in Law*. Both versions were prepared after the Supreme Court's decision in *Hamdan v. Rumsfeld* and Congress's enactment of the Military Commissions Act of 2006 in response to that decision, but before the Court ruled in *Boumediene v. Bush* that foreign nationals detained at Guantánamo had a constitutional right to seek habeas corpus. Although *Boumediene*, perhaps to an even greater degree than *Hamdi*, was heralded as a powerful victory for constitutional principles, with the benefit of hindsight it is possible to recognize the deficiencies of the decision. To begin with, access to habeas has had little practical effect on the Guantánamo detainees' quest for freedom, in large part because of the lack of clarity surrounding the scope of habeas review and the general skepticism of the judges of the District of Columbia Circuit toward detainee claims. In addition, the multivariate test devised by Justice Kennedy to determine the availability of habeas has created significant uncertainty, specifically with regard to the writ's availability in Bagram prison in Afghanistan. Moreover, although *Boumediene*, unlike *Hamdan*, dared to make a constitutional pronouncement, it nevertheless also may be regarded as a minimalist opinion, for it sought to resolve only the less controversial of the two issues examined in *Hamdan* (habeas), and through its silence perpetuated the implicit premise of *Hamdan* that military commissions are not constitutionally defective.

Guantánamo remains open in 2015, and the use of military commissions to try alleged terrorists continues under President Obama despite his campaign promise to close the prison and his aborted efforts to try some high-profile detainees in civilian courts. That this state of affairs persists despite more than a decade of litigation and several Supreme Court decisions celebrated as "landmark" civil liberties victories owes much to the Supreme Court's preference for the passive virtues of minimalism at the expense of a full recognition of its responsibility to nourish and protect the Constitution.

# Chapter 3

# THE PERILS OF MINIMALISM

Cuba is an island 112 miles off the coast of Florida. The United States freed it of Spanish dominion in the Spanish-American War of 1898 but did not take possession of Cuba as spoils of war. Rather, it contented itself with a 45-square-mile area on the southeastern corner of the island, known as Guantánamo Bay, which has been an American naval station ever since.

As a purely formal matter, the United States occupies Guantánamo under a lease, which was first executed in 1903 and modified in 1934. The lease reserves "ultimate sovereignty" in Cuba, but it has no term. The United States possesses the unilateral power to terminate the lease, and has occupied and maintained exclusive control of the territory for more than a century.

Each year the United States tenders the rent—approximately $4,000—but for decades, the Castro government has refused to accept it. The Guantánamo Naval Station has its own residences and stores, some of which are well-known American franchises, and it is separated from the rest of Cuba by an extensive fencing system. There is no exchange between the rest of the island and the U.S.-run naval station, with the exception of a handful

72

of elderly Cuban employees. Cuban law, such as it is, does not reach Guantánamo.

In January 2002, as the initial phase of the war in Afghanistan still raged, the Bush administration decided to open a prison in Guantánamo, and it has interned hundreds of men there who were captured in that war. Over the years, it has been used to detain al-Qaeda suspects seized in a wide number of countries—including Bosnia, Thailand, and Zambia—but Guantánamo remains first and foremost a prison for men captured in Afghanistan or near the border in Pakistan. None of the Guantánamo prisoners is an American citizen. At its height, between six hundred and eight hundred men were imprisoned at Guantánamo.

The United States invaded Afghanistan in October 2001 and ousted the Taliban in less than six months. Under the oversight of the United States and its allies, by the end of 2004 the Afghan people adopted a constitution and held democratic elections. At that point, the war in Afghanistan appeared at an end. Even though there is a growing insurgency in parts of that country, all claims of military exigency that might have justified the initial detention policy at Guantánamo today seem stale. It is important to remember, however, that the United States invaded Afghanistan not simply to oust the Taliban regime for supporting and protecting al-Qaeda but also, and perhaps more important, to vanquish al-Qaeda itself. This objective has not been achieved, and it is this larger conflict between al-Qaeda and the United States that has been used to justify the continuing detention of the Guantánamo prisoners.

The basic constitutional question posed by Guantánamo is whether the prisoners held there have any constitutional rights that might be protected by the courts and, if so, what those rights might be. This may not seem much of a question in many democracies throughout the world, including Israel, because they view their constitutions in universalistic terms. The guarantee of human dignity, for example, controls the actions of Israeli officers wherever they act and against whomever they act.[1] The U.S. Supreme Court moved toward such a cosmopolitan conception of the U.S. Constitution during the Warren Court era, but starting in 1990 it headed in a different direction.

The issue arose in a case involving a search of the home—in Mexico—of a Mexican citizen who had been seized—also in Mexico—by agents of the United States and who was then taken for trial to the United States.[2] The search had been conducted by American officials and was challenged as a violation of the Fourth Amendment. Chief Justice William Rehnquist, purporting to speak for a majority, wrote an opinion that espoused a more nationalist conception of the Constitution. According to him, the Constitution protected American citizens from the actions of U.S. officials no matter where they were located. It also protected foreign nationals when they were living in the United States and were part of the American political community, but the Constitution, reasoned Rehnquist, afforded no protection to foreign nationals abroad. The Bush administration's decision to transform Guantánamo into a prison rests on the assumption that it, like Mexico, is not part of the United States and that the prisoners, since they are all aliens, cannot claim the protection of the Constitution and the various legal procedures, such as habeas corpus, that could secure that protection.

For their part, the Guantánamo prisoners and their lawyers challenged the legality of their detention and thus contested the scope and force of Rehnquist's 1990 ruling. Rehnquist had emphasized the special wording of the Fourth Amendment, which speaks of "the right of the people," and thus it was not at all clear that the 1990 case applied to provisions such as the Due Process Clause of the Fifth Amendment, which protects the life, liberty, and property of "any person." A question could also be raised as to whether Rehnquist's opinion had the backing of a majority and thus governed. The crucial fifth vote came from Justice Anthony Kennedy, then a recent appointee, who said that he joined Rehnquist's opinion, but then went on to express the view that "the Government may act only as the Constitution authorizes, whether the actions in question are foreign or domestic."[3] He implied that the government might be obliged to respect certain basic rights even when acting overseas, though constitutional norms would have to be adjusted to take account of the different contexts. Kennedy thought the phrase "the right of the people" appearing in the Fourth Amendment was not a term of limitation but more a rhetorical flourish to emphasize the rights being conferred.

On two separate occasions, once in June 2004 and then again in June 2006, the Supreme Court addressed the claims of the Guantánamo prisoners. Both decisions rebuffed the Bush administration and received banner headlines in the press. Such results were indeed remarkable because a majority of the justices seemed to cut through a tradition in American history of judicial deference to the executive on military matters. Yet, on closer inspection, these victories for the Guantánamo prisoners were less momentous than they first appeared. Rather than resolving the basic constitutional claims of the prisoners, the Court based these decisions entirely on statutory grounds.

In fashioning the opinions in this way, Justice Stevens, who wrote for the Court in both instances, seemed to be pursuing a methodology—widely referred to as minimalism—that has gained currency in recent years in some corners of the liberal establishment in the United States.[4] One tenet of minimalism directs the judiciary to resolve cases on statutory grounds if at all possible, and to turn to the constitutional issues only if necessary. Those who defend this method of decision making argue that minimalism lets judges reduce the potential costs of wrong decisions. Constitutional decisions are for all time, the apostles of minimalism note, while a statutory interpretation can easily be corrected. Perhaps more important, minimalists also say that relying on statutory grounds encourages—nay, requires—the president to work with Congress to further his objectives, thereby promoting the democratic values of the nation.

To the surprise of no one, after each of the Court's decisions the Bush administration turned to Congress and quickly obtained the necessary legislative warrant for its detention program in Guantánamo. As a consequence, Congress became a full partner of the president in this front of the War on Terror. This turn of events has led me to ponder the wisdom of minimalism as a decisional strategy.

Part of my concern with minimalism is specific to the Guantánamo detainees. For years on end, they have been unable to obtain a satisfactory response to their constitutional claims. Their continued imprisonment has been the subject of a series of judicial rulings and congressional enactments, and the Court's initial decisions, couched in statutory terms that virtually invited legislative intervention, made it more difficult—not impossible, but considerably more difficult—for the Court to reach a satisfactory resolution of the ultimate constitutional issues. In this respect, the decision to proceed in two steps, as minimalism dictates, already has had enormous costs, even if the Court eventually affords the detainees all that the Constitution promises.

My concern, however, is not confined to the Guantánamo prisoners and their hardships. Minimalism can be faulted not just for the hardship it imposed upon the prisoners and government institutions but also because it is based on two theoretical misunderstandings. One relates to the Court's function. To my eyes, the Court sits not to resolve the dispute before it, which may leave the Court free to choose the narrowest ground that would serve that purpose, but rather to nourish and protect the basic values of the Constitution. The duty of the Court is to act—not minimally nor even maximally but responsibly—so as to be mindful of its role within the political system as the guardian of the Constitution.

A second failing of minimalism arises from its supposition of a necessary antagonism between constitutional pronouncements and democratic values. I maintain that democracy should not be understood as simple majoritarianism ("let the political branches have their say") but as a deep and broad-based deliberative process in which we—all of us—give content to the values that define us as a nation. Constitutional pronouncements by the Court do not prevent or even stifle such deliberations but give them a certain vitality by fully revealing the threat that is posed to our basic commitments.

## The Practice of Minimalism

One of the fundamental tenets of the U.S. Constitution is the principle of freedom. It denies the government the authority to imprison anyone unless that person is charged with a crime and swiftly brought to trial. An exception is allowed for enemy combatants seized on the battlefield. The Bush administration invoked this exception to incarcerate the Guantánamo prisoners and to hold them without criminal charges. Some prisoners claimed, however, that their imprisonment was mistaken—that they were not, in fact, soldiers of the Taliban or al-Qaeda—and sought a writ of habeas corpus in federal court in Washington, D.C., to press their claim.

The writ of habeas corpus has both a statutory and a constitutional basis. Article I, Section 9, of the U.S. Constitution identifies the terms under which habeas corpus may be suspended, and by regulating the suspension and thus presupposing its availability, it gives some measure of constitutional protection to the writ. On top of that, a federal statute specifically grants federal courts jurisdiction to issue the writ of habeas corpus.[5] In the first Guantánamo case to reach the Supreme Court—the 2004 decision in *Rasul v. Bush*[6]—the Supreme Court put the constitutional issues aside and held only that the prisoners could utilize the federal statute to adjudicate their claim to freedom. The Court did not decide the merits of the prisoners' claim to freedom, only that the federal district court had, as a matter of statutory interpretation, jurisdiction to hear that claim as long as the prisoners' custodian—the secretary of defense—was within reach of the court.

In analyzing the case in this way, Justice Stevens failed to engage the major premise that was the cornerstone of the government's argument and that had been sustained by the Court of Appeals. Relying on Rehnquist's ruling in the 1990 Mexican case, the government argued that habeas was not available because the prisoners do not possess any substantive constitutional rights that might be vindicated by the writ. They are aliens, and although aliens residing in this country may enjoy the same constitutional rights as American citizens, this cannot be said of the Guantánamo prisoners, who have no independent ties to the political community and are imprisoned abroad. Accepting the government's argument, the Court of Appeals ruled, "We cannot see why, or how, the writ may be made available to aliens abroad when basic constitutional rights are not."[7]

To his credit, Justice Stevens emphasized in his opinion in *Rasul* the special, somewhat anomalous, status of Guantánamo. Although it is not part of the United States as that term is ordinarily used, it has been under the exclusive control and authority of the United States for more than a century. Justice Stevens also listed in a single footnote, note 15, the essential claims of the prisoners—that they are not enemy combatants and have been held incommunicado for some time without being charged with a crime—and concluded by noting that if these allegations were proved true, their incarceration would be unlawful. However, Justice Stevens did not otherwise address the constitutional premise underlying the argument of the government and the decision of the lower court.

In July 2004, immediately after the *Rasul* decision, the Bush administration established a process in Guantánamo to address the claims of those prisoners who denied that they were enemy combatants.[8] Under the scheme then established, these claims are to be resolved by tribunals, referred to as Combatant Status Review Tribunals, that are staffed entirely by military officers appointed by the secretary of the navy and are governed by regulations issued by him. According to these regulations, prisoners are allowed to have only military officers with security clearance represent them in proceedings, not lawyers. The tribunals are not bound by the rules of evidence such as would apply in a court of law, and are permitted to consider any evidence—including, presumably, hearsay and the product of coercive interrogation—that the presiding officer deems relevant. The decisions are to be reviewed by a designate of the secretary of the navy. Each year, a separate military panel examines the need for continued detention of persons previously found to be enemy combatants. These decisions are, in turn, reviewed by a civilian official designated by the secretary.

The roots of this procedure can be traced to another decision handed down on the same day as *Rasul*: *Hamdi v. Rumsfeld*.[9] This case involved an American citizen who was captured in Afghanistan and held in a naval brig in South Carolina. The government accused him of being a soldier of the Taliban, even though he denied having taken up arms against the United States and claimed that he had been in Afghanistan for personal reasons. He insisted that the internal executive procedures used by the Bush administration to determine that he was an enemy combatant were insufficient under the Constitution.

Justice O'Connor announced the opinion of the Court. In it, she granted the prisoner, as a matter of due process, an evidentiary hearing on his claim to freedom. She also declared that the prisoner was entitled to access to counsel. She added, however, that the tribunal need not abide by the stringent evidentiary requirements of a federal trial. In that vein, she held that the government could rely on field records to create a presumption of lawfulness of the detentions and that the burden would be on the prisoners to rebut the presumption. Even more, O'Connor said that military tribunals might be used to hear these claims of freedom. Justice Souter, joined by Justice Ginsburg, whose votes were needed to give O'Connor's opinion majority status, refused to endorse the use of military tribunals as a substitute for habeas corpus.

Following *Hamdi*, it was unclear where the claims of freedom of American citizens held as enemy combatants might be adjudicated. Would only a federal court under a writ of habeas corpus be acceptable or would a military tribunal suffice? Despite this uncertainty, the Bush administration quickly acted on the assumption that a military tribunal was acceptable for the Guantánamo prisoners—all of whom are aliens. Indeed, since not a word in *Rasul* required the procedural apparatus that the military established in Guantánamo in July 2004, the Bush administration's decision to set up Combatant Status Review Tribunals there might be seen as a preemptive strike against the efforts of the Guantánamo prisoners to obtain access to federal habeas corpus.

At the same time that it established these tribunals, the Bush administration turned to Congress to explicitly foreclose the habeas remedy. Since the *Rasul* decision held that the jurisdictional requirements of the habeas statute could be satisfied if the custodians of the prisoners were within the reach of the district court, it was, of course, within the power of Congress to amend the statute to deny a habeas remedy to the Guantánamo prisoners. Congress exercised this power in the Detainee Treatment Act of

2005, which amended the habeas corpus statute to provide that no court shall have jurisdiction to hear "an application for a writ of habeas corpus filed by or on behalf of an alien detained by the Department of Defense at Guantánamo Bay, Cuba." [10]

The statute also gave the Court of Appeals for the District of Columbia exclusive jurisdiction to review the decisions of the Combatant Status Review Tribunals and any military commissions that might be established to try the prisoners for war crimes. Appellate review was limited to whether the tribunal had complied with the standards and procedures established by the secretary of defense, and whether those standards and procedures were consistent with the Constitution—provided, the statute was quick to add, the Constitution was applicable to such proceedings. In addition to that restrictive language, almost out of an abundance of caution, the statute declared that it should not be construed as conferring any constitutional rights on aliens detained as enemy combatants in Guantánamo.

The Supreme Court's first encounter with the Detainee Treatment Act of 2005 occurred in its June 2006 decision in *Hamdan v. Rumsfeld*.[11] At issue in that case was not so much the principle of freedom, which had been central to *Rasul*, but the requirement, also rooted in the Due Process Clause, of procedural fairness. The Court was asked whether a prisoner—in this instance, Salim Ahmed Hamdan, who was alleged to have been Osama bin Laden's bodyguard and personal driver—could be tried for war crimes by a military commission specifically established for that purpose by the president.

To stop his trial before the military commission, Hamdan had sought a writ of habeas corpus. He filed this petition before the enactment of the Detainee Treatment Act, but, as it turned out, his habeas petition was pending in the Supreme Court at the time the statute was enacted. The first question the Supreme Court had to consider, therefore, was whether the bar on habeas corpus in the statute prevented the Court from reaching the merits of the prisoner's claim.

Justice Stevens responded to this question by subtly parsing the statutory language. The Detainee Treatment Act stated that its prohibition on the issuance of habeas writs by federal courts "shall take effect on the date of enactment." [12] It also contained another, separate provision expressly stating that the rule granting the Court of Appeals for the District of Columbia Circuit exclusive jurisdiction to review final decisions of the Combatant Status Review Tribunals or military commissions should be applicable to cases pending on the date of enactment. [13] Stevens relied on this second provision relating to appellate review by the Court of Appeals, unmistakably applicable to pending cases, to infer that Congress had not intended the act's general bar on granting habeas relief to Guantánamo prisoners to apply to pending cases such as Hamdan's. [14]

The minimalism of *Hamdan* was also manifest in the way the Supreme Court ruled on the merits of the claim challenging the use of military commissions to try some of the Guantánamo prisoners for war crimes. Justice Stevens fully understood the highly irregular and exceptional nature of military commissions. They are tribunals of exigency, which should be used, in his terms, to punish an "act for which [the accused] was caught red-handed in a theater of war and which military efficiency demands be tried expeditiously." Stevens also noted that Hamdan's case did not fit this model because the Guantánamo prison was not in a theater of war and because three years had lapsed between Hamdan's capture and the filing of formal charges. These discrepancies led Justice Stevens to express the fear that for Hamdan and the other Guantánamo prisoners about to be tried, a military commission had been transformed "from a tribunal of true exigency into a more convenient adjudicatory tool." Yet, in the end, Stevens did not turn these sentiments into a principle of higher law. As minimalism dictates, he declared that the use of military commissions in Guantánamo was not authorized by statute and further that the circumstances that might allow the president, acting as commander in chief, to establish military commissions on his own—the need to establish swift and immediate justice in an active theater of war—were not present.

The most plausible source of authority for the establishment of the commissions is Article 21 of the Uniform Code of Military Justice (UCMJ), which provides that the granting of jurisdiction for courts-martial should not be construed as depriving military commissions of jurisdiction "that by statute or by the law of war, may be tried by military commissions." [15] Yet, for Justice Stevens, Article 21 did not authorize the use of military commissions but merely preserved those independently authorized by either statute or the law of war. Stevens found no other statute authorizing the use of military commissions to try the Guantánamo prisoners.

Stevens did not preclude the possibility that the president might under certain circumstances establish on his own military commissions to try war crimes. But Stevens tightly limited such an exercise of authority to "military necessity"—that is, to situations where a soldier commits a war crime in a theater of active combat, is caught red-handed, and must immediately be tried as a way of controlling the future course of ongoing military operations. Such a view of the limited jurisdiction of presidentially convened military commissions would make the use of such commissions in Guantánamo odd, particularly with respect to Hamdan, who was arrested in 2001 and not charged until 2004. Speaking more generally, Stevens concluded that conspiracy to commit a war crime (the charge against Hamdan) was not itself a war crime cognizable by the military commission established by the president on his own.

Justice Stevens not only complained of the absence of statutory authority for the Guantánamo commissions and the failure to meet the stringent conditions that allowed the president to act on his own. He also found that the procedures to be used by the Guantánamo commissions violated the requirement of Article 36 of the UCMJ that the procedures of courts-martial and military commissions be "uniform insofar as practicable." [16] In reaching this conclusion, he placed special emphasis on the fact that before a commission the accused may be excluded from the proceeding or denied access to the information used against him under a broader range of circumstances than courts-martial would allow. Justice Stevens also observed that the rules of evidence of the Guantánamo commissions were much less stringent than those of courts-martial. Before a commission, prosecutors could introduce evidence that the presiding judge deemed to "have probative value to a reasonable person," [17] a standard that seems to render admissible hearsay evidence and even evidence obtained by coercion. In addition, those convicted by a Guantánamo commission have no right to appeal to a civilian court unless they face capital punishment or imprisonment for more than ten years. However, rather than condemn these rules as a violation of the duty, rooted in the Due Process Clause, to provide fair procedures, Justice Stevens, guided by the principles of minimalism, held only that they violated the uniformity requirement of Article 36 of the UCMJ.

As an alternative ground for condemning the procedures of the Guantánamo commissions, Justice Stevens cited Article 3 of the Fourth Geneva Convention of 1949. That article, common to all of the Geneva Conventions, prohibits the execution or imposition of sentences "without previous judgment pronounced by a regularly constituted court affording all the judicial guarantees which are recognized as indispensable by civilized peoples." [18] According to Stevens, absent any pragmatic considerations that would warrant departure from court-martial practice, a military commission set up to try a particular person or group of persons, such as the Guantánamo detainees, is not a "regularly constituted tribunal" within the meaning of Article 3. Justice Stevens also condemned the procedural rules to be used by Bush's commissions that permitted the exclusion of the accused from the trial and the denial of access to evidence against him as inconsistent with the language in Article 3 requiring that the tribunal imposing sentence afford "all the judicial guarantees recognized as indispensable by civilized people." To support this conclusion, Stevens cited Article 75 of Protocol 1 of the Geneva Convention of 1949, which affirmed the right to be tried in one's presence. Stevens did, however, soften his condemnation of this procedural feature of the Guantánamo commissions by noting that it lacked statutory endorsement. In so doing, he suggested that he might acquiesce in the exclusion of the accused from trial if that exclusion was authorized by statute.

Justice Kennedy had some qualms with Stevens's analysis of these procedural issues. He respected what he called the "right of presence" but thought that the trial would have to unfold before the Court could determine whether there was any significant discrepancy between the commissions' procedures and those of courts-martial. Kennedy was also unwilling to ground the right to presence on Protocol 1 of the Geneva Convention, since the United States has refused to ratify it. In this way, Kennedy deprived another portion of Stevens's opinion—in this instance, the reference to the Geneva Convention—of majority status.

In other respects, however, Kennedy agreed with the thrust of Steven's analysis. He was of the view that the establishment of the military commissions at Guantánamo were not authorized by Congress and in fact departed in important ways from the systems of courts-martial established by Congress in the UCMJ. In identifying these departures, Kennedy stressed the structural aspects of the arrangement, such as the way the membership of the commission was composed. These departures had two consequences for Kennedy. First, they meant that the commissions could not be considered regularly constituted courts as required by the law of war (referred to in Article 21), and second, that the uniformity requirement of Article 36 was violated. Much in the spirit of Stevens, Kennedy was prepared to allow the president some slack, provided military necessity required it, but he concluded that there was no justification for such departures in this instance. Kennedy joined the crucial portions of Stevens's opinion; Ginsburg and Breyer, who had joined Stevens's opinion, also largely embraced Kennedy's opinion.

Not too much should be read into Stevens's use of the Geneva Convention, even standing by itself, as many commentators have done.[19] It did not represent a departure from the minimalist premises undergirding his opinion. Although Stevens ruled that the Fourth Geneva Convention was applicable to the conflict between the United States and al-Qaeda, he assumed that the convention was not, by itself, judicially enforceable. The relevance of the convention stemmed only from the fact that Article 21 of the UCMJ, the savings clause, conditions the use of military commissions on compliance with the law of war, which of course includes the Geneva Conventions. What rendered the procedures of Guantánamo commissions illegal for Stevens was not Article 3 common to all of the Geneva Conventions but rather Article 21 of the UCMJ.

In *Rasul*, the Court rejected an argument of the government (about the interpretation of the federal habeas statute). In *Hamdan*, the Court went a step further and impinged more sharply on the exercise of executive power. It set aside the order of the president establishing the Guantánamo military commissions on the ground that the president lacked the necessary authority for issuing such an order and that it conflicted with an existing statutory command that required the procedures of military commissions to conform, unless otherwise impracticable, to those of courts-martial. Implicit in this ruling was a constitutional judgment about the allocation of powers between the president and Congress. Although the Court did not altogether deny the president the power to establish military commissions, it strictly confined the circumstances when the president might act unilaterally and further ruled that when the president's order conflicts with a statute of Congress the congressional rule will prevail. In a sense, then, the Court made a constitutional judgment.

Yet the constitutional character of that judgment must be distinguished from a constitutional judgment that would have deemed the use of a military commission to try Hamdan a violation of due process. Although the judgment allocating power among the branches implicit in the *Hamdan* decision confers some constitutional protection on the Guantánamo prisoners, they receive that protection in only an indirect way—as though they are third-party beneficiaries of a constitutional rule allocating powers between Congress and the president. On the other hand, a due process judgment predicated on the unfairness of using military commissions the way Bush contemplated their use would make the Guantánamo prisoners direct beneficiaries of the Bill of Rights.

On the day that *Hamdan* was handed down, legislation was introduced in the Senate to respond to the decision. On October 17, 2006, only four months later, though just weeks before the midterm elections, Congress passed the Military Commissions Act (MCA) of 2006. One provision of the MCA reiterated the ban on habeas corpus and made it applicable "to all cases, without exception, pending on or after the date of enactment." [20] A second feature of the act amended Article 21 of the UCMJ in order to fully authorize the use of military commissions to try the Guantánamo prisoners. It listed the offenses that can be tried before military commissions; the list included conspiracy to violate the laws of war. The MCA promulgated a code of procedure that departed from the procedural rules used by courts-martial and that, with only some qualifications,[21] conformed to the procedural code initially prescribed by the Bush administration. Finally, the MCA removed the Geneva Convention as a bar of any sort to the president's plan. It declared that the military commissions the president established were consistent with Article 3 of the Geneva Conventions; gave the president the authority to interpret the conventions; and denied that the conventions were judicially enforceable against the United States. The Bush administration welcomed this grant of power, and a number of the Guantánamo prisoners have been placed on trial before military commissions.

In February 2007, the Court of Appeals—the very same court that had made the initial decision in *Rasul*—ruled on the legality of the Military Commissions Act of 2006. The Court of Appeals first held that, as a matter of statutory interpretation, the very same habeas petitions considered in *Rasul* and then again in *Hamdan* were now clearly and unmistakably barred by the MCA.[22] As the Court said, "it is almost as if the proponents of [the statute] were slamming their fists on the table, shouting 'when we say all, we mean all—without exception!' "[23] The Court of Appeals then went on to consider the charge that the statute was unconstitutional as an improper suspension of the writ of habeas corpus. On this question, the Court of Appeals, displaying none of the reticence of the Supreme Court, reiterated the position it had taken earlier: aliens imprisoned at Guantánamo did not enjoy any constitutional rights and thus there could be no objection to denying them access to habeas corpus.

The Court of Appeals was mindful of the anomalous status of Guantánamo as a territory over which the United States has exercised long-term, exclusive jurisdiction and control. Yet it concluded that de facto sovereignty was not sufficient. The Court of Appeals held that for constitutional purposes Guantánamo should be viewed much as we would view a foreign country, not like one of the states or a territory such as Puerto Rico. By way of support for this proposition, the Court of Appeals pointed to the legislative determination in the Detainee Treatment Act of 2005 that "the United States, when used in a geographic sense . . . does not include the United States Naval Station at Guantánamo Bay, Cuba." [24]

Lawyers for the prisoners sought review of the Court of Appeals' decision. In April 2007 the Supreme Court denied certiorari. The lawyers persisted, however, and filed a motion for a rehearing. In their response to the government's memorandum and opposition to that motion, they attached an affidavit of a lawyer who, as an army reserve intelligence officer, had served on a Combatant Status Review Tribunal at Guantánamo. This affidavit described the lawyer's experience on the tribunal and pointed to its gross procedural deficiencies. In June 2007, much to the surprise of Court watchers, the Court reversed itself.[25] It granted the motion for rehearing and the writ of certiorari. In so doing, the Court provided for itself yet a third opportunity to resolve the central question—do the Guantánamo prisoners have any constitutional rights that might be protected by a writ of habeas corpus and, if so, what might they be?—that it had avoided in 2004 and again in 2006.

## The Court as the Guardian of the Constitution

The Guantánamo prison was first opened to serve the War on Terror in January 2002. In its 2004 and 2006 decisions, the Court acknowledged that the prisoners had access to habeas corpus but refused to ground its decisions on any constitutional basis. The Court simply held that habeas jurisdiction was established by statute. The 2006 decision also relied on statutory ground in order to set aside Bush's order establishing military commissions to try Guantánamo prisoners. The Court declined to address the obvious due process objection to the use of military commissions to try persons who had been in prison for as much as four years, and far beyond any theater of armed combat. We can readily see the costs of such minimalist decisions: the cycles of litigation, the hardship on the prisoners during this period, and the resources consumed by the judicial and legislative branches. But what has been gained?

In a separate and very short concurrence in the 2006 *Hamdan* decision, Justice Breyer pointed to a possible answer. Stressing the limited nature of the Court's decision, he said that the Court had done no more than declare that Congress had failed to grant the president the authority to create the kind of commission at issue in the case, and in fact seemed to deny that authority. "Nothing," Breyer continued, "prevents the President from returning to Congress to seek the authority he believes necessary." [26] Then, to justify the value of that exercise, Breyer invoked the theme that had been made prominent by the proponents of minimalism and in much of Breyer's extrajudicial writing: democracy. [27] Judicial insistence that the president turn to Congress and gain its assent would further the democratic purposes of the Constitution.

Such a view ignores the specific democratic system—a presidential one—established by the U.S. Constitution. In a presidential system, there are two mandates from the electorate, one for the president and another for the legislature. Of course, when a measure is endorsed by both the president and the legislature, both mandates are being honored. But to insist on the priority of the decision of the legislature when it conflicts with that of the president or to require congressional authorization to use military commissions is to ignore a distinctive feature of the presidential claim to authority, one that might, seen objectively, give it priority, especially in the context of war: the president speaks for the nation as a whole. Although the members of Congress can also speak for the nation, they are elected by districts or states and are necessarily responsive to their local constituencies.

Granted, there may be offsetting democratic advantages of the legislative branch. For example, it may be easier for electors to hold individual members of Congress accountable than it is to hold the president accountable. The multitude of representatives in Congress may also make public deliberation more common, though hardly a strong institutional practice, as anyone knows who has witnessed on late-night TV many a legislator making a speech to an almost empty chamber. Account must be taken of the (promised) deliberative character of the legislative process and the ways it facilitates accountability, but the distinct electoral mandate of the president or his claim to democratic authority should not be ignored.

Even more fundamentally, it would be wrong to assume, as the proponents of minimalism do, that the democratic values of the Constitution are furthered by simply enhancing the power of Congress or of the president because of their political character. Democracy is not majoritarianism. Increasing the power of the political branches may enlarge the opportunities for the majority to exercise its will, but it does not ensure that this exercise of will is based on a consideration of all the interests affected or will entail the kind of reflection that makes such exercises of will worthy of our respect. Maybe nothing can ensure such reflection, but a robust use of the judicial power—a strong and unqualified statement of constitutional principle—often provides the foundation for such reflection and in so doing enhances the deliberative character of the majority's decision.

The Constitution vests enormous power in elected officials and requires periodic elections. It also enshrines certain basic values—free speech, religious liberty, racial equality, due process—that have long been the source of America's identity and inner cohesion. All the branches of government, including the elected ones, have the right and responsibility to interpret these values, but the Supreme Court has a special responsibility in this domain and thus might properly be considered the guardian of the Constitution. The Court is expected to protect the values of the Constitution from transient majorities and the officials who serve them, although the Court is always subject to the checks inherent in the amendment process; regulations governing the jurisdiction of the federal judiciary; loud and forceful expressions of popular and professional disapproval; and the appointments process. The Court stands above politics but is always inextricably tied to it.

The authority of the Court to set aside ordinary congressional enactments or executive decrees because they conflict with basic values does not presuppose that those who happen to be judges possess any moral expertise. Nor does it assume that the justices are the representatives of the disenfranchised, such as the foreign nationals imprisoned in Guantánamo. Rather, their claim of authority stems from the simple fact that all exercises of the power by judges are bounded by the strictures of public reason. Judges must listen to grievances they might otherwise wish to ignore, hear from all affected parties, and then give a principled response to the grievances before them.

Judges exercise their power within the context of a dispute, but we should not confuse the context in which a power is exercised with the social purposes served by the exercise of that power. The requirement that the Court exercise its power within the context of a concrete dispute is primarily based on instrumental considerations. It seeks to ensure that the Court, situated in an adversarial system and therefore dependent on it, be given a full presentation of the facts and the law. The purpose of the Court is not, however, to resolve the dispute before it but to give, through the reason of the law, concrete meaning and expression to the values of the Constitution.

The need for the Court to defend the Constitution in this way is always great, but it is even greater in times of war, especially when the war is so amorphous and ill defined and generates as much fear as a war against terrorism, where the enemy is invisible and threatens to strike at home. In the midst of such a war, fears are likely to be great, and a small group of outsiders—the prisoners in Guantánamo—can easily be made to shoulder the burden of our self-protective instincts. They are accused of being the agents of our enemy and are conveniently isolated on a distant island. In such a setting, I maintain, robust use of the judicial power—one that projects a clear, unqualified view of the requirements of the Constitution—will further, not diminish, public deliberation and thus democratic values. Such a use of the judicial power does not preclude further action by the political branches but sets the limits of that action and thus provides the framework for their continued deliberations.

Proponents of minimalism may well acknowledge the danger to our liberties from the coordinated actions of the legislative and executive branches but then seek refuge in what may be described as a two-step process—in the words of the manifesto of minimalism, *One Case at a Time*.[28] Minimalism's defenders stress that a decision grounded in a conflict with a statute does not preclude the Court from later striking down a congressional revision of that statute if the Court determines that the revision violates the Constitution. Yet those who have defended the Supreme Court's minimalism in cases such as *Hamdan*, as Justice Breyer has, on the ground that it is doing no more than requiring the president to consult with Congress and that "[t]he Constitution places its faith in those democratic means,"[29] will, I venture to suggest, be ill disposed, maybe even embarrassed, to ignore or set aside the congressional action endorsing the president's program—in particular, to try before military commissions foreign nationals accused of terrorism.

Formally, the option remains, but as a purely practical matter it has become encumbered. For an institution that values consistency, there is an inherent awkwardness in invalidating an act of Congress after declaring that "[t]he Constitution places its faith in those democratic means," especially when the congressional response to the initial decision was so predictable. The field of action has also changed. When the Court eventually does take up the issues that it has avoided—for example, is trial by military commission a violation of due process?—it will have to confront congressional action or decisions not present at the time of *Rasul* or *Hamdan*. Of course, the Court can set aside the congressional judgment, but only after it has decided that it is for itself, not Congress, to resolve these issues. Moreover, the justices, always mindful of the stature of the Court and the limits of its authority, will be keenly aware of the new institutional alignment and are likely to be humbled by it. Instead of defending the constitutional promise of due process against the unilateral actions of the executive, they might, in this second step, have to act against both the president and Congress.

## The Dilemma of Each Individual Justice

The argument against minimalism presented here is predicated on an assumption that a majority of the justices is prepared to defend the constitutional rights of Guantánamo detainees but believes that minimalist decisions better serve democratic ideals. This assumption about the disposition of a majority of the justices may be far-fetched. Indeed, minimalism may be so appealing to a portion of the liberal wing of the American academy only because the alternative I offer—a cosmopolitan conception of the Constitution and a robust articulation of the rights it confers—is no longer possible as a practical matter. This alternative vision may be unable to garner five votes. Under this assumption, minimalism is less a strategy—an active choice by the majority to disregard constitutional questions—and more a characterization or rationalization of the only result that a majority of the justices could reach. Strategy necessarily implies a choice.[30]

Of course, choice will always remain for the individual justice, and for him or her minimalism might therefore be viewed as a decisional strategy. On the issue of the availability of habeas, Justice Kennedy rejected a minimalist approach in *Rasul* and turned his back on the majority. In contrast to Stevens, who wrote for the majority, he refused to treat the Guantánamo prisoners' right to habeas as purely a matter of statutory interpretation. Speaking at the level of general constitutional principles, Kennedy viewed the Constitution as reaching the Guantánamo prisoners and insisted that there were sometimes circumstances—present in the case before him—"in which the courts maintain the power and the responsibility to protect persons from unlawful detention even where military affairs are implicated."[31] He emphasized that the United States had exercised long-term, exclusive control over Guantánamo, and that the territory was far removed from any hostilities. He was also moved by the fact that the Guantánamo prisoners were being held indefinitely—not just for weeks or months, but for years—making the administration's claims of military necessity and their objection to habeas weak. No other justice joined Kennedy's opinion. Breyer, Souter, Ginsburg, and O'Connor silently joined Stevens's statute-based opinion and acquiesced in his exercise in minimalism.

By June 2006, the time of *Hamdan*, the margins had drawn closer. John Roberts had replaced William Rehnquist as chief justice. Although Roberts did not participate in *Hamdan*, as a circuit judge Roberts had sustained the use of the military commissions.[32] More to the point, Sandra Day O'Connor had retired and was replaced by Samuel Alito, who in the *Hamdan* decision sided with Justices Thomas and Scalia in defense of executive power and would have upheld Bush's order. In *Hamdan* as in *Rasul*, Justice Kennedy wrote a separate opinion, but in this case his primary purpose was to explain why he believed that the Guantánamo military commissions were not authorized by Congress. Breyer, Souter, and Ginsburg were able to join this portion of Kennedy's opinion, as well as Stevens's opinion for the Court. (Like Souter and Ginsburg, Kennedy joined Breyer's separate concurrence.)

To conceive of minimalism as a judicial strategy, now for a hypothetical individual justice, we must assume that at least one justice in the *Hamdan* majority was inclined to find that the Guantánamo commissions were objectionable from the perspective of due process and that the prisoners could use habeas corpus to vindicate their rights. Otherwise, there would be no choice, and thus minimalism could not be conceived of as a strategy of decision. There are hints in *Rasul* and *Hamdan* that this assumption is reasonable.

In the obscure footnote in *Rasul* that I have already mentioned, Justice Stevens referred not to Rehnquist's opinion in the 1990 Mexican case but to Justice Kennedy's, in which he argued that the Constitution imposes certain minimum obligations on U.S. officials wherever they act and against whomever they act. In *Hamdan* itself, Justice Stevens attacked the rule excluding the accused from trial on the ground that it represented a departure from, in the words of the Geneva Convention, "a judicial guarantee recognized as indispensable to civilized people"—a standard not very different from due process itself. He also expressed his hostility to the temptation of the executive to use military commissions as tribunals of convenience. Perhaps one of those who joined his opinions in both cases—Souter, Breyer, or Ginsburg—believed that trial before a military commission offended the Constitution and that the prisoners are entitled to habeas corpus to protect that right.

For our imagined justice, writing a separate opinion in *Hamdan* based on constitutional considerations would not have undermined the judgment itself, for, like the statute-based decision, it would have declared that the ban on habeas by the Guantánamo prisoners was invalid and that the use of military commissions was unlawful. Only the grounds of decision would be different. An artful justice might be able to affirm his or her allegiance to both the statutory and constitutional grounds of decision—for example, by arguing that at a minimum statutory authorization is required, but a statutorily endorsed scheme would offend due process. If that option is not available and the justice feels obliged to file a separate concurrence based only upon due process, Justice Stevens's opinion might well be deprived of majority status. This would have disappointed Stevens, who was presumably anxious to speak for the Court, and thus would have strained collegial relations. Yet respectful disagreement, even to the point of depriving a colleague of the privilege of delivering a majority opinion, should never be taken as a personal offense. The duties of an officer of the Court are far too weighty.

Filing a separate concurrence might also introduce an element of uncertainty. The majority might be splintered. Some of the majority might have denied that the congressional ban on habeas applied to Hamdan's petition. Others thought it was applicable but was unconstitutional. Some of the majority might object to trial by military commissions on statutory grounds; others might object on the basis of due process. Under these circumstances, neither the president nor Congress would know whether the illegality could be cured by enacting legislation. Such uncertainty should not, however, be necessarily viewed as a fatal vice.

For one thing, our imagined justice could count on the ingenuity of the political branches to move forward in the face of whatever uncertainty he or she might create. In the *Hamdi* case, for example, the Court was badly splintered, and it was unclear whether the evidentiary hearing to which the prisoner was entitled should be held before a military tribunal or a federal court. Faced with such uncertainty, the administration entered into an agreement that allowed the prisoner to move to Saudi Arabia, provided he agreed to certain restrictions and renounced his U.S. citizenship.

Alternatively, our imagined justice might be willing to subject the political branches to legal uncertainty in order to fully express deeply held beliefs. This second, more principled stance may well be justified, or at least rationalized, on the theory that his or her job is to safeguard the Constitution and the values it embodies, not to facilitate the choices of the elected branches. More pragmatically, this justice might act on the understanding that a bold, forceful, and—let's hope—eloquent opinion articulating the underlying constitutional principles, even if joined by no other justice, would enrich the resources of the law. It would not *be* the law, but, as was the case with Justice Brandeis's separate concurrence in *Whitney v. California*,[33] it might enhance the law by introducing a new strain into the sources from which the law evolves.

A separate opinion by our imagined justice based on due process would also have made an immeasurable contribution to public discourse, including the debate occurring in the legislative chambers or the offices of the executive. It would have underscored the true stakes at issue. Had such an opinion been filed in *Hamdan*, politicians and the citizens they serve could have seen with far greater clarity that habeas corpus is a constitutional imperative and that Guantánamo military commissions are at variance not only with various statutes and maybe even international agreements, but—even more important—with the Constitution.

## Prologue to Chapter 4

Trevor Sutton

"I believe with every fiber of my being that in the long run we also cannot keep this country safe unless we enlist the power of our most fundamental values." So spoke Barack Obama in a closely followed speech on national security delivered at the National Archives in May 2009, nearly four months to the day after he succeeded George W. Bush as president of the United States. Much like his election campaign, Obama's speech was presented as a direct repudiation of the counterterrorism policies of the Bush administration. After the September 11 attacks, Obama said, "we went off course," and "made a series of hasty decisions" that had the effect of treating our enduring principles as "luxuries." He added that this "ad hoc approach for fighting terrorism" was neither "effective nor sustainable"; in its place he promised an approach that drew on our "legal tradition" of "checks and balances," the "rule of law," and "due process." The president explained that this return to core values meant a firm rejection of torture and the closing of the prison at Guantánamo Bay.

Beyond these pronouncements, however, the president's National Archives speech suggested something other than a clean break with the past. Obama said that he would seek civilian trials for alleged terrorists "whenever feasible"—hardly an unqualified commitment to principle—and noted that in some cases military commissions would be more appropriate. Even more troubling, he stated that there were a number of detainees at Guantánamo who could not be prosecuted because of "tainted" evidence, but who were still too dangerous to be released. Although the president insisted he would use "clear, defensible, and lawful standards" to justify prolonged detention, he did not hint at the content of those standards or the manner in which they would be applied.

To many, Owen Fiss included, the National Archives speech seemed less a clean break with the Bush era than a grudging prolongation of it. In this regard, this chapter, "Aberrations No More," shared in the disappointment felt by many who had hoped that Obama's election would usher in a restoration of constitutional values. Yet, unlike many of Obama's critics, Fiss sought to look beyond the shortcomings of the current president to the complicity of the other branches of government, particularly the Supreme Court, which to a greater degree than either the executive or Congress has responsibility for balancing short-term exigencies with enduring values. In that sense, the essay, originally presented as a lecture at the University of Utah in October 2010, is a natural, if regrettable, sequel to "The Perils of Minimalism." As "Aberrations No More" observes in acute detail, the Obama administration's failure to fully turn the page on Bush-era counterterrorism policies undermines the case for minimalism even more forcefully than the Bush policies themselves did. Put otherwise, Obama's record on national security offers a powerful example of how the heavy burden of protecting the country from attack can lead even the best-intentioned president to curtail civil liberties.

Looking back from the vantage point of Obama's second term, "Aberrations No More" was prescient. Guantánamo remains open, and only a handful of prisoners (none of whom could be classified as senior-level terrorist operators) have been tried in civilian courts. Khalid Sheikh Mohammed, regarded as one of the masterminds of the September 11 attacks, was slated for trial in the Southern District of New York, but the Obama administration transferred his trial to a military commission after Congress voted to block the use of federal funds to transfer detainees to the United States. The use of torture appears to have stopped, and indefinite detention without trial exists only in a legacy capacity, but, as the final chapter in this volume makes clear, the government has expanded the use of targeted killings (including of American citizens) to a degree well beyond that practiced during the Bush administration. Finally, recent disclosures have revealed that under Obama the National Security Agency has engaged in wiretapping and monitoring of electronic communications on at least as large a scale as under Bush—although unlike Bush, Obama can claim a clear statutory basis and the occasional blessing of a special intelligence court composed of federal judges. These policies were available to the Obama administration only because the judiciary failed to offer a robust and enduring defense of fundamental liberties when it reviewed similar policies under President Bush.

Somewhat unsurprisingly, a number of former Bush administration officials have recently taken to claiming that Obama's national security agenda vindicates the actions taken by his predecessor. One such official, former White House press secretary Ari Fleischer, went so far as to proclaim that Obama was "carrying out Bush's fourth term." Although such comments have an obvious political bias and fail to account for political constraints the Obama administration confronted after the 2010 midterm elections, they are not wholly without basis. Whether one sees Obama's national security decisions as driven by conviction or by political expedience, the continuities with Bush's War on Terror are plain.

# Chapter 4

# ABERRATIONS NO MORE

S eptember 11, 2001, marked the beginning of a new era in American law. Combating terrorism became a matter of great public urgency, and as part of that endeavor, policies have been pursued that compromise once-sacred principles of the Constitution. These policies were initiated by President George W. Bush, but with some exceptions other branches of government soon endorsed them. Remarkably, they are now being continued by President Barack Obama.

Although terrorism did not begin on 9/11, the attacks on that day were distinguished by the magnitude of the death and destruction that they caused. Those attacks also had the threatening quality of a foreign invasion. Important sites in the United States—the World Trade Center and the Pentagon (and, if the terrorists had had their way, the Capitol or the White House)—were struck by foreign nationals acting on directions from abroad. Moreover, the events of 9/11 became a public spectacle. Scenes of airplanes crashing into the World Trade Center and the collapse of the towers were caught on video and frequently replayed in later years. The messages conveyed and the fears aroused by these images were further reinforced in the decade that followed by bombings in London, Madrid, Amman, Mumbai, and Bali; attempts to blow up two airplanes on their way to the United States; and the failed plot to detonate a car full of explosives in Times Square. As a result, starting on September 11, 2001, and continuing to this day, terrorism acquired an immediacy and reality for Americans that it never had before.

The government's response to the attacks of 9/11—Bush's announcement of a "War on Terror"—also endowed the events that occurred on that day with special significance. This declaration of war was intended to mobilize the American people, and it had that effect. It prioritized the need to respond to the risk of terrorism and prepared the public for the sacrifices that such a response would entail. In that respect, Bush was following the practice of earlier presidents who had declared a "War on Poverty," a "War on Drugs," and even a "War on Cancer," but there was one important difference—Bush soon employed the military to achieve his objectives.

## Bush's War

In the fall of 2001, Bush determined that al-Qaeda, a far-flung organization that operates in secret, was responsible for the 9/11 attacks. He then began what can properly be regarded as a war against al-Qaeda. He unleashed the military force of the United States and charged it with the task of capturing or targeting Osama bin Laden and other leaders of al-Qaeda. At the same time, Bush ordered the invasion of Afghanistan, then controlled by the Taliban, on the theory that a symbiotic relationship existed between the Taliban and al-Qaeda. In March 2003, the president broadened the United States military operations in the Middle East and invaded Iraq, then controlled by Saddam Hussein and the Baath Party. Although the 9/11 terrorist attacks were not the basis of that military endeavor, terrorism, sometimes at the hands of al-Qaeda, was a consequence of the invasion of Iraq and the occupation that inevitably followed.

In his War on Terror, Bush instituted a number of practices that violated principles long viewed as hallmarks of our constitutional tradition. One such principle is the prohibition of torture. This prohibition is rooted not only in an international treaty and a federal statute implementing that treaty, but also in the Fifth and Eighth Amendments to the U.S. Constitution, part of the Bill of Rights. Soon after 9/11, however, the White House turned to lawyers within the executive branch for legal opinions that narrowed the definition of torture to allow the use of interrogation techniques such as waterboarding—to induce the fear of imminent death by drowning—that are almost universally condemned as torture.

During this same time, suspects were secretly sent to other countries, such as Syria and Egypt, that routinely torture their prisoners and subject them to abuses that would qualify as torture even under the Bush administration's narrow definition. This practice, known as extraordinary rendition, and more properly seen as a form of outsourcing,[1] is as much a violation of the rule against torture as when officials of the United States engage in torture themselves.

Bush also instituted a detention policy that threatened another principle of our constitutional order—what I have called the principle of freedom. This principle prohibits the executive from incarcerating anyone without charging that individual with a crime and swiftly bringing him to trial. There are exceptions to this principle, including one for war. Under this exception, the executive is allowed to detain enemy combatants captured on the battlefield and to hold them for the duration of hostilities. Bush invoked this exception and then construed it in a way that threatened to undermine the very values that the principle of freedom seeks to protect.

Bush did not confine himself to imprisoning persons seized in Iraq, Afghanistan, or even the mountainous region between Afghanistan and Pakistan. Rather, he treated the entire world as if it were a battlefield, even to the point of seizing persons within the United States, including American citizens, and treating them as enemy combatants. Bush also refused to place any temporal limits on this policy of imprisonment without trial and was prepared to incarcerate persons for prolonged, indefinite periods of time—maybe for life. Although he said he would hold these individuals only until the end of the War on Terror or, more modestly, until the end of the war against al-Qaeda, the end of this war is not readily foreseeable. Extending the exception to the principle of freedom for wartime captures to a never-ending war of this sort threatens to undermine the principle itself.

All of the prisoners subject to Bush's detention policy were held incommunicado, but sometimes a friend or relative, or even a volunteer lawyer, discovered a prisoner's whereabouts and filed a petition of habeas corpus on his behalf. These petitions claimed that the prisoner was not in fact an enemy combatant, and thus there was no legal authority for the executive to detain him, even under the rule allowing wartime captures. Nevertheless, the Bush administration resisted any factual inquiry by the judiciary into the merits of these claims.

For prisoners who were American citizens and who were thus held in prisons within the United States, the government sought to limit the evidentiary inquiry by the federal judiciary.[2] The government insisted that an affidavit filed by an official in the Department of Defense explaining the basis for the incarceration should be accepted at face value and treated as sufficient for detaining the prisoners. The government maintained that there could be no judicial probe into the adequacy of the affidavit and no opportunity for the prisoner to offer evidence to substantiate his claim that he was not an enemy combatant.

For foreign nationals being held abroad, including those at Guantánamo, the government took the position that these prisoners had no right to habeas corpus whatsoever. According to the government, foreign nationals held abroad had no constitutional rights, including the right to personal freedom, and thus the writ of habeas corpus served no function.

Although the Bush administration claimed that it had the right to hold anyone it classified as unlawful enemy combatants for prolonged, indefinite periods, it also claimed the right to place some on trial for their actions on behalf of al-Qaeda or the Taliban. Some of these individuals were to be tried in ordinary civilian courts. One, an American citizen named John Walker Lindh, who had been captured in Afghanistan and acknowledged that he had fought for the Taliban, was charged in federal court and accused under federal criminal statutes of attempting to kill American personnel. The administration also used civilian courts to indict or try a number of persons accused of being agents of al-Qaeda who had been arrested and imprisoned in the United States. One was an American citizen seized at O'Hare Airport in Chicago; another was a citizen of Qatar who had been studying in the United States. Bush did not, however, limit himself to the use of civilian courts. In November 2001, he issued an executive order authorizing the use of military commissions to try terrorists.[3] By 2005, the administration determined that twenty detainees being held in Guantánamo were to be tried by military commissions established pursuant to the president's order.

In the midst of an ongoing conflict, military commissions have been convened on the battlefield to try enemy soldiers accused of war crimes. Now and then, we departed from this tradition of using military commissions, but only in exigent circumstances. For example, in World War II, a military commission was used, with the reluctant approval of the Supreme Court, to try Nazi soldiers who had entered the country for purposes of sabotage.[4] Bush's decision to use military commissions in Guantánamo built on this precedent. However, the prescribed procedures for the military commissions he created ignored the intervening advances in our understanding of due process that occurred during the Warren Court era. Bush's plan also vastly expanded the jurisdiction of military commissions by contemplating their use to try a group of prisoners that had been incarcerated for years at Guantánamo, far from any battlefield. Nor did Bush confine the commissions to trying offenses that were proscribed by the laws of war. In this way, Bush effectively transformed the military commission from a tribunal of necessity to one of convenience, giving the prosecution advantages that are anathema to the constitutional dictates of due process.

Under Bush's scheme, trials of Guantánamo prisoners were to be carried out by military officers subject to supervision by an official in the Department of Defense.[5] The rules of evidence permitted the introduction of a wider range of hearsay evidence than would be allowed in federal court. Any evidence that had probative value was admissible. There were no protections against the use of confessions obtained by coercion or even torture. The accused could be convicted on the basis of evidence presented secretly to the tribunal—in other words, evidence which neither the accused nor his counsel had the chance to hear or rebut. The accused's choice of counsel also was strictly circumscribed. In addition, Bush's commissions compromised the accused's right to a speedy and public trial by a jury of their peers.

In conducting his War on Terror, Bush also showed little respect for the protection of privacy guaranteed by the Fourth

Amendment. In the immediate wake of 9/11, he authorized the National Security Agency (NSA) to tap telephones without prior judicial authorization.[6] These taps were aimed at international telephone calls between persons in America and individuals abroad suspected of having ties to al-Qaeda. In 1967, when the Supreme Court ruled that wiretapping was the functional equivalent of a search and thus subject to the warrant requirement of the Fourth Amendment, it reserved the question of whether such a rule would extend to cases of national security.[7] The case before the Court involved telephone calls of a suspected gambler. In 1972, the Supreme Court extended the warrant requirement of the Fourth Amendment to a prosecution involving the bombing of a CIA office in Ann Arbor, Michigan.[8] In that case, the Supreme Court reserved yet another question, specifically whether the warrant requirement should apply to wiretaps aimed at obtaining foreign intelligence.

Unprepared to wait for further clarification by the Supreme Court, in 1978 Congress passed a statute—the Foreign Intelligence Surveillance Act (FISA)—that required warrants for wiretaps seeking foreign intelligence and established a new tribunal with streamlined procedures for obtaining such warrants.[9] These warrants were to be issued by a tribunal that operated in secret and whose judges were appointed by the chief justice. To obtain such a warrant, the government did not have to show probable cause that a crime was committed, but only that the target was an agent of a foreign power and that the purpose of the interceptions was to obtain foreign intelligence. Bush's NSA wiretapping program violated the very terms of the 1978 statute and, even more fundamentally, the constitutional principles that the statute sought to further. A warrant requirement creates a check on arbitrary executive action and, to that end, protects the right of private communication so essential to the development of the human personality and political freedom.

## The Complicity of the Other Branches

Some have depicted the five practices that I have identified—interrogation under torture, imprisonment without trial, denial of habeas corpus, unfettered use of military commissions, and warrantless wiretapping—as entirely the work of Bush and his close circle of advisers. So characterized, these practices have been denounced as excesses of Bush's unilateralism and a violation of separation of powers, which at least from one reading should have required collaboration among the three branches of government. There is an element of truth to this charge—in conducting his War on Terror, Bush made extravagant claims about the power of the presidency—but such a charge should not obscure a deeper and more fundamental truth: although the president led the way, the other branches were complicit in this assault on the Constitution. At issue, therefore, was not simply separation of powers but the constitutional principles prohibiting torture, protecting personal freedom, ensuring fair procedures, and guaranteeing privacy.

In December 2005, Congress passed the Detainee Treatment Act.[10] One part of that statute, spearheaded by Senator John McCain, prohibits American officials from inflicting torture wherever they might act and against whomever they act. Bush fiercely resisted this measure as it made its way through Congress, and when he eventually signed the bill he issued one of his most notorious signing statements.[11] In it, Bush called attention to the fact that the McCain measure provided no remedy for the enforcement of the ban on torture. The president also said that he was signing the bill into law with the understanding that he would not allow it to compromise his duties as commander in chief, suggesting that he would engage in the prohibited action—torture—if, in his judgment, it were a military necessity.

This assertion of his power as commander in chief was an

affront to the constitutional allocation of power. The Constitution grants Congress authority to share in the regulation of the activities of the armed forces.[12] Even more striking, Bush's assertion of power gave no recognition to the fact that the McCain measure was only a codification of the ban on torture rooted in the Fifth and Eighth Amendments—in fact, the statute borrowed some of the language of the Eighth Amendment. These constitutional provisions unequivocally limited the president's power as commander in chief. Bush's signing statement disputed not only the power of Congress but the constitutional tradition that subordinates all executive action, even the exercise of an enumerated power, to the Bill of Rights.

The other provisions of the Detainee Treatment Act of 2005 posed no such confrontation with the president. Rather, the act affirmed Bush's program of executive detention. The act specifically denied the writ of habeas corpus to all the prisoners at Guantánamo.[13] It also acknowledged, and thus approved, the system of military tribunals—the so-called Combatant Status Review Tribunals—established on the island in July 2004, more than two years after the prison was opened, to hear claims of prisoners who denied any connection to al-Qaeda or the Taliban or any other terrorist organization. These tribunals were staffed by military officers operating under the most lax evidentiary rules, and there was no provision for legal representation of the prisoners. Under the 2005 statute, review of the decisions of the Combatant Status Review Tribunals was confined to the Court of Appeals for the District of Columbia Circuit, and the grounds available to it for review were restricted. The factual basis for a Combatant Status Review Tribunal's decision could not be questioned in any way.

The Military Commissions Act of 2006 also reaffirmed Bush administration policies. It expanded the 2005 ban on the writ of habeas corpus by extending the ban to all unlawful enemy combatants, regardless of where they might be held, and by making it clear that the ban was applicable to all pending cases.[14] In addition, the 2006 act authorized the president to use military commissions to try so-called unlawful enemy combatants, and thus endorsed the position Bush had taken in his November 2001 executive order. Admittedly, Congress rejected some of the procedures originally contemplated by Bush when he issued his executive order. Congress gave the accused the right to hear the evidence against him and placed limitations on the use of confessions obtained through torture. Congress also required that the accused had to be notified in advance that hearsay was to be used. Still, the essential due process defects of military commissions remained: trial by military officers, supervision by a political appointee, permissive evidentiary rules, no right to a jury trial, and no right to a speedy or public trial. Moreover, like Bush's initial executive order, the 2006 act attempted to punish offenses, such as giving material support to a belligerent, that were not proscribed by the laws of war.[15] And, as was true of the executive order, the 2006 act confined the use of military commissions to the trial of foreign nationals, which not only raised questions of equal protection but testified to the second-class character of the justice the commissions were likely to render— it was not good enough for Americans.

Not long after passing the Military Commissions Act, Congress also gave the president the authority to conduct wiretaps without court authorization. Although the NSA warrantless wiretap program was authorized by Bush immediately following the 9/11 attacks, it was not publicly disclosed until December 2005. In the period immediately following that disclosure, many complained that the NSA program violated the warrant requirement established in 1978 under the Foreign Intelligence Surveillance Act. The attorney general insisted otherwise but, even more audaciously, claimed that the president's action was within his powers as commander in chief and thus could not be limited by Congress.[16]

In January 2007, the attorney general announced that the president was voluntarily, as a matter of policy, abandoning the NSA program.[17] In April, the administration turned to Congress for authorization of the surveillance conducted under that program. In August 2007, Congress passed legislation—the Protect America Act—that allowed the executive to wiretap, without warrants, telephone calls abroad to persons suspected of al-Qaeda ties.[18] In July 2008, another statute—known as the FISA Amendments Act of 2008—was enacted that extended the authorization of the 2007 act for warrantless wiretaps.[19] The FISA Amendments Act also protected the telephone carriers who had participated in the NSA program from any liability for their wrongdoing.

In each of these measures—the Detainee Treatment Act of 2005, the Military Commissions Act of 2006, and the authorization for warrantless wiretaps of the 2007 and 2008 acts— Congress endorsed a number of Bush's counterterrorism policies that offended the Constitution. The Supreme Court's endorsement was more oblique and harder to discern, but nevertheless important—and deeply disturbing. Even where the Court rebuffed the government, its defense of the Constitution was weak and compromised.

In June 2004, the Supreme Court ruled in *Hamdi v. Rumsfeld* that an American citizen who had allegedly fought for the Taliban was entitled, as a matter of due process, to an evidentiary hearing on his claim that he had not taken up arms against the United States.[20] This victory was compromised, however, when Justice O'Connor, writing for the Court, fashioned the particular procedural rules to govern these hearings.[21] She further compromised her commitment to due process when she declared—now for only four justices—that the required evidentiary hearing need not be held before a federal court sitting in habeas, but instead could be conducted by a properly constituted military tribunal. Indeed, it was this pronouncement that guided the Department of Defense, anxious to defeat any claims to habeas, to establish the Combatant Status Review Tribunals on Guantánamo in July 2004, only a month after the Court's ruling. The secretary of defense must have reasoned that if a military tribunal was good enough to determine whether an American had taken up arms against the United States, it was certainly good enough for foreign nationals.

In *Rumsfeld v. Padilla*, a companion case also involving an American citizen—who was seized in Chicago, transferred to New York, and then held in a naval brig in South Carolina as an enemy combatant—the Supreme Court refused to pass on the merits of his habeas petition.[22] The opinion was written by Chief Justice Rehnquist. Clinging to the most arcane technicality, Rehnquist ruled that the prisoner should have filed his petition in the South Carolina, rather than the New York, federal district court.

This ruling was handed down in June 2004, almost three years after the War on Terror had begun and after the prisoner had been held incommunicado for more than two years. Subsequently, the prisoner filed a habeas petition in the South Carolina district court, and that court granted it.[23] However, that decision was reversed by the United States Court of Appeals for the Fourth Circuit.[24] The prisoner then sought review by the Supreme Court, but when the moment came to respond to the prisoner's application for certiorari—and in an obvious attempt to avoid Supreme Court review of its policy of imprisonment without trial—the Bush administration reversed course and charged the prisoner with a crime in a Florida district court. On April 3, 2006, the Supreme Court failed to confront this transparently evasive strategy and denied the prisoner's application for certiorari.[25]

The Court's policy of avoidance also governed its treatment of the Guantánamo prisoners' attempts to obtain habeas corpus. The U.S. Court of Appeals for the District of Columbia had embraced the administration's position and denied the Guantánamo prisoners the writ on the ground that they had no constitutional rights. However, rather than address this ruling in any direct way, the Supreme Court, in a June 2004 ruling, held that under the very terms of the governing statute, habeas was available to Guantánamo prisoners as long as the jailor (in this instance the secretary of defense) was within the jurisdiction of the habeas court.[26]

Congress responded to this interpretation of the habeas statute in the Detainee Treatment Act of 2005, in which it amended the habeas statute to deny the writ to the Guantánamo prisoners and make the Combatant Status Review Tribunals their exclusive remedy.[27] In June 2006, the Court once again avoided deciding whether the Guantánamo prisoners had a right to habeas corpus that was protected from legislative encroachment by the Constitution. Rather, the Court held, through a strained interpretation, that the ban on habeas of the 2005 statute did not apply to a case such as the one then before it, which had been pending at the time of enactment.[28]

In October 2006, as part of the Military Commissions Act, Congress once again amended the habeas statute. It made the ban on habeas applicable to all persons held as unlawful enemy combatants, regardless of where they might be held, and also made it abundantly clear that the ban was applicable to all pending cases "without exception."[29] In reviewing this measure in a case arising from Guantánamo, the court of appeals acknowledged the applicability of the ban on habeas to the case before it, even though it had been pending at the time of enactment. The court went on to uphold the ban, once again denying that the Guantánamo prisoners had any constitutional rights that might be protected by the writ.[30] Finally, in June 2008—more than six years after the prison opened—the Supreme Court ruled in *Boumediene v. Bush*[31] that the Guantánamo prisoners were entitled, as a constitutional matter, to have their imprisonment reviewed by a writ of habeas corpus. But the majority opinion, written by Justice Kennedy, failed to address the view of the court of appeals that denied the protection of the Bill of Rights to foreign nationals being held abroad.

Justice Kennedy's opinion in *Boumediene* depicted the provision of the Constitution protecting the writ of habeas corpus as an instrument of separation of powers.[32] He saw separation of powers as furthering freedom in general, but on his account freedom was only a residue.[33] Freedom was not a right directly conferred on the Guantánamo prisoners by the Constitution or Bill of Rights but was derived from any habeas court decision holding that a prisoner was not an enemy combatant and thus could not be lawfully imprisoned by the executive.[34] Justice Kennedy did not declare that the Guantánamo prisoners enjoyed the protection of the Bill of Rights—protections that might enable a Guantánamo prisoner determined in a habeas proceeding to be an enemy combatant to challenge prolonged detention without trial or the use of military commissions to try him for whatever he had done in the war, or to protect against the use of so-called "enhanced interrogation techniques" (torture). Remarkably, all of that was left for yet another day.

The limitations of the *Boumediene* decision were also evident in the test Kennedy announced for determining when habeas would be available. He did not find, as he might have, that the writ must be available whenever or wherever a prisoner is held in a secure detention facility by an American official but rather made his decision turn on a multivariate test. According to Kennedy, the availability of the writ depended on (1) the citizenship of the prisoner, (2) the prisoner's status, (3) the adequacy of the process through which his status was determined, (4) the nature of the site of apprehension, (5) the nature of the site of detention, and (6) the practical difficulties in resolving the prisoner's claim of freedom.[35] Of course, we have become accustomed in the law to multivariate tests, but usually, as with the famed *Matthews v. Eldridge*[36] test, the various factors are meant to pursue or serve a single unifying principle. Some factors identified in *Boumediene*, by contrast, bore little relation to the separation-of-powers principle that was allegedly the foundation of the decision. As a result, no one could tell how the test might apply to other detention facilities abroad, such as the one maintained by the United States at the Bagram Air Field, an air force base in Afghanistan, which was also used to detain suspected terrorists and, at the time, held close to six hundred prisoners.

## The War on Terror, Continued

On November 4, 2008, only months after the *Boumediene* decision, Barack Obama was elected president of the United States. There was reason to believe that Obama might repudiate many of the Bush policies that offended the Constitution: Obama had campaigned on a platform that promised change, and many understood that promise to reach Bush's counterterrorism policies. Obama gave further credence to this hope when, in his inaugural address, he rejected the notion that the fight against terrorism required us to betray our ideals. For the most part, however, Obama has not been true to his promise. Although he withdrew the last combat troops from Iraq in August 2011 and is scheduled to end the U.S. military presence in Afghanistan by the end of 2015, and although he has been meticulous in avoiding the use of the phrase "War on Terror," Obama has frequently declared that we are at war with al-Qaeda and the Taliban, and in the name of these wars has continued many of the unconstitutional policies of Bush.

As his first piece of business, Obama issued an executive order banning torture.[37] He thus reaffirmed the constitutional principle codified by McCain's addition to the Detainee Treatment Act of 2005 and removed the doubt created by the statement Bush had made on signing that act. Obama also minimized the risk of torture by issuing orders that same day closing the secret prisons maintained abroad by the CIA—the so-called black sites[38]—and requiring the CIA to follow the Army Field Manual when interrogating suspects.[39]

Yet Obama quickly brushed aside calls for criminal prosecutions and truth commissions to investigate the abusive interrogation practices of the previous administration. After a public outcry, his attorney general opened an investigation on a CIA interrogator accused of going beyond agency guidelines.[40] The alleged crime was not waterboarding, which appears to have been authorized by higher officials—perhaps, if his memoir is to be believed, by Bush himself. Rather, the agent was accused of threatening a hooded and shackled prisoner with imminent death first by revving an electric drill near the prisoner's head and then by cocking a semiautomatic handgun in the same position. The investigation of this rogue agent was opened in August 2009 and came to naught. For the most part, the president has insisted, even with as gross an offense as torture, that he is interested in the future, not the past, without understanding that how one treats the past partly determines what will happen in the future.[41]

Obama can also be faulted for seeking to block any judicial inquiry into the practice of extraordinary rendition, even in cases in which it is alleged that the suspected terrorist in the custody of the United States was handed over to a foreign ally for interrogation under conditions of torture. In two notable instances, one in the Ninth Circuit and the other in the Second Circuit, the Obama administration sought to block judicial inquiries into renditions conducted by the Bush administration. These proceedings were brought by victims of rendition and were pending before appellate courts when Obama took office. In one, Obama's lawyers relied on the state-secrets doctrine, transforming what was originally an evidentiary privilege into a de facto grant of immunity to the CIA.[42] In the other, his lawyers claimed that any judicial inquiry into the practice of extraordinary rendition would compromise the executive's authority over military and foreign affairs.[43]

In contrast to Bush, Obama has been reluctant to treat the United States as part of the battleground against al-Qaeda and the Taliban. Accordingly, he placed within the ambit of the criminal justice system two terrorist suspects who were seized in the United States on his watch. One was an American citizen attempting to detonate a bomb in Times Square[44] and the other a citizen of Nigeria attempting to detonate a bomb on a Northwest Airlines flight as it was about to land in Detroit.[45] Yet Obama invoked the war exception to the principle of freedom as the basis for continuing the imprisonment without trial of prisoners being held in Guantánamo and at the Bagram Air Field in Afghanistan. Bush had claimed this power as commander in chief. Anxious to avoid the unilateralism of Bush, Obama did not invoke his authority as commander in chief to justify this policy but relied instead on the statute passed by Congress immediately after 9/11, which did no more than authorize the president to use force in responding to the terrorist attacks on that day.

Although on occasion Bush tried al-Qaeda suspects in civilian courts, he also claimed the authority to try some before military commissions and did so without announcing the criteria to govern the choice between tribunals. Obama has claimed the same authority. Obama made headlines when he first announced that he would try the alleged mastermind of 9/11, Khalid Sheikh Mohammed, in the Southern District Court of New York,[46] but the controversy that erupted over this announcement should not blind us to the fact that Obama is prepared to try some of the Guantánamo prisoners before military commissions and, in fact, is now trying Khalid Sheikh Mohammed in that way. Unlike Bush, Obama announced criteria for governing the choice of tribunal, but these criteria were stated at such a high level of generality as to compromise their capacity to constrain that choice.

As a senator, Obama voted against the Military Commissions Act of 2006, which not only barred habeas corpus but authorized the use of military commissions to try foreign nationals being held as unlawful enemy combatants.[47] As president, Obama sponsored the Military Commissions Act of 2009.[48] Admittedly, the principal purpose of this legislation was to strengthen the evidentiary rules governing military commissions. Under this statute, all coerced testimony was barred, the accused was given a reasonable opportunity to obtain evidence and witnesses, the government's obligation to disclose exculpatory evidence was expanded, and the accused was given the right to examine any evidence offered at trial. Moreover, the political officer convening a military commission was prohibited from punishing members of the commission for any of their rulings.

Still, the basic structural shortcoming of the commission—trial by military officers—persists. Indeed, the 2009 act, building on Bush's initial executive order of November 2001 and the Military Commissions Act of 2006, represents a further institutionalization of military commissions as an irregular alternative the executive might choose—based on criteria we will never know—for the prosecution of unlawful—or now unprivileged—enemy combatants. Much like the 2006 act and Bush's November 2001 executive order, the 2009 act defined the offenses that could be tried before a commission to include crimes, such as giving material aid to a belligerent, that could not properly be considered crimes under the laws of war.[49] The irregular nature of these military commissions was underscored by a provision in the 2009 act, also present in the 2006 act and the 2001 executive order, confining them to the trial of foreign nationals.

Obama has sought to follow through on his promise to close Guantánamo. In December 2009, he announced his plan to transfer the remaining Guantánamo prisoners to a prison in Thomson, Illinois. This plan encountered congressional resistance and has not yet been implemented. It should be emphasized, however, that once Obama decided, as he did in May 2009, to continue the practice of using military commissions for the trial of some of the Guantánamo prisoners and to continue the policy of holding other Guantánamo prisoners for prolonged, indefinite detention without trial, the closing of Guantánamo has become a gesture of doubtful significance. Guantánamo became an object of public controversy and disapprobation not just because it was viewed as a site where prisoners were tortured but also because Bush had planned to use military commissions to try some of the prisoners being held there and to continue the imprisonment of others being held there without affording them a trial of any type.

The notoriety of Guantánamo had also arisen because Bush insisted that it lay beyond the reach of habeas corpus. It had become something of a legal black hole.[50] The *Boumediene* decision, in June 2008, relieved Obama of the need to take a position on the availability of the writ of habeas corpus to the Guantánamo prisoners—the Supreme Court rejected Bush's position—but Obama has tried to limit the scope of that ruling, and in so doing further denied the act of closing Guantánamo of much of its meaning. Obama's lawyers argued in open court that the *Boumediene* decision should be confined to Guantánamo alone and that the prison at Bagram—to which terrorism suspects from the four corners of the earth had been brought—was beyond the reach of the Constitution.

The district court rejected the stark position of Obama. It applied the *Boumediene* criteria to Bagram and found that habeas is available to those prisoners who were not Afghan citizens.[51] However, the court of appeals, also applying the *Boumediene* criteria, reversed this decision and denied habeas to any of the Bagram prisoners.[52] Three years later, following further proceedings in the district court on remand, the court of appeals reaffirmed its position.[53] Such protracted litigation is not at all surprising, given the multivariate test Justice Kennedy laid down in *Boumediene*, but what is remarkable and disturbing is that Obama denied that habeas is available for the prisoners of Bagram, just as Bush had for the Guantánamo prisoners.

Finally, account must be taken of Obama's position on the warrantless wiretaps that began during the Bush era. Bush claimed the authority to institute such surveillance as an incident of his power as commander in chief and insisted that, as such, he was free to disregard the obligation to obtain a warrant imposed by FISA. Obama did not claim such executive prerogatives, nor was there any reason for him to do so. In the Protect America Act of 2007, Congress authorized the president to engage in such eavesdropping, and this authorization was extended in the FISA Amendments Act of 2008. As a senator, Obama voted against the 2007 act. He fought the grant of immunity to the carriers eventually contained in the 2008 act, but in the end he voted for the measure. Upon assuming office, Attorney General Eric Holder indicated that he would vigorously defend the 2008 act's constitutionality. In 2013 Holder obtained a ruling from the

Supreme Court that denied standing to probable victims of the surveillance and, in so doing, effectively insulated the statute from judicial review.[54]

## The Creation of a New Normal

Although the differences between Bush and Obama must be noted and acknowledged, the essential truth is one of continuity. Obama has sought to block judicial inquiries into extraordinary rendition. Obama has continued the policy of imprisonment without trial. Obama has sought to deny the writ of habeas corpus to the prisoners now being held in Bagram. Obama has continued to use military commissions to try terrorist suspects. And Obama has continued the policy of warrantless wiretaps. Obama sometimes announced these policies with reluctance, which was never Bush's style, but in the end Obama overcame this reluctance and chose to sacrifice principle.

The reasons for Obama's perpetuation of Bush's policies are hard to fathom. Maybe Obama learned things about the nature of the terrorist threat that he did not know before. Maybe Obama compromised on these issues of principle in order to gain support for a number of his domestic policies—health care or economic recovery. Or maybe Obama has been unable to resist the momentum achieved by the Bush policies once they were, for the most part, endorsed by Congress and condoned by the Supreme Court. We do not know and we are likely never to know. Our concern should be, however, not with the reasons for Obama's actions but rather with the consequences of his action, which are unmistakable and troubling.

In the immediate wake of 9/11 and the beginning of the War on Terror, many of the abuses of the Constitution that I have identified were seen as aberrations, perhaps unilateral excesses of Bush and his close circle of advisers. Soon these practices received the endorsement of Congress and often the acquiescence of the Supreme Court. Now they have been endorsed by the new president, a lawyer who professes to be dedicated to the Constitution and the highest ideals of the nation. As a result, the transgressions of the Bush era, rather than being denounced as unworthy of our Constitution, have been institutionalized. They have become the official policies of our government and are routinely defended as constitutional. The transgressions we suffer today will inevitably determine what is permissible in the future. They have shaped our understanding of what is acceptable, and may well serve as precedents for a less reluctant president.

Continued in this way, unconstitutional policies initiated by Bush have taken on a life of their own and have become durable features of our legal order. As such, they betray the proudest ideals of the nation, undermine one of the pillars of our self-understanding, and deny us—all of us, including Obama—the right to speak of the example of America as we once did—as a beacon for all the world.

## Prologue to Chapter 5

Trevor Sutton

Many of the legal issues addressed in these essays were matters of genuine first impression for American jurists—and indeed for the majority of American lawyers and legal academics, including Owen Fiss. It is true that the United States' long history of armed conflict contains episodes that informed the judiciary's assessment of the Bush administration's War on Terror. Nevertheless, none of the seminal Supreme Court decisions relating to the executive's wartime actions, such as *Ex Parte Milligan*, *Ex Parte Quirin*, and *In Re Yamashita*, supplied a clear precedent to resolve the central questions examined by the Supreme Court in its review of the Bush administration's counterterrorism policies; nor have they provided an easy answer for the controversial counterterror programs of the Obama administration, such as the targeted killing of American citizens affiliated with overseas terrorist groups.

But such questions were not novel to the entire world. One country in particular, Israel, has for much of its modern history struggled to balance its need for security with its belief in human rights, civil liberties, and the fundamental dignity of the individual. In Israel, perhaps to a greater degree than in any other nation, the judiciary is routinely asked to adjudicate between these powerful considerations. As in the United States, on especially sensitive or intractable issues, Israel's Supreme Court often has final—or at least a very influential—say.

That Israel's Supreme Court has come to occupy a pivotal role in the country's public life and served as a beacon to many courts throughout the world owes much to the country's most famous jurist, Aharon Barak. This chapter, "Law Is Everywhere," discusses some of Barak's seminal decisions weighing security against fundamental rights. These decisions are an important part of Barak's legacy, but they are only one part. Even before he became president of the Supreme Court, Barak made major contributions to Israeli jurisprudence. The title "Law Is Everywhere" is meant to capture Barak's universalist vision of the reach of legal norms, and echoes Barak's famous assertion that "the world is filled with law," a belief that received its fullest treatment in Barak's 2008 book, *The Judge in a Democracy*. Consistent with this vision, under Barak's influence the Supreme Court revolutionized traditional Israeli standing doctrine to eliminate the "particularized" or "personal" injury prong so familiar to students of American civil procedure. According to a series of decisions penned by Barak over the course of the 1980s and 1990s, a plaintiff in an Israeli court needed to show only that a violation of the law has occurred, and that the plaintiff's suit for redress is in the public interest.

"Law Is Everywhere" first appeared in the *Yale Law Journal* in 2007 as a tribute to Aharon Barak on his retirement. The essay was not the product of distant admiration. Fiss and Barak have been intellectual companions and personal friends for many decades, and some have said that the legal philosophy captured in Fiss's *The Law As It Could Be* is the one that best approximates

Barak's ideas about the role of law in society. This shared vision is all the more extraordinary when one considers that Barak did not have the luxury of advocacy without consequence; his lofty political perches required him to have the courage of his convictions. Such courage is all the more remarkable in a country like Israel, where the threat of political violence is far more pervasive and acute than in the United States, and where under certain circumstances the legislature can overrule a decision of the Supreme Court if it feels the Court has overstepped its bounds.

# Chapter 5

# LAW IS EVERYWHERE

Aharon Barak was born in Lithuania in 1936. He was one of the few who miraculously survived the slaughter of Jews in that country during the Second World War—he and his mother hid in the walls of a neighbor's house, while his father was able to continue laboring in the ghetto. Barak moved to Israel with both his parents after the war, became a professor of law at Hebrew University in 1968, and later served as dean of the law faculty. From 1975 to 1978 he was the attorney general of Israel. In 1978, Barak was appointed to the Israeli Supreme Court and then received special dispensation from the Court to serve as a legal adviser to Prime Minister Menachem Begin at the Camp David peace talks with Egypt that occurred in September of that year. Barak became president of the Israeli Supreme Court in 1995, and he retired from that Court on his seventieth birthday, in September 2006.

Barak's rulings, particularly those involving issues of national security, have been heralded throughout the world and teach an important lesson on how to be faithful to the rule of law in the face of a terrorist threat. Living through the post–9/11 era in the United States and taking account of the constitutional wrongs to which we have become so accustomed makes those rulings all the more remarkable. He safeguarded basic liberties in a context in which the threat to national security was as great as, if not greater than, the threat facing the United States.

We in the United States have the benefit of geographic distance. Iraq and Afghanistan are geographically remote. It may be that al-Qaeda has agents within the United States, but its nerve center is located half a world away—somewhere in the mountains between Afghanistan and Pakistan. Israel's enemies, such as Syria and Iran, are its neighbors, and terrorist organizations have their centers on Israel's borders—Hezbollah in Lebanon and Hamas in Gaza.

The suicide bombings in Israel and the rockets of Hezbollah and Hamas may not have the same quality of spectacle as the 9/11 terrorist attacks on the United States, but they have been more pervasive and have wrought death and destruction on an enormous scale, especially given the small size of the country. The threat of terrorism is part of the fabric of everyday life in Israel.

Some of the acts of terrorism Israel has encountered are fueled by the same kind of inchoate hatred that impels al-Qaeda. Others have a discrete strategic objective: to bring an end to Israeli occupation of the territories it acquired at the end of the 1967 war and to create a Palestinian state in them. Still others, for example the terrorist attacks associated with Hezbollah and Hamas, seek to eradicate Israel as a nation and establish a Palestinian state stretching from Jordan to the sea. The attacks of al-Qaeda on the United States on 9/11 cannot plausibly be regarded as having such grandiose ambitions, nor could any of the sporadic terrorist attacks or attempted attacks that occurred over the past decade.

The pleas of military necessity confronting Barak were more pressing than those faced by the U.S. president and other branches of government in the post–9/11 era, and the sources upon which claims of rights rested were more elusive. As Barak acknowledged, he had to develop "constitutional law without a constitution."[1] Israel has no written constitution. At the time of its founding, plans were made for the formulation and adoption of a constitution. Indeed, its Declaration of Independence promised that a constitution would be adopted no later than October 1, 1948. But those plans never came to fruition. So Barak, following in the tradition of his predecessors, constructed many of the governing principles of Israel—its body of constitutional law—as an elaboration of Israel's foundational aspiration, set forth in the Declaration of Independence, to be a free and democratic society. Such a rationalistic endeavor is also the core of the process that has given content and life to the American constitutional tradition, but the American Supreme Court has enjoyed the comfort of a sturdy source of authority—the written Constitution of 1787 and all its amendments.

Israel is governed through a parliamentary system, which among other things means that it is committed to the principle of legislative supremacy. Once the plan to adopt a written constitution failed, the Knesset (the Israeli parliament) began enacting a series of statutes known as the Basic Laws, which purport to set forth the governing principles of Israeli society. For Israel's first forty years, the Basic Laws primarily addressed the structure and organization of government powers. In 1992, however, the Knesset took a new turn and adopted a Basic Law guaranteeing human dignity and freedom. This law can properly be seen as part of the human rights tradition and resembles the U.S. Bill of Rights in both the generosity of its spirit and the generality of its language. Since 1992, this Basic Law has functioned for Justice Barak much as a written constitution, with one important exception: the supremacy of the legislature is preserved.

In a well-known 1995 decision, Justice Barak held that because the Basic Laws were passed by the Knesset sitting as a constitutional assembly, they took precedence over ordinary legislation, even if that legislation was adopted after the enactment of the Basic Laws.[2] Yet the legislature remains supreme. The Knesset possesses the power to amend any Basic Law in order to allow a statute that would otherwise be invalid because of a conflict. Generally, a Basic Law can be amended by a simple majority of the members of the Knesset present, although certain provisions of some of the Basic Laws—not the one on human dignity—stipulate that an amendment requires an absolute majority of all members of the Knesset or a supermajority.

Israel is a small country of around 7 million people, covering a compact geographic area roughly the size of New Jersey. Its political culture is characterized by vibrant public discussion (to understate the matter). Barak's decisions are widely known throughout the nation and remain a subject of great controversy. Some attempts have even been made to overturn them. Once, the minister of justice proposed amending the Basic Law on human dignity in order to overturn a decision—one of Barak's last—that invalidated a statute that had exempted the state from compensating Palestinians in designated zones in the Occupied Territories for injuries caused by Israeli security forces, even if the injuries did not relate to military operations aimed at suppressing terrorism.[3] Yet, so far, none of these efforts has succeeded, which is a testament both to Justice Barak and to the strength of the country's foundational commitments.

Barak's constitution is one without borders. It binds Israeli officials wherever they might be and protects citizens and noncitizens alike. Its overarching aim is to protect human dignity, which Barak sees as lying at the foundation of democracy and as the source of rights people are owed simply by virtue of their humanity. The depth of his commitment to human dignity is most clearly revealed in his decision denying the military the authority to subject anyone, including Palestinians or even suspected members of Hamas or Hezbollah, to harsh and aggressive interrogation techniques that he regarded as torture.[4] Impelled by respect for the dignity of all persons, Barak fashioned a prohibition of torture that is as absolute as the one found—at least before 9/11—in the U.S. Constitution.

Some commentators have called into question the absolute nature of this prohibition by imagining a scenario in which the only way to avoid a great loss of human life and other disastrous consequences is through torturing a prisoner. In this scenario, a bomb of enormous power is ticking away in a city and only the prisoner knows where it is located. In his ruling banning especially aggressive interrogation techniques, Justice Barak confronted this dilemma, even though the facts before him did not require him to do so, and he held that even in such a dire context a prior authorization of torture would be unconstitutional. The offense to human dignity would be too gross.

Barak acknowledged that, at a criminal trial after the fact, the guard who tortured the prisoner in this imagined scenario might—only might—be able to assert the defense of necessity and on that ground be exonerated. Some have criticized him for this concession. These critics fail to account for the fact that even the most absolute of rules are often tempered in their application. In the United States, for example, someone who tortured a prisoner to save innocent lives or the destruction of a city could assert a necessity defense or, more likely, trust a sympathetic jury to nullify the law through a general verdict of "not guilty."

For the most part, Justice Barak's principles are not absolutes like the prohibition of torture but rather seek an accommodation of conflicting values or, as he has put it, "clashing considerations."[5] In that sense, they are like the Fifth Amendment's requirement of due process or the Fourth Amendment's protection against unreasonable searches. The terms "due" and "unreasonable" necessarily entail a consideration of conflicting values, and as a result the liberties that these amendments promise are especially vulnerable in times of stress, when military necessity is to justify a sacrifice of individual freedom. For that reason, Barak's work is especially instructive because he has sought to create a distinctive judicial method—call it a jurisprudence—that acknowledges military necessity without permitting it to overwhelm fundamental freedoms.

This method accounts for two of his most important rulings on terrorism. One required the Israeli military to reroute the security fence that it was building between itself and the Occupied Territories to prevent the infiltration of suicide bombers and other terrorists.[6] The other—the so-called targeted killing case—limited the power of the military to kill persons who are civilians but who are suspected by the military of engaging in terrorist activities in Israel.[7]

Like any good judge, Barak began his analysis in these cases with an acknowledgment of the values—all the values—at stake in the controversy. He recognized the interest served by the government's action as well as the harms that would likely be inflicted by the proposed action. He accepted that national security—the survival of the nation and the protection of the lives of Israeli citizens—was a compelling justification for government action. But he also maintained that respect for human rights and human dignity were pillars of democracy and could not be casually brushed aside.

Although many jurists have faced similar dilemmas, Barak's distinctive contribution has been to place limits on the deference due to the military. In his opinions, he drew a vital distinction between the assessment of military needs and the question of whether the military action is normatively justified given its impact on fundamental values. He was prepared to defer to the government in its assessment of military needs but saw it as the essence of his job to determine whether the pursuit of those needs unjustifiably interfered with the exercise of a protected liberty or a fundamental value.

In the case regarding the construction of a security fence, for example, those contesting the route of the fence offered evidence—experts with considerable military experience—to demonstrate how the military's needs could be satisfied by building the fence along a line other than the one proposed. Yet Justice Barak was unprepared to second-guess the military on that score, and regarded the military's judgment on how to satisfy its needs as determinative. He took this view not simply because of the military's expertise on issues of national security but rather, and perhaps more fundamentally, because the military alone is responsible for the technical quality of its actions. By contrast, Barak reserved for the judiciary the function of determining whether the infringement of basic rights would be so great as to bar the military from acting as it wished. There was to be no deference in the realm of values. That judgment, in his view, belonged to the judiciary.

We in the United States have a strong tradition—especially evident in the post–9/11 era—of judicial deference to military authorities, but we fail to make Barak's distinction. Our deference goes not just to the military's technical assessment of the needs of national security but also to the question of whether, given the harm to fundamental values, its proposed actions are normatively justified. By granting the executive wide latitude both in its pursuit of its objectives and in its determination that those objectives merit sacrificing basic freedoms, the American judiciary allows the executive to strike the balance between military necessity and fundamental values. Such blanket deference overlooks the genuine danger to fundamental values posed by a political agency's response to perceived military needs or external dangers. It is true that in a presidential system, such as that of the United States, the executive and the legislature have independent sources of legitimacy, and thus the legislature can act as a check on the executive. Yet as the enactment of the Detainee Treatment Act of 2005, the Military Commissions Acts of 2006 and 2009, and the 2008 amendments of the Foreign Intelligence Surveillance Act illustrate, the legislature can also be complicit in the transgression of basic liberties in times of war. In this respect, judicial deference to the executive of the type Barak opposed is no more justified in a presidential system than in the Israeli parliamentary system.

In her opinion in *Hamdi v. Rumsfeld*, Justice O'Connor was explicit about the need for deference to the executive in fashioning procedural rules for adjudicating a claim to freedom by any individual—even a citizen—accused of being an enemy combatant. She was willing to place on the prisoner the burden of proving that the military's field records were mistaken, and she would have allowed military tribunals to decide the merits of that claim. A similar deference was manifest in the U.S. Supreme Court's refusal to force the government to charge persons held for prolonged periods, as well as in the lower courts' decisions not to give redress to victims of extraordinary rendition or even to inquire into the merits of their allegations. I suspect that the fear of interfering with the executive's capacity to conduct foreign affairs also explains the Supreme Court's 2013 decision denying standing to challenge the 2008 FISA amendments to persons whose telephone calls were likely to be intercepted under that measure.

Not only has Barak rejected this kind of blanket deference as a dereliction of what he understands to be the duty of a judge, he also has identified with greater clarity than any American jurist the appropriate inquiries for determining when a government action that affects fundamental values is justified. These inquiries, which he generally refers to as the "proportionality test," examine both the instrumental and the substantive rationality of the government's action. Justice Barak pursued these inquiries in all manner of cases, especially in recent years, but they had their greatest force in his rulings on national security. For that reason, they are especially illuminating in gauging the American response to terrorism in the post–9/11 era.

The instrumental inquiry concerns the relation between means and ends. It asks whether the means chosen by the government are rationally related to the end and, more important, whether the chosen means are the least restrictive alternative. Barak requires that the means be narrowly tailored to achieve their purpose, fitting, to use his metaphor, as closely as a suit might fit a body.[8] The sacrifice of fundamental values must be kept to an absolute minimum. This means that if the government has an alternative way of meeting its needs that entails less of a sacrifice in fundamental values, the original, more burdensome actions will not be allowed.

In the targeted killings case, for example, Barak fully appreciated the danger of terrorist attacks but sought to carefully cabin the power of the military to kill suspected terrorists. He drew a sharp line between enemy combatants and civilians, and was wary of placing civilians who were suspected of terrorism in yet a third category—unlawful combatants—that would afford neither the protections given to combatants nor those given to civilians. Although the laws of war allow the military to kill combatants in the course of armed conflict, civilians are fully protected. Civilians forfeit this protection when they participate in hostilities, such as terrorist attacks, but Justice Barak stringently defined the conditions for such forfeiture. Links to or membership in a terrorist organization were not sufficient. The person targeted, according to Barak, had to take a direct part in hostilities and was vulnerable to attack only while engaged in such hostilities. Even then, the military had the obligation to pursue only the least harmful means and could not kill the suspected terrorist if arrest and trial were feasible. As Barak reasoned, "among the military means, one must choose the means whose harm to the human rights of the harmed person is smallest." [9]

The U.S. Supreme Court, under the rubric of strict scrutiny, has required that when a fundamental value such as free speech or racial equality is threatened, the government must use the least restrictive means available to pursue its end—or, to use another formulation, governmental interference with a privileged value must be no greater than necessary. Unfortunately, however, the Court applies strict scrutiny only intermittently, and hardly ever in the context of war. Perhaps most famously, the Supreme Court did not insist upon the least restrictive means or least harmful alternative in the *Korematsu* case, even though in that decision the Court announced—for the very first time—that racial classifications should be strictly scrutinized.[10] *Korematsu* gave constitutional legitimacy to the mass relocation of persons of Japanese ancestry in the western states during the Second World War. Although the Court said that it was applying strict scrutiny to the relocation program, it nevertheless deferred to the government's assessment of the need for such a policy and, more importantly, it never considered whether less harmful alternatives were available.

The second type of inquiry in Barak's decisions—an inquiry that could be characterized as an investigation into substantive rationality—asks whether the harm of the government action is disproportionate to the benefit that might be achieved from it. In other words, even if the government's action serves compelling interests and the means used are rationally connected to the pursuit of those interests and in fact represent the least restrictive alternative, the government's action will nevertheless be deemed unjustified and thus unlawful if the harm it inflicts is disproportionately greater than the gains that it might achieve. Aside from some concurring and dissenting opinions by Justice Breyer,[11] there is no trace of this proportionality requirement in the decisions of the U.S. Supreme Court, certainly not in the context of war, and yet Justice Barak routinely and successfully applied it in a wide range of cases in which fundamental values were at stake.

In fact, proportionality was the linchpin of Barak's opinion in the case of the security fence. Although he accepted the military's claim that its proposed lines for the security fence would be the most effective in saving the lives of Israeli citizens and that any redrawing of the lines would result in increased loss of life from terrorist attacks, he nonetheless ordered sections of the fence built along a different line in order to reduce the harm to Palestinians that would result from the division of their communities and separation from their fields and places of work. The harm of the lines proposed by the military was deemed disproportionate to any advantages that might be achieved in terms of security. Put another way, Barak was prepared to sacrifice the military objectives—to risk Israeli lives—in order to avoid the greater harm to the Palestinian communities that would have resulted from the erection of the security barrier as originally planned. His intention was not to demean the importance of the military objective but to find a way to accommodate two compelling, albeit conflicting, values.

In all this—his refusal to defer to the military in the trade-off of values, his insistence on the least restrictive alternative, and, finally, his application of the requirement that the harm to fundamental values not be disproportionate to the gain in security—Justice Barak held firm in his attachment to the law and the belief that the law is the embodiment of reason in the service of humanity. His method was to demand, systematically and relentlessly, that any sacrifices of rights required by a proper regard for human dignity be fully and rationally justified. In so doing, Barak revealed a deep and profound commitment to reason—the common element that unites his life as a professor and as a judge and that defines his unique place in Israeli society and the world legal community. For him to declare, as he has done on many occasions, that "law is everywhere" [12] is to invite us to imagine that every aspect of our public life, even war, should be governed by reason, and reason alone.

Aharon Barak and I are the closest of friends, but I have often wondered in private: Isn't it remarkable that in such a small corner of the world, so often racked by violence and religious passions, a modern-day apostle of the Enlightenment has risen and taken a place not just in the history of Israel but of all mankind?

# PART II

# THE NEW NORMAL

# Prologue to Chapter 6

Trevor Sutton

"I don't want these individuals to die," President Obama said at an emotional press conference held in April 2013, following media reports of a hunger strike by more than one hundred prisoners held at the detention facility in Guantánamo Bay, Cuba. "I am going to go back at this," he promised, alluding to his unfulfilled 2008 campaign pledge to close the prison and end the practices that made it infamous. "I am going to get my team to review everything that is currently being done in Guantánamo," he continued, adding: "I am going to reengage with Congress to try and make the case that [Guantánamo] is not in the best interests of the American people."

It is possible to take the president's emotion at face value and still deem him primarily responsible for what is occurring at Guantánamo. This, in fact, is the view expressed by Owen Fiss in this chapter, "Imprisonment Without Trial," which describes how and why President Obama perpetuated one of the most controversial of the Bush administration's counterterrorism policies: prolonged, indefinite detention without trial of any type. The essay, which first appeared in an abbreviated form in *Slate* and later in full in the *Tulsa Law Review*, revisits many of the themes and events discussed in previous essays, but brings to them a new theoretical rigor through an elaboration of what Fiss has called the principle of freedom. In Fiss's view, this principle, which represents the collective operation of several constitutional provisions, overrides the various statutory and practical arguments in favor of prolonging the imprisonment without trial of foreign nationals held at Guantánamo.

Two applications of the principle of freedom discussed in the essay deserve special mention. The first is the incompatibility between the principle and what Fiss calls the "bifurcated exclusionary rule," under which tainted evidence may be used as the basis for perpetual incarceration but not for a criminal trial. The second is the principle's requirement that incarceration be conditioned on a criminal trial presided over by an independent judge. In Fiss's view, oversight of executive action determining that the prisoner remains a threat to the United States—even if this oversight is conducted by an Article III judge—does not satisfy this requirement.

These two applications are noteworthy because they illustrate the perils of administrative solutions to constitutional wrongs. This is the central message of "Imprisonment Without Trial," which demonstrates how even the most well-intentioned president can inadvertently entrench unconstitutional practices if he takes primary responsibility for protecting the rights of unpopular groups. As the essay makes clear, judges can transcend political inertia in a way that officials of the executive branch often cannot.

In the end, the president's solution to the hunger strike was to permit the military to force-feed prisoners through the application of physical restraints and feeding tubes. One can only imagine the anguish the president must feel in knowing that his attempts to solve the problem of Guantánamo have created the need for such grotesque practices. At one point in his career, Obama taught constitutional law, and he should not have been surprised to learn that the dignity of the individual is secured not through Article II of the Constitution, but rather the Bill of Rights.

# Chapter 6

# IMPRISONMENT WITHOUT TRIAL

The Constitution is a broad charter of governance. It establishes the institutions of government and places limits on their exercise of power. For the most part, the Constitution speaks in broad generalities, and over the last several hundred years many principles have been developed to give specific content to these generalities.

Some of these principles, such as the one requiring separation of powers, are inferred from the general structure of the Constitution. Others, among them antidiscrimination or its alternative, the antisubordination principle, are rooted in a specific provision such as the Equal Protection Clause and are meant to give further content to those provisions.

Both types of principles are supposed to guide government officials in discharging their duties, and, if required, they can be enforced against these officials by the judiciary. These principles are as endowed with the authority of the Constitution as are the words on the parchment, though they present themselves to us as an interpretation of those words and can be criticized and, if need be, reformulated in ways that, short of an amendment, the words on the parchment cannot.

One such principle—I refer to it as the principle of freedom— has been violated by the Bush administration and, more recently, by the Obama administration in their fight against terrorism. This principle denies the government the power to imprison anyone without charging that individual with a specific crime and swiftly bringing him to trial. The principle of freedom is implicit in the provision of the Constitution that limits the power of Congress to suspend the writ of habeas corpus—the means by which the legality of imprisonment can be tested.[1] More importantly, the principle should be seen as a gloss on the Fifth Amendment, which denies government the power to deprive anyone of "life, liberty, or property without due process of law."

At its core, the principle of freedom denies the government the power to deprive an individual of his liberty without charging that individual with a specific crime and producing evidence of guilt in open court. It also requires the government to give the accused an opportunity to cross-examine the witnesses who testify against him, and to present his own witnesses.

Many of the procedural protections required by the principle of freedom have instrumental value: they are considered the best means available for arriving at the truth of the matter. They also reflect elemental notions of fairness and are thus one source of the government's legitimacy. They put the government to the burden of proving its charges in open court and give the accused, who is also protected by a presumption of innocence and the right to trial by jury, a reasonable opportunity to defend himself. The underlying assumption is that a government willing to abide by these limitations is likely to win the respect and admiration of its citizens.

Like many constitutional principles, the principle of freedom has a limited number of exceptions. War is one. The Constitution recognizes the authority of the United States to engage in war, and the principle of freedom has been adjusted to accommodate the necessities of combat. In the throes of war, the government is allowed to capture enemy soldiers and imprison them without a trial for the duration of the hostilities. Both Bush and Obama have made claim to this exception to the principle of freedom and have insisted on the authority to imprison for prolonged, indefinite periods of time anyone that they determine has fought for the Taliban or al-Qaeda.

## The Taliban and the Geneva Convention

The continued detention of persons accused of fighting for the Taliban presents a special set of problems arising from the Third Geneva Convention of 1949. This treaty, having been ratified by the Senate, operates within this sphere of authority allowed by the Constitution and should thus be seen as a secondary constraint on the authority of the government to imprison without trial. Under the Third Geneva Convention, enemy combatants can be held for the duration of a war and are to be repatriated at the conclusion of the hostilities.[2] The convention also implicitly provides that enemy combatants cannot be prosecuted simply for fighting, although they can be prosecuted for war crimes.[3] The United States is a signatory of the treaty and is constrained by it whenever the belligerent is also a signatory.

In the fall of 2001, shortly after the terrorist attacks on September 11, the United States launched a war against Afghanistan. At that time, the Taliban, essentially a political organization of religious fanatics, controlled the government of Afghanistan and used its power to support and harbor al-Qaeda. The United States invaded Afghanistan when its government refused to turn over Osama bin Laden, then the leader of al-Qaeda. The Taliban fighters taken into custody in the course of this war are protected by the Third Geneva Convention simply by virtue of the fact that both the United States and Afghanistan are signatories to the treaty. The fact that the United States had previously refused diplomatic recognition to the Afghan government when it was controlled by the Taliban did not preclude the applicability of the convention.

At an early stage in the war, President Bush declared that all who fought for the Taliban were unlawful enemy combatants.[4] By that he meant that members of the Taliban were not entitled to any of the protections of the Third Geneva Convention. So denied the protection of the treaty, the Taliban fighters could, according to Bush, be prosecuted for fighting or, alternatively, held for prolonged indefinite periods of time, even for life, without placing them on trial. Moreover, under this doctrine there was no obligation at the conclusion of the war to repatriate the prisoners who had fought for the Taliban. President Bush did not in any way recognize the principle of freedom as a limitation of his power.

Late in 2001, a young American citizen—John Walker Lindh, who admitted to having fought for the Taliban but denied any connection whatsoever to al-Qaeda—was captured by United States forces in Afghanistan. Soon thereafter he was prosecuted in federal district court in Virginia for being part of a conspiracy to kill American soldiers. Lindh argued that the prosecution contravened the Third Geneva Convention, since he was being prosecuted simply for fighting. The district court denied Lindh's motion to dismiss and in so doing lent support to the doctrine propounded by the Bush administration that treated all Taliban fighters as unlawful enemy combatants.[5] After Lindh's motion to dismiss was denied, Lindh pleaded guilty to one of the charges and was sentenced to twenty years' imprisonment in a maximum-security facility in Arizona. The plea agreement provided that if, for any reason, the sentence were to be set aside, Lindh would once again be classified as an unlawful enemy combatant and thus could be imprisoned without trial for an indefinite period of time, presumably even for life.

The Third Geneva Convention sets forth four conditions that must be met in order for an irregular militia to be brought within its protection. The fighters must (1) wear uniforms or some designation; (2) carry their arms openly; (3) be subject to a command structure; and (4) not commit war crimes. The district court took liberty with the text of the convention when it used these criteria to determine whether the Afghanistan army—not some irregular militia—was entitled to the protection of the treaty. By its very terms, the convention applies to "Members of the armed forces of a Party to a conflict."[6] It is generally understood that the convention provides no protection to spies and saboteurs, in part because they do not wear uniforms, but Bush sought to expand the use of that exception to cover the entire armed forces of Afghanistan under the Taliban regime. Unfortunately, the district court endorsed Bush's policy.

The district court can also be faulted for the evidentiary basis it relied on in applying the Geneva Convention criteria to the Afghanistan army. For example, in determining whether the fighters had committed war crimes, the district court looked to practices of the Taliban that had brought it to power rather than the way it fought the war against the United States. To compound the error, the district court rested its judgment on books (one of which happened to be published before the war in Afghanistan began), not evidence on the record. Admittedly, a trial on how the entire Afghanistan army fought the war might prove to be a difficult, if not impossible, task, but it is a consequence of Bush's extension of the exception for spies and saboteurs to the Afghan army.

President Obama has been careful to avoid using the nomenclature of unlawful enemy combatants, but he appears to be pursuing the same policy as Bush with regard to the Taliban. On May 21, 2009, in a speech at the National Archives, Obama announced his strategy for dealing with the prisoners still being held at Guantánamo. By way of example, he listed among those to be held indefinitely without trial a prisoner who "had commanded Taliban troops in battle."[7] Obama said that this prisoner was being held for his "past crimes"[8] but never specified what those crimes were. If the Taliban prisoners being held at Guantánamo had violated the laws of war—by killing civilians, for example—then they should be tried for that crime. However, if their only crime was fighting against American soldiers, as was arguably true of the unnamed Taliban commander mentioned by Obama, then under the terms of the Geneva Convention, they should be turned over to the Afghanistan government, which would then be responsible for determining their fate.

The obligation of repatriation stems from the fact that we are no longer at war with Afghanistan, but rather are a vital (if increasingly frustrated) partner of the country's government. That war ended by at least 2004, when the Taliban were routed, a new constitution was adopted for the country, elections held, and a new government installed. In fact, a second round of national elections was held in August 2009 and another in 2014. The United States and a limited number of NATO forces are still, as of this writing, operating in Afghanistan, but they are now doing so at the behest of the Afghan government, helping to reconstruct the nation, suppress the resurgence of the Taliban, and pursue al-Qaeda.

Inevitably, repatriation is a long, arduous process. It does not occur overnight. What is striking about Obama's May 2009 National Archives speech is that he did not acknowledge the obligation to repatriate Afghan soldiers, including the one he described as having led troops in battle. In fact, in announcing that such prisoners will remain incarcerated for indefinite periods of time without trial, Obama appears to have repudiated such an obligation.

In a speech to the American Society of International Law on March 25, 2010, Harold Koh, the legal adviser to the Department of State, described recent attempts to improve the detention facilities in Afghanistan. He spoke glowingly of the Department of Defense's efforts "to prepare the Afghans for the day when we turn over responsibility for detention operations."[9] There was no recognition, however, of the obligation to repatriate the Afghan soldiers, nor any indication that these new detention facilities would be used for the Guantánamo prisoners who had fought for the Taliban and who, Obama had declared, would be subject to indefinite, prolonged imprisonment without trial.

In the same speech, Koh reminded his audience of the conflict in Afghanistan and characterized the military operation in that country that began in 2001 as a war against the Taliban, not against the Afghan government. Such a characterization has enabled the administration to ignore the 2004 transfer of sovereignty and to treat the battle against the Taliban in Afghanistan today not as an effort to suppress the insurgency but as a continuation of the war that began in 2001. From my perspective, however, such a characterization of the initial military invasion is ill-advised, as wrong as would be an attempt by the administration to characterize the invasion of Iraq in March 2003 as a war against the Baath Party and not against Iraq. Such a characterization would postpone indefinitely the obligation of repatriation, suspending it until all insurgencies are suppressed, and would thus run counter to the humanitarian purposes underlying the Geneva Convention. In any event, characterizations of the invasion of Afghanistan in that way would be of no help to the administration in justifying the detention of the Taliban prisoners subject to the policy announced by Obama in his National Archives speech, for they did not participate in the insurgency, nor could they have—for years on end they have been imprisoned at Guantánamo. They stand accused of fighting against U.S. forces when we invaded the country in the fall of 2001 and, according to Obama, are being held for their "past crimes."

## Al-Qaeda and the Principle of Freedom

Al-Qaeda cannot possibly claim the protection of the Third Geneva Convention. All of its soldiers are unlawful—or, perhaps more properly, unprivileged—enemy combatants. This, remember, was the same classification President Bush (and, by implication, President Obama) applied to the Taliban. While the argument for placing the Taliban outside the reach of the convention was founded on a strained interpretation of a provision of the treaty concerning irregular militias, there is a much more straightforward argument for reaching the same conclusion for al-Qaeda. For the most part, the convention constrains the United States only when a belligerent is a signatory, and al-Qaeda is not such a signatory, nor could it be, for it is a far-flung international terrorist organization that operates in secret and does not (yet) lay claim to any national territory. The convention provides that a signatory may be bound by the convention in its relationship to a non-signatory, but only if the non-signatory acts in accordance with the requirements of the convention[10]—a condition al-Qaeda most assuredly does not satisfy.

Even though executive action toward al-Qaeda is not constrained by the treaty (nor perhaps by customary humanitarian law), it nevertheless remains subject to the Constitution and to the principle of freedom in particular—unless, of course, the action fits within the exception allowed for war. The Bush administration took the position that al-Qaeda was responsible for the 9/11 attacks, and for that reason it launched a war against al-Qaeda. Obama has meticulously avoided using Bush's mantra of the "War on Terror," but he has repeatedly declared, "We are at war with al-Qaeda."[11]

Although the campaign against al-Qaeda may be character-ized as a war, thereby allowing the United States to target or cap-ture al-Qaeda fighters, it is no ordinary war, and the exceptions to the principle of freedom must be adjusted accordingly. In its fight against al-Qaeda, the Bush administration was prepared to treat the entire world as a battlefield and insisted that the prerog-atives of the United States as a belligerent allowed it to seize and perhaps even target members of al-Qaeda anywhere they could be found, be it at O'Hare Airport, in the streets of Milan, or at a university in Peoria, Illinois. However, by acknowledging this prerogative, we undermine and endanger the very nature of civ-ilized life as we know it and defeat the values that underlie the principle of freedom.

To guard against such a danger, it became necessary to cali-brate the concept of the battlefield and to distinguish between active theaters of armed conflict (so-called hot battlefields) and other locations where suspected terrorists might be found. Sus-pects not residing within an active theater of armed conflict can of course be apprehended outside of it, but only through the ordinary processes of the law, not the kind of action typically undertaken by the military on a battlefield.

Analogous restrictions must be placed on the authority of the United States to imprison individuals accused of having links to al-Qaeda, even if they were captured on the battlefield and al-legedly engaged in armed conflict. In this case, the restrictions must be temporal in nature and reflect the potentially unending character of the war against al-Qaeda. Much of our military ac-tion has been aimed at capturing or killing Osama bin Laden. That objective was achieved on May 2, 2011, but it has not brought an end to the war against al-Qaeda. Other leaders have emerged, and once they are captured or targeted, others will emerge. Account must also be taken of the fact that al-Qaeda has units throughout the world that are capable of acting on their own.

Accordingly, just as it is unthinkable to treat as a battle-field every place on earth where al-Qaeda fighters might be, it is unthinkable to allow the government to hold al-Qaeda suspects until the war between the United States and al-Qaeda has ended—a time that we cannot readily foresee. The justification for continued detention might be the same—preventing alleged fighters from returning to the battlefield—but the consequences would be radically different. To allow persons accused of being al-Qaeda soldiers to be imprisoned for the duration of hostilities would constitute such an enormous expansion of the exception to the principle of freedom as to undermine the principle itself and deny the values it serves.

The Bush administration was, of course, allowed some lee-way when it began its war against al-Qaeda and captured persons it believed were members of al-Qaeda. It soon became clear, however, that the administration was prepared to incarcerate suspects seized far from an active theater of armed conflict and to do so for a prolonged period of time, maybe forever, without ever placing them on trial. Some of these prisoners were held in naval brigs in South Carolina and Virginia. For the most part, however, they were imprisoned at Guantánamo Naval Station in Cuba.

The prison in Guantánamo was opened in January 2002 and over the years between six hundred and eight hundred prisoners were incarcerated there at one time or another. Some of these prisoners were accused of fighting for the Taliban, but most were accused of having links to al-Qaeda. During this period, some were transferred to other prisons and others were released due either to diplomatic pressure or to decisions by military tribunals established by the Department of Defense in July 2004. (The tribunals are part of the government's strategy to deprive the Guantánamo prisoners of access to federal courts to advance their claim of freedom through the writ of habeas corpus.) In January 2009, when Obama took office, Guantánamo had 240 prisoners, some of whom had been incarcerated there for as long as seven years.

Upon taking office, President Obama signed an executive order requiring that the prison at Guantánamo be closed in one year's time, but it remained unclear what might happen to the prisoners still confined there. Accordingly, in his National Archives speech in May 2009 he announced a tripartite policy—free those who had succeeded in their petitions for habeas corpus, place others on trial before either military commissions or civilian courts, and continue the imprisonment without trial for the group that remained. At the time of the speech approximately fifty individuals fell within this third category.[12] Admittedly, it is sometimes difficult to know when a detention will be brief enough to be justified by the necessities of war and thus allowed by the exception to the principle of freedom, but not in this instance.

To Obama's credit, he, unlike Bush and his defenders, appears to be using the power to imprison without trial only reluctantly. When he announced the policy in May 2009, Obama called the prospect of prolonged, indefinite incarceration without trial "one of the toughest issues we will face."[13] Yet, rather than honor the principle of freedom, Obama continued Bush's policy of indefinitely imprisoning some Guantánamo detainees and declared by way of justification that they "cannot be prosecuted."[14] He did not explain why trials were not an option. Certainly it cannot be the case that U.S. law is incapable of dealing with al-Qaeda agents or terrorism in general. Bush tried and convicted a number of al-Qaeda terrorists during his tenure, and Obama has put a number on trial too, as well as attempting to try the alleged mastermind of the 9/11 attack, Khalid Sheikh Mohammed. At first, Mohammed was to be tried before a civilian court in Manhattan, but in the face of congressional opposition and, eventually, legislation prohibiting transfer of any of the Guantánamo prisoners to the United States even for trial,

Obama decided in the spring of 2011 to have him tried before a military commission at Guantánamo.

In announcing his decision to continue Bush's policy of imprisonment without trial, Obama explained that "in some cases" the evidence is "tainted," and by that he presumably meant that the evidence against the prisoner was obtained through torture. This kind of evidence has long been subject to an "exclusionary rule," often affirmed by Obama, that prohibits the use at trial of evidence that has been acquired through torture and is thus in violation of the Constitution and federal statutes. So if the policy of imprisonment without trial stemmed from the tainted quality of the evidence against the prisoner, Obama effectively had bifurcated the exclusionary rule: evidence secured through torture cannot be used at trial, but it can be used as the basis for incarcerating a suspect, even for the rest of his life.

Such a bifurcated exclusionary rule would create all the wrong incentives. Government interrogators will know that a confession secured through torture may serve as the basis for prolonged incarceration, despite the fact that upon taking office Obama issued an order banning torture.[15] The bifurcated rule would also compound the wrong suffered by the Guantánamo prisoners who were tortured and are now being held indefinitely without trial: first they were subject to excruciating pain, and now the fruits of that abuse will keep them in prison with no end in sight. The Constitution should not allow any deprivation of liberty to be based on evidence procured through torture, regardless of whether that deprivation is the result of a trial or a presidential decision.

Alternatively, the concern animating Obama's, and before him Bush's, unwillingness to go to trial may not have been the use of tainted evidence but a fear that the trial would result in the disclosure of secret evidence—for example, the identity of undercover agents. The government is, of course, entitled to a measure of secrecy, but that should not justify—and in fact never has justified—imprisonment without a trial. In a good number of criminal prosecutions touching on national security, defendants have sought information that the government deems top secret. Courts have been more than capable of accommodating these concerns, typically by examining the evidence in private outside the presence of the accused or his lawyer and evaluating its relevance to the case.[16] If the judge determines that the evidence is important, the government can make it available to the accused, offer a substitute, or drop the case. The remedy has never been to suspend the trial and incarcerate the prisoner indefinitely.

Nor can the policy of imprisonment without trial be justified as preventing some extraordinary harm, such as the detonation of a radioactive bomb. One al-Qaeda operative—Jose Padilla—who was taken into custody in 2002 at O'Hare Airport in Chicago as he alighted from a flight that originated in Pakistan, was accused of such a crime. He was accused not in the formal sense of the term, but rather in a press release issued by the Department of Justice.[17] After seven years' imprisonment, the government finally brought Padilla to trial—but for an entirely different crime.[18] No other al-Qaeda suspect, not even any of those held at Guantánamo, has been accused of a crime of equivalent potential destructiveness. Even if one were, the burden would remain on the government to prosecute that individual for that crime, even if it carried a risk of acquittal.

In defending his initial decision to place Khalid Sheikh Mohammed on trial before a civilian court in Manhattan, Eric Holder, Obama's attorney general, sought to minimize the risk of an acquittal and in so doing produced an even more barbarous offense to the principle of freedom. Testifying before a Senate committee, Holder suggested that even if Mohammed were acquitted at trial, he could be imprisoned indefinitely, even for life, as an unprivileged or unlawful enemy combatant.[19] Such a policy would make the trial pointless and defeat the very values the principle of freedom seeks to further. Indeed, imprisonment after acquittal would be far worse than imprisonment without trial. The exceptions to the principle of freedom must be narrowly cabined to protect the values furthered by the principle and, in any event, cannot be adjusted on a case-by-case basis to reflect the president's assessment of the gravity of the threat posed if the prisoner is acquitted, or much less allow the president to imprison the accused after he has been acquitted.

Many have criticized President Bush's conduct of the War on Terror as an exercise of excessive unilateralism. They faulted him for acting on his own without seeking the involvement or concurrence of the other branches of government. Fully aware of this line of criticism, President Obama declared in his National Archives address, in May 2009, that "in our constitutional system prolonged detention should not be the decision of any one man,"[20] and then went on to promise to develop a system that involved "judicial and congressional oversight" of his decision to incarcerate someone as an enemy combatant.[21]

On September 24, 2009, Obama announced that he would not turn to Congress for establishing the promised oversight system.[22] He said that support for his action was already provided by the Authorization for the Use of Military Force (AUMF),[23] a statute passed by Congress immediately after September 11. On March 25, 2010, the legal adviser to the Department of State also made reference to this statute in defending the administration's detention policy before the American Society of International Law.[24] Yet these references to the AUMF seem inapposite. The AUMF authorized the president to use whatever force was necessary to apprehend and bring to justice whoever he determined was responsible for the September 11 attacks. As such, the statute gave legislative authorization for the war against al-Qaeda and against Afghanistan for harboring and sheltering al-Qaeda.

In technical terms, the AUMF provided the congressional declaration of war required by the Constitution. Yet it in no way functioned as the kind of oversight system Obama initially promised, which of necessity would be concerned with the prolonged detention of particular individuals.

On March 7, 2011—almost two years after his National Archives speech—Obama issued an executive order establishing an oversight system that sought to address the plight of particular individuals who were imprisoned but never tried. This oversight system is neither judicial nor legislative, as originally promised, but is lodged in the executive branch. It vests power in a board consisting of senior officials from six government departments and offices—the Departments of State, Defense, Justice, and Homeland Security, the Office of the Director of National Intelligence, and the Office of the Chairman of the Joint Chiefs of Staff—to determine whether the continued detention of each prisoner "is necessary to protect against a significant threat to the security of the United States." [25] This board's determination is subject to a veto by the heads of the various departments and offices. If the board determines that a prisoner no longer remains a threat to the United States, and if that determination is allowed to stand, the secretary of state and secretary of defense are, by the terms of the executive order, required to make "vigorous efforts" to arrange for the prisoner's transfer to another country. Obama's new oversight system can thus be seen as a specially designed parole procedure, with a number of drawbacks—it is subject to control by political appointees, and the prisoners have never been tried or adjudged guilty of any crime by a court of law.

Others who have defended imprisonment without trial, such as David Cole,[26] have proposed an oversight system that would be less politically sensitive and would in fact make the judiciary primarily responsible for case-by-case assessments of the basis of the executive's decision to detain an individual. The federal judiciary sitting in habeas might be utilized for this purpose, where the judge would have to determine whether there was a reason to imprison the individual in the first place (was he an enemy combatant?) and then whether there were still reasons to detain him (is he a threat to the United States?). Such a scheme would be a great improvement over Obama's administrative parole system, but it still would not satisfy the principle of freedom, which requires not simply oversight by the judiciary but a trial determining the guilt or innocence of the accused.

The procedures governing a trial seek to protect the innocent by casting the burden of proof on the government and controlling the discovery and admission of evidence. Theoretically, these procedures can be replicated in an oversight system, but as a practical matter they are likely to be watered down. Otherwise, there would be no point to the exercise—avoiding a trial. Moreover, the allocation of power entailed in an oversight system is necessarily—as a theoretical matter—quite different from that in a trial. For one thing, the jury would be supplanted. In addition, when compared to cases tried without a jury, the responsibility of the judiciary would be diluted. In a trial without a jury, the task of the court is not to decide whether the government has good reason to believe that the suspect has committed a crime, as it would under a system of oversight, but to decide whether, in fact, the accused is guilty of the crime charged. In such a trial, the responsibility for determining guilt and thus to deprive an individual of his liberty is not shared with the executive but rests entirely on the shoulders of the judiciary, as due process of law requires.

## The Scope of Obama's Policy

In analyzing the policy of imprisonment without trial, I have treated Obama's stance as a continuation of Bush's. There are, however, two differences between Bush's and Obama's respective positions, both of which stem from the circumstances under which Obama announced his policy, though it remains to be seen whether these differences are of any significance.

One difference arises from the number of persons affected by the policy. Obama announced his policy in the context of deciding the fate of some of the prisoners being held at Guantánamo. At the time there were about fifty such prisoners who would be subject to the policy. There were also indications that the policy would be applied to prisoners being held at Bagram Air Field in Afghanistan.[27] Although the vast majority of the prisoners once held there—approximately six hundred—have been turned over to the Afghan government, we still have custody of a good number of them. They should be added to the ones at Guantánamo, in gauging the scope of Obama's policy. Still, the number of persons to whom Obama's policy applies is limited. Moreover, Obama's policy does not have the open-ended quality of the policy Bush announced, which applied to all al-Qaeda and Taliban fighters, regardless of where they are captured or incarcerated.

The essentially vestigial quality of Obama's policy is underscored by his treatment of Umar Farouk Abdulmutallab, a Nigerian citizen accused of trying to detonate a bomb on a Northwest flight as it was about to land in Detroit on Christmas Day 2009. Abdulmutallab was accused of being an operative of al-Qaeda, trained by the organization in Yemen, but he was immediately brought within the ambit of the criminal process, not treated as an enemy combatant.[28] Similarly, Ahmed Abdulkadir Warsame, a Somali national accused of working with al-Shabaab and al-Qaeda, was captured by the U.S. military in the Gulf region on April 19, 2011. He was questioned for intelligence for over two months and then turned over to civilian law enforcement agents, and was arraigned in the Southern District of New York on July 5, 2011.[29]

These developments strike me as an encouraging turn of events, but there is still reason to object to the detention policy announced by Obama in his National Archives speech. The offense to the principle of freedom and the rule of law does not turn on the number of persons affected. Moreover, President Obama's policy, even if embraced reluctantly and confined to a limited number of those imprisoned by the previous administration, will define what the government is allowed in the years ahead. It will lend a measure of legitimacy to Bush's action and will have the inevitable effect of normalizing what should be seen as an offense to the Constitution.

Another circumstance limiting the scope of Obama's policy is the fact that all the prisoners at Guantánamo and Bagram are foreign nationals. Initially, it was unclear whether Obama believed that the policy could extend to American citizens. A brief filed around the time of the National Archives speech stated that the policy of imprisonment without trial was to apply to "persons," with no distinction between American citizens and foreign nationals.[30] In 2010, Obama seemed to honor the principle of freedom in his treatment of Faisal Shahzad, a naturalized American citizen. Shahzad was arrested by civilian law enforcement officials, swiftly charged, and then brought to trial in federal court for attempting to detonate a bomb in Times Square.[31] Yet that case did not necessarily indicate that Obama opposed imprisoning any American without trial. After all, his treatment of Shahzad was no different from that afforded to the Nigerian national Umar Farouk Abdulmutallab. However, at the end of 2011, more than two years after his National Archives speech, Obama went out of his way to draw a distinction between American citizens and foreign nationals. "I want to clarify," he declared, "that my Administration will not authorize the indefinite military detention without trial of American citizens."[32]

In this declaration, Obama broke from Bush. President Bush

was prepared to treat all al-Qaeda and Taliban fighters, including American citizens, as unlawful enemy combatants who could be imprisoned indefinitely without trial. This was evident in the cases of John Walker Lindh and Jose Padilla. It was also evident in the case of Ali Saleh Kahlah al-Marri, a citizen of Qatar who had lawfully been admitted to the United States for educational purposes. Al-Marri was taken into custody while enrolled as a student at Butler University in Peoria, Illinois, and, on the basis of alleged al-Qaeda links, was imprisoned as an unlawful enemy combatant in a naval brig in South Carolina for six years. As in the case of Jose Padilla, the government eventually changed its strategy. While a petition for certiorari was pending before the Court, and for the obvious purpose of mooting Supreme Court review of its detention policy, the government charged al-Marri with a specific crime, to which he later pleaded guilty.[33]

The imprisonment of any American citizen brings into play the Non-Detention Act of 1971, which provides that no American citizen can be detained without authorization of Congress.[34] This statute was enacted as a belated repudiation of the internment of citizens of Japanese ancestry during World War II. The 1971 measure might be seen as a watered-down version of the principle of freedom—watered-down because it applies only to citizens; requires a grant of authority from Congress, not a trial; and seeks to protect the authority of Congress rather than personal liberty.

The force of the Non-Detention Act was further reduced by the Supreme Court's decision in *Hamdi v. Rumsfeld* in 2004.[35] In an opinion by Justice Sandra Day O'Connor, four justices ruled that the statutory authorization required by the 1971 act could be found in the AUMF—the statute passed immediately after 9/11 that authorized the use of force to respond to the terrorist attack on that day and that functioned as the declaration of war against Afghanistan. The Court did not rule on the government's further contention that even if the AUMF did not satisfy the requirement of the 1971 Non-Detention Act, the 1971 act did not provide any protection for American citizens who had been captured in an active theater of war.

In truth, the primary protection for the personal liberty of American citizens is not the 1971 Non-Detention Act or any other statute, but rather the principle of freedom as embodied in the Constitution. This principle's protections are not confined to American citizens; they apply to citizens and noncitizens alike. The primary textual source of the principle is the Due Process Clause, which by its very terms protects the liberty of "any person," and this provision should be seen as limiting the authority of United States officials wherever they act and against whomever they act.

As a general matter, the Due Process Clause and perhaps the Bill of Rights as a whole should not be read as a testamentary document distributing property or benefits (individual rights) to privileged classes of persons (American citizens) but as promulgating general norms defining the authority of U.S. officials. Although foreign nationals may not be part of the political community—the "We the People" that endows the Constitution with democratic legitimacy—the Constitution represents the political community's definition of the standards of conduct that it expects of its officials wherever they act and against whomever they act. Accordingly, even though Obama's policy of imprisonment without trial appears to be confined to persons who are not American citizens or those not lawfully admitted to the United States, as is true of the persons still incarcerated in Guantánamo or Bagram, it would, I contend, violate the Constitution and be as clear a breach of the rule of law as was Bush's.

At the time of Obama's National Archives speech, the Supreme Court had already handed down its decision in *Boumediene v. Bush*. The Court concluded in that case that the statute banning the writ of habeas corpus for persons determined by the executive to be unlawful enemy combatants was unconstitutional. Justice Anthony Kennedy spoke for the Court, and in doing so he carefully avoided any broad pronouncements on the rights possessed by foreign nationals. He ruled that the Guantánamo prisoners were entitled to the protection of the provision of the Constitution limiting the powers of Congress to suspend the writ of habeas corpus but saw that provision as serving separation of powers and announced a multivariate test to determine its applicability. As he said, "[W]e conclude that at least three factors are relevant in determining the reach of the Suspension Clause: (1) the citizenship and status of the detainee and the adequacy of the process through which that status determination was made; (2) the nature of the sites where apprehension and then detention took place; and (3) the practical obstacles inherent in resolving the prisoner's entitlement to the writ." [36] The application of this test will vary from case to case; in fact, the Court of Appeals for the District of Columbia decided that under the *Boumediene* test the Suspension Clause did not reach prisoners at Bagram Airfield, a U.S. military base in Afghanistan, largely because the base was located in a theater of armed conflict.[37] But from the very terms of the test itself and its initial application, it is clear that the benefit of the Suspension Clause is not confined to United States citizens or even foreign nationals who are incarcerated within the sovereign territory of the United States.

*Boumediene* recognized that the essential function of the writ is to guard against arbitrary action by the executive. In the specific context of that case, the action in question was the detention of persons who denied that they had ever taken up arms against the United States. *Boumediene* does not preclude, however, and the principle of freedom requires, that the writ be available to guard against another form of arbitrary action by the executive: the failure to place on trial individuals who have been accused of terrorism and who have been incarcerated for prolonged periods of time—in some cases, for more than a decade. A habeas proceeding authorized by *Boumediene* may find the prisoner seeking the writ to have fought for al-Qaeda and thus properly classified as an unprivileged enemy combatant but then go on to decide that under the principle of freedom the continued detention of this individual can be authorized only if he is tried and convicted of some specific crime. The constitutional right to freedom must, of course, accommodate claims of military necessity, but never in a way that relieves the judiciary of its duty to scrutinize these claims with care and to limit the sacrifice of freedom to the smallest possible domain.

## Prologue to Chapter 7

Trevor Sutton

The idea that torture has no place in a civilized society emerged in the Enlightenment and is as old as the American Republic itself. The framers' ban on "Cruel and Unusual Punishments," enshrined in the Eighth Amendment, was not an abstract concern: European monarchies routinely and openly prescribed torture-based punishments into the eighteenth century. Even after torture came to be regarded as a barbaric practice in the West, some governments—Imperial Russia in particular—continued to torture dissidents, radicals, and terrorists behind closed doors.

Although the United States never reached the depravity of the tsars, it is a sad truth that during the eighteenth and nineteenth centuries federal and state officials engaged in practices that today seem self-evidently cruel and unusual. These practices did not take the form of criminal sanctions, where the text of the Eighth Amendment was clearly prohibitive, but rather occurred in the context of police interrogation. This was especially the case in the South during the antebellum and Jim

Crow eras, where violence was an essential element of racial oppression. Of course, in the cities of the North, too, use of the "third degree" against criminal suspects was routine for much of American history.

Over the course of the twentieth century, the systemic use of pain-based interrogation techniques in the United States ebbed considerably. Today, there exist statutory prohibitions on torture at both the state and federal levels, and at the level of international law the United States has ratified the United Nations Convention against Torture. Many actors contributed to this decline in officially sanctioned brutality, including civil rights activists, elected officials, the press, and public commissions of inquiry—most famously the Wickersham Commission created by President Herbert Hoover. Nevertheless, the role of the courts in ending torture was essential. Of key importance is the celebrated 1936 case *Brown v. Mississippi*, in which the Supreme Court unanimously found that a confession extracted through police violence—specifically, flogging—could not serve as evidence of guilt, and that a conviction on such grounds violated the Due Process Clause of the Fourteenth Amendment. Another important development was the 1952 case *Rochin v. California*, in which the Court overturned the conviction of a defendant who had been forced to vomit up narcotics against his will, on the reasoning that such conduct "shocks the conscience."

That the federal judiciary played an important role in limiting the use of torture by state agents is not surprising: many of the scenarios under which official torture commonly arises relate to areas of governance traditionally subject to judicial oversight, such as police interrogation and criminal punishment. But the kind of executive action examined in this chapter, "Torture and Extraordinary Rendition," does not fall within these comfortable bounds. Rather, the essay discusses torture carried out by U.S. officials outside U.S. territory, or by foreign governments on behalf of the United States, to collect intelligence about foreign extremist organizations suspected of plotting terrorist attacks.

Although the parallels between official torture in the counterterrorism context and its use in purely domestic contexts seem obvious, the judiciary has been reluctant to extend the prohibition of torture into the realm of national security. This wariness, documented in "Torture and Extraordinary Rendition," is lamentable but not wholly unexpected. From as early as the *Insular Cases*, the federal courts have approached extraterritorial application of the Constitution with caution. But with respect to victims of torture committed outside the United States, the judiciary has avoided reaching even this question of extraterritorial reach, and has instead ruled against the victims on the basis of discretionary doctrines of abstention—specifically, an extension of the state secrets privilege, and a novel reading of the "special factors" exception to the availability of damages under a *Bivens* action. As the essay observes, both of these bases for dismissal are framed so broadly that they could easily "degenerate into a free-floating political question doctrine" barring review of any suit that touches on the political branches' foreign affairs and war powers.

This refusal on the part of the judiciary to adjudicate questions of fundamental rights through self-imposed procedural obstacles bears a striking resemblance to an earlier concern of Owen Fiss: the Burger and Rehnquist Courts' paring back of the structural injunction, and with it the role of the federal courts in redressing civil rights violations, through judicially created rules of abstention. The Supreme Court's retrenchment on injunctive relief in the final decades of the twentieth century was presented as exercises in humility and comity, but its effect was hardly modest: it served to marginalize the role of the judiciary in one of its areas of core competence. The same critique can be leveled at the judicial hand washing discussed in "Torture and Extraordinary Rendition." In Fiss's view, torture, like racial segregation, is too grave an offense to constitutional values to entrust its prohibition to the political branches.

On December 9, 2014, the nation was delivered a chilling reminder of the consequences of unquestioning deference to the executive's national security policies. On that day, the Senate Select Committee on Intelligence publicly released a formerly classified report on the CIA's interrogation and detention program under the Bush administration. The report described the deliberate and systematic use of physical and mental torture against suspected terrorists in U.S. custody, including waterboarding, prolonged placement in painful "stress positions," and a practice known as "rectal feeding," in which liquids are pumped into an individual's large intestine via a tube inserted into the rectum. The Senate report was greeted with widespread outrage and may well lead to a tightening of the legislative and policy regimes prohibiting torture. But as Fiss makes clear in his essay, even robust oversight by Congress is no substitute for open and public trials and an independent, assertive judiciary willing to protect fundamental rights even in times of exigency. Whether the executive and Supreme Court will permit the judiciary to play such a vital role is, lamentably, very much an open question.

# Chapter 7

# TORTURE AND
# EXTRAORDINARY RENDITION

In this essay, I focus on one of the most egregious of all abuses associated with the War on Terror—the policies and practices that put into doubt America's commitment to prohibiting torture. The ban on torture is embodied in a number of international instruments, most notably the 1984 Convention against Torture,[1] signed by the United States in 1988, and also in the criminal statutes enacted to implement that treaty.[2] Yet it is important to understand, so that we can be clear about the magnitude of the wrong, that the rule against torture did not await the arrival of the 1984 convention and its implementing statutes; it is rooted in the Constitution itself.[3]

The Eighth Amendment prohibits cruel and unusual punishments, and torture would surely meet the standard of cruel and unusual. Although some may claim that torture inflicted for the purpose of extracting information from a person held in custody might not be deemed a "punishment" and thus is beyond the scope of the Eighth Amendment, I insist that such conduct is prohibited by an implicit premise of the Eighth Amendment. Certainly, if we cannot torture someone who has been judged to have broken the law, we cannot torture someone who we only suspect has broken the law or who we believe is in possession of information that might enable us to prevent or punish unlawful acts. Immanent in the Eighth Amendment is a principle—let us call it the dignity principle—that denies state officers the power to treat inhumanely anyone in their custody.

A similar regard for human dignity can be found in the Fifth Amendment. In the broadest of terms, that amendment denies the state the authority to deprive any person of "life, liberty, or property without due process of law." This norm has been construed to prohibit not just unfair procedures but any state action that shocks the conscience or offends an elemental regard for the humanity of persons in state custody. The phrase "shocks the conscience" was used by the Supreme Court to denounce police action that consisted of pumping the stomach of a suspect.[4] The substantive dimensions of due process have also been manifest in decisions striking down laws that denied parents the right to send their children to private schools[5] and, more recently, that denied consenting adults the right to engage in intimate sexual conduct.[6]

As an expression of the dignity principle, the constitutional ban on torture of the Fifth and Eighth Amendments is an absolute. It focuses on the intrinsic quality of the state practice—its sheer inhumanity—and does not vary according to the putative value of the information sought. The constitutional ban on torture cannot be overridden or relaxed because the interrogator believes he might be able to extract information that will save an innocent life or, for that matter, countless lives. The harm to our cherished values would be far greater than the benefit that might possibly be obtained. At issue is nothing less than the ideals that define us as a nation.

## Bush on Torture

President George W. Bush declared that he was opposed to torture, yet he governed in a way that put his underlying commitment in doubt. He declared his opposition to torture in 2004,[7] almost three years after he announced the War on Terror, in September 2001, and did so in a most defensive manner—in response to a public outcry, initially provoked by the publication of the Abu Ghraib photographs and then compounded by the leak of internal memoranda of the Department of Justice and the Department of Defense that took the proverbial "gloves off" government interrogators.[8]

The first of these memoranda was prepared by John Yoo and signed by Jay Bybee.[9] Bybee was then an assistant attorney general in charge of the Office of Legal Counsel and Yoo was a member of his staff. The memorandum was sent to the White House in August 2002. The infliction of physical pain, Yoo and Bybee said, amounted to torture only when it was "equivalent in intensity to the pain accompanying serious physical injury, such as organ failure, impairment of a bodily function, or even death."[10] This requirement was derived not from an understanding of judicial doctrine regarding the range of permissible interrogation techniques but rather from an extraneous source—regulations defining the conditions for paying medical benefits. In fact, it was in direct contradiction with the federal statute prohibiting torture, defined as an "act committed by a person acting under the color of law specifically intended to inflict severe physical or mental pain or suffering," including threats of imminent death.[11]

The Department of Defense memorandum, prepared by William Haynes, then general counsel of the department, and dated November 27, 2002, sought to establish guidelines for interrogating prisoners being held at Guantánamo Bay.[12] It divided a broad range of interrogation techniques into three categories. The practices in the first two categories, which included round-the-clock interrogations lasting up to twenty hours and the use of stress positions such as standing for up to four hours, were deemed lawful and available to the Guantánamo interrogators. The third category included practices generally understood to be torture, including waterboarding, a technique that used a wet towel and dripping water to induce the perception of suffocation or drowning. Haynes said that the practices in this third category were forbidden "as a matter of policy . . . at this time," though he was quick to add that they "may be legally available."[13] Secretary of Defense Donald Rumsfeld approved Haynes's recommendations with a handwritten note on the Haynes memorandum indicating, "I stand for 8–10 hours a day. Why is standing limited to 4 hours?"[14]

The announcement of the guidelines proposed by Haynes and approved by Rumsfeld provoked controversy within the military. As a result, a high-level working group was assembled in the Department of Defense, and on April 16, 2003, Secretary Rumsfeld issued a new directive identifying the interrogation techniques that would be allowed at Guantánamo. Seventeen of those techniques were allowed by one of the Army Field Manuals then in force. Seven techniques went beyond the manual, and in so doing once again put the rule against torture in doubt.[15] To further loosen the reins, Rumsfeld's directive acknowledged at various points that some had contended that the techniques authorized were inconsistent with protections afforded to POWs under the Third Geneva Convention. The secretary instructed the interrogators to take into consideration such contentions, while at the same time insisting that the Guantánamo detainees were not POWs but unlawful enemy combatants whose treatment was not governed by the Third Geneva Convention but only by the lesser requirement of humane treatment imposed by the Fourth Geneva Convention.

Torture is not self-defining, and for that reason disagreement will inevitably arise as to whether a particular interrogation technique constitutes torture. The abuse of the Constitution implicit in the Defense and Justice memoranda that I just described did not arise from the very understandable need to provide guidelines for interrogators but from the content of those guidelines and a desire to allow aggressive—indeed coercive—treatment of prisoners, without any regard for their dignity. Although our knowledge of the actual practices employed by government interrogators during the Bush years remains fragmentary, in no small part due to the administration's own actions,[16] the available evidence indicates that they fully understood the message being conveyed—almost everything was on the table.[17]

In the case of the CIA—which was not covered by the Army Field Manual or even Rumsfeld's guidelines for Guantánamo but only by the Yoo-Bybee memorandum—the offense to the Constitution entailed in the practices allowed by these memoranda was especially blatant. According to a December 2007 television interview with a CIA agent, the CIA used waterboarding against a high-level al-Qaeda operative, and did so under circumstances that made it clear that this was not the unruly action of agents under stress.[18] The CIA interrogators in the field were in constant and immediate communication with the deputy director for operations in Washington, who determined whether so-called enhanced interrogation techniques were to be used, against whom, and with what degree of intensity. No wonder Michael Mukasey refused, in his confirmation hearings to be attorney general, which occurred shortly before the December 2007 television interview, to say whether waterboarding was torture.[19] Had he done so, he might have politically committed himself to prosecuting some CIA agents and their supervisors.

The Bush administration not only sought to avoid the force of the prohibition of torture by manipulating the definition of the practices covered, it denied that the president is bound, as a matter of law, by that prohibition, and in doing so harked back to a conception of presidential power long identified with the Nixon White House. In the late 1970s, President Richard Nixon, in an effort to defend the action that led to his impeachment and eventual resignation, publicly maintained that the president is entitled to disobey the law whenever he determines it is for the good of the nation. If the president does an act, he said, it is not illegal. History judged this view harshly, but it was taken as an article of faith in certain circles, which included Vice President Dick Cheney, and it became an organizing theme of the Bush presidency—most remarkably even in the debates over torture.

This conception of almost unlimited presidential power was defended by the Department of Justice and its Office of Legal Counsel. The 2002 Yoo-Bybee memorandum mentioned above not only offered a contrived definition of torture, it put into question whether the president, acting as commander in chief, was bound by that prohibition. In making this claim, Yoo and Bybee treated the rule against torture as nothing more than a congressional command.

Yoo and Bybee have a skewed conception of presidential power. Although the president, as commander in chief, might be deemed to have whatever authority is needed to prosecute a war successfully, account must also be taken of the constitutional grant of authority to Congress over military matters. The constitutional vision is one of shared powers. Article I grants Congress the power to define and punish "[o]ffenses against the Law of Nations," "[t]o make Rules concerning Captures on Land and Water," and "[t]o make Rules for the Government and

Regulation of the land and naval Forces." The making of such rules would surely include the power to determine how individuals who are detained by the military should be treated or interrogated. Of course, conflicts between those who share power may sometimes arise. The error of Yoo and Bybee, however, was to assume that in the case of such conflicts the president as commander in chief should prevail over Congress. They gave no reason for that view, nor is one readily apparent.

The inadequacy of Yoo and Bybee's view of presidential power is even more apparent once we acknowledge that the prohibition of torture is not based only on a statute but also is rooted in the Fifth and Eighth Amendments, for all exercises of the powers of the president, like those of any branch of government, must comply with the Bill of Rights. This basic proposition of constitutional law is implicit in the very institution of judicial review, which empowers the judiciary to set aside measures of the president or Congress that might be within their enumerated powers but are inconsistent with the Bill of Rights.

The understanding of presidential power propounded by Yoo and Bybee in 2002 even survived the repudiation of their contrived definition of torture. In December 2004, in the wake of the public outcry surrounding the leak of the original Yoo-Bybee memorandum, the Department of Justice issued another memorandum on torture.[20] This new memorandum explicitly repudiated Yoo and Bybee's definition of torture, stating that all that is required to constitute torture is severe or extreme pain; however, it did not withdraw or in any way modify the Yoo-Bybee view of presidential power. The new memorandum said it was unnecessary to address the issue of presidential power because the president had publicly declared, as a matter of policy, his opposition to torture.

In fact, President Bush's actions regarding the Detainee Treatment Act of 2005 put his stated opposition to torture very much into question.[21] He fiercely resisted the enactment of the provision, spearheaded by Senator John McCain, that codified the constitutional ban on torture. Upon signing the act into law, the president explained that he was signing the measure with the understanding that the statute did not create or confer a private right of action on victims of torture.[22] He also said that he intended to construe the statute in a way that was consistent with his constitutional powers as commander in chief and his duty to protect the nation against future terrorist attacks. The legal effect of this so-called signing statement was unclear, but its political implications were not. It was widely understood to indicate that President Bush did not believe himself bound by the measure and that, if military necessity dictated, he would allow prisoners to be tortured as part of an interrogation process.

## Rendition to Torture

In keeping with its expansive view of executive power, the Bush administration further offended the Constitution by engaging in a practice—known as extraordinary rendition—that involved torture, though by foreign nations. Rendition occurs when the United States, acting pursuant to an extradition treaty, sends an individual to another country to stand trial for some particular crime. Rendition becomes "extraordinary" when transfer occurs outside of the framework of an extradition treaty and when the purpose of the transfer is not to enable the country to which the individual is transferred to place the individual on trial but rather to interrogate him and extract information of use to the United States. The predicate of such a transfer is that the nation receiving the prisoner will use aggressive and brutal interrogation techniques—torture—that United States agents are not prepared to use. Although this practice antedates the Bush administration and its War on Terror, it was used with notable frequency in the Bush years—there are some indications that it was used hundreds of times during this period.[23]

The fact that extraordinary rendition entails "outsourcing" torture, to use Jane Mayer's term,[24] is of no legal or moral significance. If the Constitution prohibits United States officials from engaging in a certain practice, then it also prohibits those officials from creating an arrangement whereby officials of another nation perform the prohibited action. Imagine prison officials who do not actually torture prisoners in their custody but turn the prisoners over to other inmates to do what is forbidden to the officials. These prison officials can be faulted not just for the transfer but also for the torture that occurred through the arrangement they created.[25] The dignity principle immanent in the Fifth and Eighth Amendments binds the United States and all those who act on its requests and in its interests.

A more difficult legal question presented by extraordinary rendition concerns the territorial reach of the constitutional ban against torture. Americans are fully protected by the Constitution no matter where they reside. Yet they have not been the target of extraordinary rendition, nor have aliens who are residents of the United States. With one possible exception, extraordinary rendition has been used only against foreign nationals living abroad—for example, a German citizen traveling in Macedonia was seized by CIA officials and taken to Afghanistan, and an Egyptian citizen was kidnapped by CIA agents on the streets of Milan and taken to Egypt.

The one possible exception to this rule concerns the extraordinary rendition of Maher Arar. He was seized by immigration officials on September 26, 2002, at JFK Airport, held virtually incommunicado for twelve days in nearby detention facilities, and then sent to Syria via Jordan for, as he alleges, the specific purpose of interrogation under conditions of torture. Arar brought a suit in federal court to test the legality of his rendition. That suit was soon dismissed on the pleadings by the district court, and the dismissal was affirmed by a three-judge panel of the Court of Appeals for the Second Circuit. The Second Circuit then decided to hear the case en banc. The en banc argument was held on December 9, 2008, in the closing days of the Bush administration. Obama took office on January 21, 2009, and some had hoped that he might change the government's position in that case. That did not occur, however, and on November 2, 2009, the Second Circuit sitting en banc sustained the position originally taken by the Bush administration. It affirmed the district court's dismissal of Arar's suit, thereby depriving Arar of any opportunity to prove his case at trial or even to begin discovery.[26]

Arar had only the most fleeting connections to the United States. He was born in Syria, and by virtue of that birth is a citizen of Syria. He moved to Canada with his family as a teenager and continued to reside there. At the time of his arrest in 2002 he was thirty-three years old and had become a naturalized citizen of Canada. Arar had been vacationing with his family in Tunisia and was arrested when he was returning to Canada for business. His itinerary took him from Tunisia to Switzerland and then on to JFK, where he was to take a flight to Montreal. Transit passengers at JFK need to clear customs, and upon presenting his passport to an immigration official, Arar was arrested. The arrest was based on a tip (which was later proved to be false) from the Royal Mounted Police of Canada that identified Arar as a member of a terrorist organization.

After his brief detention in the United States, Arar was flown to Syria, where he was imprisoned for ten months in a grave-like cell measuring six feet long, seven feet high, and three feet wide. He alleged that during his first twelve days in Syria he was interrogated for some eighteen hours a day and severely beaten. The interrogation ceased when Canadian officials who had learned of his presence in Syria interceded on his behalf. Yet

Arar remained incarcerated for nine more months, at which time Canadian officials were able to secure his release.

From my perspective, Arar's imprisonment and interrogation, if established at trial, violate the U.S. Constitution. This conclusion is not derived from the fact that Arar, unlike the German or Egyptian citizens, was arrested on United States soil and imprisoned in the United States for a number of days before being sent by United States agents to Syria. On my view, his entitlement to the protection of the Constitution derives from the more general notion that the Fifth and Eighth Amendments and their ban on torture are applicable to the officers of the United States and their agents wherever they act and against whomever they act.

Recall that the Fifth Amendment purports to protect any "person." The Eighth Amendment is cast as a flat prohibition with no effort to delineate the group of persons protected, and it too should be understood as defining the authority of U.S. officials. More fundamentally, my reading of the Fifth and Eighth Amendments derives from the underlying value at issue—a just and proper regard for the dignity of each person held in state custody. Human dignity is violated whenever someone is tortured, regardless of where the torture takes place. A violation of the Constitution and the basic charter of this nation occurs when the persons responsible for the torture are U.S. officials or agents acting on their behalf.

This broad understanding of the Constitution is reflected in the provisions of the Detainee Treatment Act of 2005, which prohibits torture by U.S. officials wherever they act and against whomever they act. It is also reflected in the federal statute criminalizing torture; it specifically prohibits torture by U.S. officials acting outside the country.[27] Of like import is the 2008 decision of the Supreme Court invalidating a 2006 statute denying habeas corpus to the Guantánamo prisoners (all foreign nationals).[28] Admittedly, the Court in that case did not determine what substantive rights the Guantánamo prisoners had, but the very act of extending the constitutional protection of habeas corpus to these prisoners necessarily implies that they had some constitutional rights—the most basic—otherwise the writ would be of no utility.

This interpretation of the recent Supreme Court decision accords with a constitutional tradition reaching all the way back to the early 1900s and cases involving the territories the United States acquired as a result of the Spanish-American War. One of these cases posed the question of whether the Sixth Amendment guarantee to trial by jury was applicable in the Philippines, which was then being held as a colony.[29] The Supreme Court concluded that the Bill of Rights was not in its entirety applicable to the administration of an unincorporated territory such as the Philippines.[30] Yet the Court qualified that holding by declaring that U.S. officials were bound always to respect the fundamental rights of all persons living in the territory.[31] Among the most basic or fundamental of all rights is the right against torture.

In an unincorporated territory such as the Philippines, the United States is sovereign. Similarly, the United States could be deemed to exercise a de facto sovereignty over Guantánamo. No such claim could be made about Syria, where Arar had been transferred and interrogated. Yet it is difficult to understand why the geographic site of the torture—whether it took place on American soil, at Guantánamo, or in Syria—has any significance in determining the applicability of the Fifth and Eighth Amendments' ban on torture. What makes the constitutional ban on torture applicable is the fact that the torture is inflicted by U.S. officials, or agents acting on their behalf. The dignity principle that drives the interpretation of the Fifth and Eight Amendments seeks to provide protection to persons, not places.

The Second Circuit did not take issue with this elemental proposition of constitutional law. Instead, it focused on the remedy Arar sought. Ordinarily, the victim of a constitutional wrong seeks an injunction—a court order backed by the contempt power—to prevent the recurrence of that wrong. In such cases, however, the availability of the injunctive remedy requires some showing that the wrong is likely to recur. Arar, now safely in Canada and out of the reach of the U.S. officials responsible for his rendition, could not make such a showing. So Arar asked for a declaratory judgment and damages—a declaration that he was wronged and compensation for that wrong.

Every lawsuit rests on a legal claim. When an injunction is sought, the Constitution itself provides the claim, without the need for any congressional authorization. The same rule applies to declaratory judgments. Although a congressional statute passed in the 1930s made the declaratory remedy available to federal courts,[32] the cause of action or claim underlying the request for that remedy, much like that for an injunction, arises from the Constitution itself and does not need congressional authorization.

In the 1971 *Bivens* decision,[33] the Supreme Court extended this same principle to actions for damages, though with one qualification. The Court held that a claim or cause of action underlying a request for damages for a constitutional wrong arises from the Constitution itself unless there are some "special factors" that might make it appropriate to require congressional authorization. In the *Arar* case, the Second Circuit treated the foreign policy and military ramifications of extraordinary rendition as such a "special factor" and on that ground disallowed Arar's claim for damages. The judges were mindful of the Detainee Treatment Act of 2005 and the ban on torture spearheaded by Senator McCain but thought that act insufficient to provide the congressional authorization for awarding damages that they insisted upon.

In demanding this congressional authorization, the Second Circuit underscored the political character of Congress.

However, unless the "special factors" exception to the *Bivens* rule is going to degenerate into a free-floating political question doctrine, long discredited by the Supreme Court, it is not clear why the characterization of Congress as a political institution constitutes a reason for the judiciary to await congressional authorization before allowing damages for the violation of a constitutional right. Although there is a long-standing tradition of the judiciary's deferring to the executive in matters of foreign and military policy, that deference is not owed to Congress and does not in any way depend on the nature of the remedy sought. In fact, this deference might be due to the executive even if Congress passes a statute authorizing suits for damages.

Wholly apart from the question of whether a statute is needed under the terms of *Bivens* to create a claim for damages, the government sought to defeat Arar's claim for damages by invoking what has become known as "qualified immunity." According to this privilege, damages will be awarded only if it can be shown that the officials being sued violated a right that had been clearly articulated at the time they acted. The Second Circuit, sitting en banc, meticulously avoided any reliance on this doctrine, but it was invoked by the government, and in the earlier phases of the case served as an alternative basis for the decision. The government did not deny that the right against torture in some general sense had the requisite clarity, only that it was uncertain that the right extended to foreign nationals who were tortured on foreign soil by foreign officials. Accordingly, there would be no point, the government argued, in judging the constitutionality of the extraordinary rendition Arar suffered because, even if it were unconstitutional, damages could not be recovered by Arar due to the qualified immunity enjoyed by the U.S. officials who sent Arar to Syria.

As a general matter, the qualified immunity doctrine invoked by the government serves two purposes. It avoids the unfairness of holding the government liable for damages for conduct that was not understood to be unlawful at the time it was undertaken, and it avoids creating disincentives for the government to take forceful and innovative action in a context where the legality of the proposed action is uncertain. I am doubtful that either purpose would be furthered by a ruling that put under the protection of qualified immunity the extraordinary rendition Arar suffered. Although there has been no clear ruling on the legality of the rendition that occurred in this case, it should be clear to government officials acting in good faith that their actions ran afoul of the Constitution, given the universality and force of the norms and laws against torture. This is especially true in light of the fact that the Convention against Torture prohibits the United States from sending any alien back to his country of origin if there is any chance that he might be tortured.

More important, even if Arar's claim for damages was correctly dismissed without reaching the merits, either because of the qualified immunity doctrine or because of the *Bivens* exception for special factors, his claim for a declaratory judgment remains unaffected. A declaratory judgment does not require any congressional authorization and does not penalize any past act. It simply declares the law. It is an exercise of the core judicial function. A declaratory judgment would enable the judiciary to remove any lingering uncertainty about the legality of the practice of rendering a suspect to another country for torture, and in that way it would restore the sovereignty of the Constitution.

The Second Circuit held otherwise and dismissed Arar's claim for a declaratory judgment on the theory that he lacked the standing required by Article III of the Constitution. Anxious to establish that a declaratory judgment would confer a concrete benefit on Arar, his lawyers artificially defined the declaration sought. The complaint did not seek a declaration of the unconstitutionality of the rendition to which Arar was subjected, but rather asked the court to declare invalid the removal order that was issued against him (in order to effectuate the rendition). Such a declaration, Arar's lawyers reasoned, would confer a concrete benefit on Arar and give him standing to seek a declaratory judgment. The Second Circuit denied, however, that a declaration of the invalidity of the removal order could, in fact, be of any benefit to Arar. He had been designated a member of a terrorist organization, and as long as that designation stood, the court reasoned, he could be denied permission to enter the country, and if so a judgment invalidating the removal order would not confer a concrete benefit on him.

Arar's lawyers fell into a trap of their own devising. The focus of the request for a declaratory judgment should not have been on the removal order but on the practice of extraordinary rendition itself—the torture of a foreign national by a foreign government at the behest of U.S. officials. Rule 54(c) of the Federal Rules of Civil Procedure gives a court the authority to enter any order that is just,[34] and Arar's claim should not be precluded by the strategic decision—possibly a blunder—of his lawyers.

The concrete harm that Arar suffered should be sufficient to give him standing to obtain a declaratory judgment on the legality of his rendition. Although all of us suffer when someone is tortured, since the basic law of the nation is compromised, the victim of the rendition suffers in a distinct and very particularized way. His personal suffering constitutes an injury in fact and as such should entitle him to invoke the power of the federal judiciary. As a purely formal matter, such a declaratory proceeding would constitute a "case" or "controversy" within the meaning of Article III of the Constitution. The policy objectives served by the standing requirement are also satisfied. There is nothing abstract or academic about the controversy, and Arar would have every incentive to make certain that the contentions of law and fact are vigorously presented. In fact, the claim tendered is the same as would be presented in any injunctive proceeding—the government acted in violation of the Constitution—and respects the inherently legal function of the judiciary: to say what the law is.

Concrete benefits, in contrast to concrete harm, should not also be required for standing, but even if they are, they can be found in Arar's case. A declaratory judgment would not contain the material component of a damages award, but, much like a damages award, it speaks both to the world and to the victim. It says to all the world that the government violated basic norms of the legal order—the Fifth and Eighth Amendments. It also addresses the victim of the rendition and tells him in a direct and personal way that he has been wronged—senior U.S. officials violated the basic law of their nation in sending him to Syria for interrogation under conditions of torture. Such a statement may have as much meaning to the victim and give him as much satisfaction as an award of damages. It helps restore his self-worth. It speaks to his soul, not his pocketbook, but there is nothing in Article III and its standing requirement that prioritizes the material over the spiritual.

In dismissing Arar's suit, the Second Circuit relied on a doctrine—the "special factors" exceptions to *Bivens*—that is rooted in the fact that Arar sought damages. The government also invoked the rule conferring qualified immunity, and that rule also is confined to damage suits. However, a number of lawsuits brought by other victims of extraordinary rendition in other circuits have been dismissed on the basis of yet another doctrine—the state secrets doctrine—and this doctrine is not tied to the damages remedy. It is as applicable to suits seeking a declaratory judgment or injunction as it is to suits for damages, and it arises from the very understandable need to conduct some of the business of government in the dark.

The state secrets doctrine was first announced in a 1953 case involving a tort suit against the United States for a death arising from the crash of a military airplane.[35] As part of the discovery process, the plaintiff sought internal government documents relating to the construction of the plane, and the Supreme Court upheld the refusal of the government to surrender those documents on the ground that such disclosure would compromise important state secrets. The plaintiff was allowed to continue his litigation, although without the benefit of certain information in the possession of the government.

As originally crafted, the state secrets doctrine arose in a tort suit and operated only as an evidentiary privilege. In the post–9/11 era, it has been used to defend against suits charging violations of fundamental rights. In that context, the doctrine has been transformed into a de facto grant of immunity. This most notably occurred in the Fourth Circuit decision dismissing a suit brought by a German citizen allegedly subject to extraordinary rendition.[36] According to the complaint, this individual was captured by the CIA in Macedonia, then transferred to a prison in or near the Bagram Air Field in Afghanistan. He was held there for months and allegedly tortured. The CIA allegedly then flew him to Albania, where he was left on the highway. The Fourth Circuit felt that any inquiry whatsoever into the rendition would compromise the secrecy of the CIA's operations and on that ground affirmed a dismissal of the suit on the pleadings. The court did not require the defendant to identify with any particularity the items of evidence that it wished to withhold from the plaintiff and thus exclude from discovery or trial. Rather, the court reasoned that dismissal would be justified if there were "a reasonable danger" that the litigation would expose military, diplomatic, or intelligence matters, as would indeed be true of almost any suit against the CIA.[37]

In so expanding the state secrets doctrine from an evidentiary privilege into this de facto grant of immunity, the court threatened the rule—long the hallmark of our legal system—that subjects all government officials, even the CIA, to the Constitution, and entrusts the judiciary with the task of determining whether these officials have violated the Constitution. A lawsuit challenging the legality of a rendition serves both private and public purposes. It gives a concrete benefit to the plaintiff, in the form of either damages or a declaration that he was wronged. At the same time, the lawsuit serves noble public purposes—it is the mechanism by which these officials are held accountable, and the sovereignty of the Constitution preserved. Relying on the state secrets doctrine in its new and expanded form any time a clandestine agency such as the CIA is charged with violating the Constitution would, in effect, place that agency beyond the reach of the Constitution.

Claims of secrecy are commonplace in criminal prosecutions—the paradigmatic public lawsuit. In that context, the government has been given two options: either make the evidence (or its equivalent) available to the defendant or drop the prosecution altogether. In the civil context, especially when a request for a declaratory judgment is at issue and the public nature of the lawsuit is most manifest, a similar procedure can be fashioned. First, the government must identify with some specificity the evidence it wishes to maintain in secrecy. Second, the judge must determine, in camera if necessary, whether the need for secrecy is justified. Third, if the judge decides that the need for secrecy is legitimate, he or she must then go on to determine how central or indispensable the evidence is to the plaintiff's claim or the defendant's defense. Of course, if it is not central to the plaintiff's claim or the defendant's defense, and the government's claim

for secrecy is well grounded, then the information can be with-
held and the plaintiff should be allowed to move forward with
his case.

To take one remarkable example, the Ninth Circuit dismissed
a lawsuit against a private transport contractor allegedly used by
the CIA in an extraordinary rendition even though it conceded
that the plaintiff could prove the prima facie elements of his
claim and the defendant could make a valid defense without the
evidence the government wanted to withhold.[38] Disregarding its
responsibility to hold the government accountable for violating
fundamental rights, the court justified its dismissal of the suit on
the grounds that "litigating the case to a judgment on the merits
would present an unacceptable risk of disclosing state secrets."[39]
The duty of the court is to manage the lawsuit to prevent such
a risk from ever materializing, not to turn that risk into a shield
that would protect the defendant from liability.

Of course, situations may arise where the evidence is essential
to the plaintiff's claim or the defendant's defense and the claim
of secrecy is justified. This may be so, for example, when the
evidence sought would disclose the identity of an undercover
agent of the CIA. In those cases, the government should be presented with two options that are analogous to the ones provided
in a criminal case: either disclose the evidence or, if the plaintiff
can establish a prima facie case, allow the entry of a default judgment against it. In providing the government with these options,
the judge, as in a criminal case, will respect the government's insistence on secrecy but at the same time will require it to bear the
consequences of its action and thus prevent the state secrets doctrine from becoming a de facto grant of immunity. Holding the
CIA and other government agencies accountable to the Constitution is as urgent a public undertaking as providing the accused
in a criminal trial with access to all the evidence in the possession
of the government that might be of benefit to him or her.

The state secrets doctrine, as was true of the doctrines limiting the liability of government officials for damages (*Bivens* special factors or qualified immunity), might well be seen as technical encrustments by a judiciary reluctant to second-guess the executive on foreign and military matters. The decisions of the circuit courts may have been couched in terms of these formal doctrines, but the governing impulse may well have been derived from the constitutional tradition that calls for judicial deference to the executive in cases that involve foreign and military matters. Such a view may explain, but certainly does not justify, the decisions of the lower federal courts summoned to examine renditions to torture.

Admittedly, the executive possesses a special competence in defining the foreign policy objectives of the nation and how those objectives might be pursued. The executive also has special competence in determining how a war should be fought—what military action is required for a victory. Yet the executive has no special competence when it comes to determining whether the challenged action, even if it is of a military nature or implicates foreign policy, comports with the fundamental values of the nation.[40] Indeed, such a normative determination is the essence of the judicial function—to determine whether extraordinary rendition, even if fully required by foreign policy or military objectives, is consistent with the dictates of the Fifth and Eighth Amendments. On that issue, the executive is likely to have a view, but it is owed no deference. The authority of the judiciary over such normative questions arises not from the personal virtues of those who happen to sit on the bench but from its political insularity and the strictures of public reason that govern all exercises of the judicial power—the need to listen to all those aggrieved, to try questions of the law and facts in open court, and to justify its decision on the basis of principle.

## Obama's Policies

On January 20, 2009, the Bush presidency drew to a close. On assuming office, President Obama immediately issued executive orders addressing some of the abuses of the previous administration. He confined the CIA, at least until further study, to interrogation techniques set forth in the Army Field Manual; closed the secret prisons, the so-called black sites, maintained by the CIA; and required the closing of Guantánamo in a year's time.[41] These actions were applauded—quite properly so—because they had the inevitable effect of minimizing the risk of torture. "Black sites" and "Guantánamo" entered the legal lexicon as prisons in which foreign nationals were abused and maybe even tortured. Moreover, having the CIA governed by the Army Field Manual will, at least nominally, place off-limits the "enhanced interrogation techniques" the agency had used during the Bush era.

Apart from these initial measures, the signals sent by the new administration on the issue of torture were decidedly more mixed. To his credit, President Obama maintained, as he did throughout his campaign, that he was opposed to torture.[42] In his first address to a joint session of Congress, he spoke inspirationally of the example of America, and once again declared his opposition to torture.[43] His nominee for attorney general, Eric Holder, in a clear attempt to distance himself from Bush's last attorney general, Michael Mukasey, declared in his confirmation hearing, without the least hesitation, that waterboarding is torture.[44]

On the other hand, President Obama did not issue an order barring extraordinary rendition. At his confirmation hearing to become the director of the CIA, Leon Panetta equivocated on whether extraordinary rendition would be used by his agency in the future. He said he was unprepared to send someone to another country "for the purpose of torture or actions by another country that violate our human values," but he also said that he might be prepared to return the person seized "to another country where they prosecute them under their laws." [45] He failed to guarantee that the person subject to the rendition would have judicial procedures available to make certain that he would not be tortured, and this failure may have made the distinction he drew illusory in practice.

Even deeper misgivings relate to the unwillingness of Obama to take appropriate corrective action for the constitutional wrongs, such as rendition to torture, that occurred during the Bush years. He had a clear opportunity to alter the government's position in the Arar case and chose not to do so. Similarly, in arguments before the Ninth Circuit in the suit against a CIA contractor implicated in extraordinary rendition, Obama's lawyers relied on the state secrets doctrine and thus seemed prepared to confer de facto immunity on the CIA for constitutional wrongs as gross as those entailed in extraordinary rendition. [46]

At his first press conference, President Obama was asked to comment on Senator Patrick Leahy's proposal for the establishment of a truth commission. He then said that he was more concerned with the future than with the past. [47] Fully in accord with this sentiment, Leon Panetta announced at his confirmation hearing that CIA agents who had engaged in torture, including waterboarding of suspected terrorists, would not be criminally prosecuted. [48] Acting under public pressure, in August 2009 Attorney General Eric Holder formally opened an investigation to determine whether a rogue CIA agent who had tortured prisoners should be criminally prosecuted. This agent was not accused of waterboarding but of threatening imminent death by revving a drill near the head of a hooded and shackled prisoner. In the end, the attorney general decided not to prosecute this agent.

The willingness of Obama to speak only to the future was ill-conceived. He also had a duty to seek an accounting for the wrongs of the past. He should have prosecuted those who engaged in practices clearly understood to be torture and, on top of that, allowed those who were in fact tortured to pursue civil remedies. In these civil cases, the government was, of course, entitled to defend itself on the merits of and contest the factual allegations and assertions of law that should have been contested, but it should not have hid behind the technical doctrines—such as the state secrets doctrine, the special factors exception to *Bivens*, or the privilege of qualified immunity—that enabled the judiciary to avoid reaching the merits.

The initiation of criminal proceedings and allowing the judiciary to reach the merits of a civil suit such as Arar's would have provided a measure of justice to the victims of torture, and not so incidentally would have lent credence to President Obama's lofty rhetoric about the future. It would have brought to light the way the Constitution had been abused and would have enabled the public to confront and acknowledge the violations of the Constitution committed in its name. The public would have been given an opportunity to say "Never Again."[49] These criminal and civil proceedings would also have allowed the judiciary to affirm the dignity principle and the constitutional norms to which it gives life, and to declare—in bold and clear terms—that these norms apply to American officials and their instrumentalities wherever they act and against whomever they act.

# Prologue to Chapter 8

Trevor Sutton

Nearly all of the major legal controversies that arose out of the Bush and Obama administrations' national security policies revolved around constitutional provisions that govern core functions of the criminal justice system, such as searches and seizures, executive detention, methods of interrogation, and procedural fairness in determinations affecting personal liberty. But the collateral effects of the War on Terror on our constitutional tradition have not been confined to these provisions. As the following essay demonstrates, the government's efforts to eradicate extremism worldwide have had a corrosive effect on a constitutional right that might at first seem remote from counterterrorism policy: freedom of speech.

Unlike the other essays in this volume, this chapter, "Criminalizing Political Advocacy," which was originally delivered as the Arlin M. and Neysa Adams Lecture in Constitutional Law at Temple University, focuses on one recent Supreme Court decision, *Holder v. Humanitarian Law Project*, and deals exclusively with First Amendment jurisprudence. But this narrow scope should not mislead the reader into thinking that the essay is thematically unlike the rest of the book. To the contrary, "Criminalizing Political Advocacy" offers a compelling case study of a theme that appears frequently in these pages: that war tends to corrode constitutional rights, and that long wars pose especially grave threats to those rights because their duration can turn aberrations into a new normal. The essay also offers a crisp illustration of how responsibility for such "debasement" (to use Fiss's word) of the Constitution falls on all three branches, not simply on the executive.

On some level, it is far from surprising that the right to free speech should come under pressure during wartime. Divided nations rarely win wars, and speech that might seem benign during times of peace can take on the appearance of an existential threat at the onset of armed conflict. American history provides many examples of this tendency. In 1798, before the Bill of Rights was even a decade old, the Federalist Congress passed the Alien and Sedition Acts, which criminalized speech critical of the government as the nation prepared for war with France. This pattern repeated itself numerous times in the two centuries that followed, particularly during and in the immediate wake of the First World War, when the Supreme Court twice upheld enforcement of the Espionage Act of 1917 to prohibit leafleting. However, since the First World War, the Supreme Court has erected substantial barriers protecting free speech, even in the wartime context. As a consequence, free speech protections during the Vietnam War were especially robust, as the example of the Pentagon Papers case, *New York Times v. United States*, illustrates.

To date, the statute upheld in *Holder v. Humanitarian Law Project* is the only constraint on general advocacy of violence to survive a challenge since the 1969 decision in *Brandenburg v. Ohio*, which limited restrictions on speech in the name of public

safety to situations where such speech was likely to incite or produce "imminent lawless action." The statute in *Humanitarian
Law Project* made it a crime to "knowingly provid[e] material
support or resources" to designated foreign terrorist organizations—a phrase that was construed to cover speech and that the
plaintiffs argued violated the First Amendment because it criminalized political advocacy. Chief Justice Roberts, writing for a
6–3 Court, rejected this argument on a theory that the statute
contemplated two kinds of speech, one "coordinated" with a
terrorist organization and one "independent" of it. Roberts proceeded to find the statute's ban on "coordinated" speech constitutionally sound, even if the speech in question endorsed only
the lawful, nonviolent aims of a designated organization.

This holding generated considerable controversy across the
political spectrum. The *Washington Post*, which often takes a
hawkish line on national security issues, wrote that the Court
had "go[ne] too far in the name of fighting terrorism." Eugene
Volokh, a law professor with libertarian leanings, called the
opinion "somewhat troubling." But perhaps the most piquant
observation came from David Cole, a law professor and a lawyer for the plaintiffs in the case, who observed in an op-ed piece
for the *New York Times* that three former Bush officials, including Attorney General Michael Mukasey, Secretary of Homeland
Security Tom Ridge, as well as Rudolph Giuliani, the former
mayor of New York, all appeared to have committed a federal
crime when they spoke at a conference organized by supporters of an Iranian opposition group that the State Department
had designated a terrorist organization. "The risk that speech
advocating peace and human rights would further terrorism is so
remote," Cole wrote, "that it cannot outweigh the indispensable
value of protecting dissent."

One peculiarity of *Humanitarian Law Project* is that, although
the statute under scrutiny in the case can correctly be viewed as

an outgrowth of the War on Terror, the case itself concerned advocacy on behalf of two organizations—separatist groups in Turkey and Sri Lanka—with no meaningful connection to al-Qaeda or to any other entity connected to the September 11 attacks or at war with the United States. The decision thus enables us to see that, in the long run, disregard for constitutional principles during wartime has grave consequences not only for the nation's enemies but for the people as a whole.

# Chapter 8

# CRIMINALIZING
# POLITICAL ADVOCACY

In the years following the September 11, 2001, attacks, combating terrorism became a matter of great public urgency, and as part of that endeavor we adopted a number of policies that have compromised important constitutional principles. Many of these policies pertain to the treatment of suspected terrorists who were captured as part of the War on Terror. Some of these prisoners have been subjected to interrogation techniques that might properly be considered torture. Some are being tried by military commissions. Still others are being held for prolonged, indefinite periods of time without being charged with a crime or allowed the writ of habeas corpus or any other means to test the legality of their imprisonment.

The challenge to our constitutional order has not been confined to the policies governing suspected terrorists in our custody. In the immediate wake of the September 11 attacks, President Bush authorized the National Security Agency (NSA) to use wiretaps without seeking court authorization.[1] These taps were used to monitor calls made by Americans to persons abroad suspected of having ties to al-Qaeda. The existence of this program was disclosed in December 2005 and soon became the subject of great public controversy and a number of lawsuits. In January 2007, President Bush discontinued this program as a matter of policy. Later that year and again in 2008, President Bush obtained congressional authorization for such warrantless wiretaps, embraced the law as constitutional, and declared that warrantless wiretaps are an essential tool in the fight against terrorism.

The 2008 congressional grant of authority removed the conflict between the executive's action and the Foreign Intelligence Surveillance Act (FISA) of 1978. It did not, however, overcome the objection to the NSA program based on the Fourth Amendment, which requires that, as a general matter, wiretaps need to be authorized by a court and based on probable cause. The warrant requirement seeks to curb arbitrary action of the executive and thereby protect the privacy and communicative freedom of all Americans, most immediately journalists, who often develop their stories through telephone calls to a large network of persons in the Middle East—some of whom may be thought to have ties to al-Qaeda.

This essay focuses on a related threat to our constitutional order—the curtailment of freedom of speech in the name of fighting terrorism. Specifically, my subject is the Supreme Court's 2010 decision in *Holder v. Humanitarian Law Project*,[2] which upheld the authority of Congress to criminalize political advocacy on behalf of foreign terrorist organizations. Like warrantless wiretapping, the risk of a criminal prosecution for political advocacy—for example, an utterance by an American citizen in an American forum that a foreign terrorist organization has a just cause—poses a threat to our democracy, but the danger is greater. The risk of warrantless wiretapping inhibits speech; the risk of a criminal prosecution is likely to stop it altogether.

A focus on the *Humanitarian Law Project* decision will also enable us to assign responsibility more accurately for the debasement of the Constitution in the post–9/11 era. We will be able to see more clearly than we could through an analysis of the policies governing the treatment of prisoners, or even the NSA wiretapping program, that the threat to our liberty derives not just from President Bush's unilateral excesses, but also from policies that have been defended and perpetuated by President Obama and embraced by the other branches of government, including the Supreme Court.[3] All three branches share responsibility for the abuses of the Constitution that we now confront.

## The Statute

Terrorism—acts of violence in the pursuit of some political goal—is the subject of a vast panoply of criminal statutes. Killing civilians or high-level government officials is always illegal. Congress decided, however, that such statutes were not sufficient, and a strategy was devised—first enacted in 1994, and later amended in 2001 and again in 2004—to combat organizations that nourish, support, and direct terrorist activities.[4] Congress hoped that isolating and starving these organizations would lessen the risk of terrorism.

The statute at issue in *Humanitarian Law Project* applies only to foreign, as opposed to domestic, terrorist organizations. The statute does not define the word "foreign," but presumably it requires that the organization be based abroad and that its membership be largely constituted of foreign nationals. Some organizations that meet this requirement, such as al-Qaeda, may pose threats to targets within the United States, as manifested by the attacks of 9/11. But others, such as the PKK (Kurdistan Workers Party) in Turkey or the Tamil Tigers in Sri Lanka—the specific organizations involved in *Humanitarian Law Project*—are not likely to pose such a threat because their acts of violence are confined to the territories in which they are based. Congress's interest in regulating such organizations may stem from a desire to protect individual American citizens traveling abroad who might become victims of the terrorist activities of these organizations. Or Congress may have sought to further foreign policy objectives of the United States by helping allies—such as Turkey or Sri Lanka—in their effort to combat terrorism occurring within their borders.

In pursuit of these aims, Congress established a procedure in the executive branch for designating certain organizations "foreign terrorist organizations." [5] The power to make this designation is vested in the secretary of state, who is to make his or her decision on the basis of an administrative record. This record essentially consists of a compilation of information prepared by a special office within the Department of State. The secretary of state is required to consult with the secretary of the treasury and the attorney general, and the administrative record may include information from their departments. The alleged terrorist organization and its members are not given any notice of this proceeding and thus do not have an opportunity to participate in the proceeding in any way.

Seven days before announcing a decision, the secretary of state must advise a select group of congressional leaders of the intention to designate a group a foreign terrorist organization. The secretary must then publish the designation in the Federal Register, at which time the designation takes effect. An organization designated a foreign terrorist organization can seek judicial review of the secretary's determination in the Court of Appeals for the District of Columbia Circuit, but that review is limited to determining, on the basis of the administrative record, whether the secretary's action is arbitrary and capricious or otherwise exceeds his or her authority. The secretary may supplement the administrative record by submitting to the Court of Appeals classified information, which can be examined in chambers and out of view of the attorneys for the designated organization. Otherwise, there is no evidentiary hearing in the Court of Appeals and no opportunity for the designated organization to supplement the administrative record in any way.

The designation procedure established by Congress is the prelude to the key operative provision of the statute.[6] This provision bans "material support" to a designated foreign terrorist organization and subjects those who violate the ban to up to fifteen years in prison. Here, it is important to note an ambiguity in the word "material." It may mean "tangible" and thus include the provision of physical objects such as computers or mobile phones or guns or even funds. "Material" also means "important" or "significant," and it is this meaning of the word that enables the statute to reach political advocacy.

The statute lists the various ways support might be given to a designated organization, and in 2004 the statute was amended to include the provision of "services" on that list.[7] In *Humanitarian Law Project*, the government contended that political advocacy—for example, a speech by an American citizen to a group of American citizens defending the goals of the organization—should be considered a service. The Court, in an opinion by Chief Justice Roberts, agreed with this reading of the statute.[8]

Some, but not all, organizations that engage in violent terrorism also provide a wide range of peaceful or humanitarian services. Although members of such organizations may kill civilians or high-level government officials, they may also distribute food to the needy. This duality of function does not appear to be true of al-Qaeda, the principal focus of the United States' War on Terror. It is true, however, of Hamas, Hezbollah, and the two organizations that were the specific subjects in *Humanitarian Law Project*—the PKK in Turkey, seeking autonomy and cultural rights for the Kurds, and the Tamil Tigers in Sri Lanka, recently annihilated by the Sri Lankan government but which had for decades sought autonomy for Tamils on the island.[9]

A question therefore arose before the Court as to whether it should make any difference if the defendants provided material support to the peaceful or humanitarian—as opposed to the violent—activities of the organization. Roberts read the statute as containing a universal ban on support, making no difference whatsoever whether the support, worldly or otherwise, is given to the organization to further its peaceful or humanitarian as opposed to its violent activities.[10] All support is criminally proscribed.

When the material support consists of money, one can well understand Congress's insistence on a universal ban. Money is fungible. Money given for humanitarian purposes, such as for buying food, might well be used to purchase arms. Even if the money is used for buying food, it would free up financial resources that might then be used for the violent activities of the organization. However, a policy of compartmentalization is far more plausible when the support consists of political advocacy that benefits the organization. Congress might well have been concerned with the speech that extolled the violent activities of the group but not the humanitarian.

In a crucial turn of the argument, the chief justice refused to read the statute in such a way as to allow any compartmentalization, even in the context of advocacy.[11] A speech extolling only the humanitarian projects of the organization or defending the justness of the organization's goals, Roberts reasoned, might lend legitimacy to the organization and thereby help it solicit funds or recruit members that might then be used to further the organization's violent activities. Roberts also maintained that Congress might have feared that exempting any speech from the criminal ban of the statute would jeopardize our relations with the foreign nation trying to suppress the organization, even if it is assumed that the support entailed in the speech was a benefit only to the organization's humanitarian activities. For example, at one point Turkey was at war with, and determined thoroughly to defeat, the PKK and the achievement of its separatist goals, and in that spirit may have tried to deny any support to any of the PKK's activities, even those that are wholly peaceful. And, according to Roberts, Congress, anxious to foster international cooperation with an ally such as Turkey, may have authorized the secretary of state, through the exercise of the power to designate the PKK a foreign terrorist organization, to support that endeavor.

Although Roberts read the statute in such a way as to deny the compartmentalization of the violent and humanitarian activities of a designated organization, he did, in fact, recognize one limitation in the material-support statute as it applies to political advocacy. This limitation—so central to Roberts's opinion—is premised on the distinction between independent and coordinated advocacy. Coordinated advocacy consists of advocacy that occurs in coordination with, or at the direction of, a designated terrorist organization, while independent advocacy remains a residual category—all advocacy that is not directed by, or coordinated with, a designated terrorist organization. Roberts read the statute to cover only coordinated advocacy. He insisted, "Under the material-support statute, plaintiffs may say anything they wish on any topic. They may speak and write freely about the PKK and [the Tamil Tigers], the governments of Turkey and Sri Lanka, human rights, and international law. They may advocate before the United Nations." [12] The catch, however, is that in Roberts's opinion the statute allows individuals to engage in such advocacy only if it is independent, as opposed to coordinated, advocacy.

Roberts maintained that the distinction between independent and coordinated speech is implicit in the term "services"—the category of material support that brings political advocacy within the reach of the statute. I am doubtful of this reading. According to Roberts, a service to an organization is an activity done for the benefit of the organization. Yet independent advocacy extolling the justness of an organization's claim can be as much a service to the organization—a benefit done for, or conferred on, the organization—as coordinated advocacy. What moved Roberts to make the distinction between independent and coordinated advocacy, to my mind, is not the word "services" but a view of the Constitution—a view that remains to be examined. This view holds that coordinated advocacy on behalf of a foreign terrorist organization is not protected by the First Amendment.

## The Court's Decision and the Free Speech Tradition

A constitution establishes the structure of government and identifies the lawful means by which grievances are to be aired and social changes are to be effectuated. Violence is not one of those means. There is thus no constitutional interest in protecting violence as an instrument of change, and it is difficult to understand why a constitutional guarantee of freedom of speech, even one as absolute as the First Amendment, should protect speech urging others to engage in violence. However, starting in the period following World War I, and inspired by the dissents of Justices Holmes and Brandeis, the Supreme Court began to place limits on statutes that criminally proscribed the advocacy of violence. The purpose of this doctrine was not to protect the advocacy of violence in and of itself but to protect criticism of society so radical or far-reaching that it can only be implemented, so its proponents believe, through violent means. Radical criticism often operates, as Harry Kalven once put it, as the major premise upon which the advocacy of violence rests.[13]

This effort to place bounds on the censorship of the advocacy of violence had its ups and downs during the twentieth century but reached something of a resting point in 1969 in the Supreme Court's decision in *Brandenburg v. Ohio* [14]—a case that, to borrow a phrase made popular in Roberts's confirmation hearing, may be a "super precedent." [15] *Brandenburg* involved not a foreign but a domestic terrorist organization—the Ku Klux Klan— that held a rally on an Ohio farm at which there was advocacy or at least talk of violence. The Court held that an Ohio criminal statute proscribing the advocacy of violence could not, consistent with the First Amendment, be applied to the Klan members as long as the Klan's advocacy was not directed "to inciting or producing imminent lawless action and [was not] likely to incite or produce such action." [16] A distinction was thus drawn between incitement to violence and the general advocacy of violence, with the state censor confined to proscribing incitement.

Of course, general advocacy can lead to violence, but this contingency was seen as a risk that had to be suffered in order to ensure the robustness of public debate. In that respect, as others have observed,[17] *Brandenburg* followed from the Supreme Court's 1964 decision in *New York Times Co. v. Sullivan*,[18] which, in order to create more "breathing space" for the press, enlarged the risk of defamation that public officials must suffer. *Sullivan* required public officials seeking to recover damages for defamation to prove that the alleged defamatory statement was false and, even more decisively, that the speaker knew or had reason to know that it was false. There could be no recovery for the kinds of slips or errors inevitable in aggressive reporting or the rough and tumble of heated debate. The right of public officials to recover for damage to their reputations had to be limited, the Court reasoned, to make certain that debate on issues of public importance remains "robust, uninhibited and wide open." [19]

The political advocacy at issue in *Humanitarian Law Project*

—for example, a speech supporting the PKK—cannot possibly be regarded as incitement to violence or imminent lawless action. Suppose the advocate says that the platform of the PKK is just, or even goes so far as to argue that the justness of its demands entitles it to use violence. Such utterances may lend legitimacy to the PKK and help in its efforts to raise funds and to recruit members who might be willing to engage in violent action. In that way, such advocacy may be part of the causal chain that leads to violence. Yet the same could be said of the general advocacy of violence protected by *Brandenburg*—it too makes violence more likely. However, we protect the general advocacy of violence in order to preserve the radical critique upon which it is premised. Political advocacy that benefits or is made on behalf of a designated terrorist organization should also be protected so long as it cannot be regarded as an incitement to violence.

Admittedly, under the terms of the statute, the ban on political advocacy applies only to advocacy that benefits a foreign, as opposed to a domestic, terrorist organization. It is important to understand, however, that this ban applies to speakers who are Americans addressing their fellow citizens or their representative institutions for the purpose of changing the policy of their government toward such an organization. Criminalizing political advocacy on behalf of foreign terrorist organizations strikes a blow to American democracy, which in our times has become, as it must, increasingly cosmopolitan and concerned with foreign nations and foreign organizations.

Roberts virtually conceded that independent advocacy supporting a designated terrorist organization is protected by the First Amendment. Trying to assure his audience, he disclaimed any intent to allow Congress to criminalize independent advocacy: "[W]e in no way suggest that a regulation of independent speech would pass constitutional muster, even if the Government were to show that such speech benefits foreign terrorist organizations."[20] Yet it is difficult to understand why an advocate loses the protection of the First Amendment because his speech is coordinated with, or even made at the direction of, a designated organization.

We may have greater respect for an individual who takes it upon himself to speak out on issues of public importance and who acquires on his own the information needed for such speeches than we would for a person who speaks at the direction of an organization or who gets all his information from that organization. The independent speaker often strikes us as the more admirable person. But the democratic theory of the First Amendment—dedicated to preserving the vitality and robustness of public debate—requires that the focus be on the listeners and their need for information and critical perspectives, not on the moral qualities of the speaker. The character of the speaker—his independence—might make a difference in the listener's evaluation of the speech, but, while such a concern may justify requiring the speaker to disclose the nature of his tie to the organization, it does not justify a flat prohibition on speaking.

Protecting the independent speaker in the way that Roberts promised might lessen the loss to democracy attributable to the ban on the coordinated speaker. As long as the independent speaker is protected, some views about the justness of the designated organization's cause, or its use of violence, might reach the public. That contingency does not, however, render the loss to democracy from a ban on coordinated speech de minimis, and, in fact, there is every reason to believe that the loss is substantial. Although globalization and recent advances in the technologies of communications enhance the capacity of Americans independently to acquire information about foreign organizations, some degree of coordination or contact with these organizations still seems essential for Americans to develop well-informed opinions about these organizations and the United States' policy toward them.

There is, moreover, no reason to assume that the loss arising from the ban on coordinated advocacy will—as a purely quantitative matter—be compensated for by the available independent speech. Granted, free speech doctrine has long been concerned with the availability of alternative channels of communication and has tolerated closing one channel (handing out leaflets inside a shopping center) when another appears available (handing out the leaflets at the entrance to the shopping center).[21] But it has never tolerated a ban on one speaker on the ground that another might take his place.

First Amendment analysis depends not only on the quality and quantity of speech at issue but on the danger the speech presents to society. Roberts viewed sympathetically Congress's decision to ban advocacy so long as it was coordinated on the theory that such speech might legitimate the designated organization and thus enhance its capacity to pursue violent activities.[22] I do not dispute the capacity of political advocacy to legitimate an organization and thus to enhance the danger of violence. My claim, rather, is that this risk of legitimation is never constitutionally sufficient to justify censorship; the First Amendment demands that the remedy be more speech, not censorship. If, however, this danger of legitimation is sufficient to justify censorship, as Roberts suggests, it is difficult to understand why it is not sufficient to justify the censorship of independent political advocacy, which also might legitimate the designated organization and its activities and set in motion a causal chain leading to violence. In terms of assessing or weighing the social danger arising from speech, there is no reason to distinguish between independent and coordinated political advocacy. Both present the same danger to society.

After ruling that the statute covered coordinated but not

independent political advocacy, Roberts manifested a rare commitment to the passive virtues and gave the statute as applied to coordinated advocacy what might, at first, seem a reprieve. He suggested that what was wrong with the First Amendment claim against the ban on coordinated advocacy was its generality rather than its merits.[23] This reprieve was, in my opinion, only an illusion. Although Roberts was reluctant to say whether plaintiffs had sufficient ties to the designated organization to fall within the statutory ban, the entire opinion emphasized the distinction between coordinated and independent advocacy and was structured to deny that coordinated advocacy is protected by the First Amendment. Indeed, he wrapped up his First Amendment analysis with this peroration:

> Given the sensitive interests in national security and foreign affairs at stake, the political branches have adequately substantiated their determination that, to serve the Government's interest in preventing terrorism, it was necessary to prohibit providing material support in the form of training, expert advice, personnel, and services to foreign terrorist groups, even if the supporters meant to promote only the groups' nonviolent ends.[24]

At the outset of his opinion, Roberts identified the unusual procedural posture of the case. The Court was not being asked to review a criminal conviction for a violation of the statute; it was reviewing a request for an injunction against the enforcement of the statute. He also noted that there were two groups of plaintiffs seeking an injunction, one involving the PKK, the other the Tamil Tigers. The PKK plaintiffs, according to Roberts, alleged that, in addition to having an interest in training members of the PKK to use international law for the peaceful resolution of their disputes and to petition the United Nations for relief, they wanted to "engag[e] in political advocacy on behalf of Kurds who live in Turkey." [25] The other group of plaintiffs alleged that, in addition to wanting to help the Tamil Tigers present claims to international agencies for tsunami-related relief and negotiate a peace agreement with the Sri Lankan government, they wanted to "engag[e] in political advocacy on behalf of Tamils who live in Sri Lanka." [26] In commenting on this second branch of the case, Roberts noted, as this group of plaintiffs conceded before the Court, that the recent military defeat of the Tamil Tigers rendered moot their claims relating to the tsunami relief and peace negotiations, but not the one about political advocacy. Quoting from the plaintiffs' brief, Roberts said, "[p]laintiffs thus seek only to support the [Tamil Tigers] 'as a political organization outside Sri Lanka advocating for the rights of Tamils.' " [27]

The anticipatory quality of the relief plaintiffs sought raised a question of whether the case was justiciable. Should the Court address the plaintiffs' free speech claims on the merits or require them to await a criminal prosecution and then seek review of the conviction? Fully in accord with the tradition that seeks to minimize the loss of speech arising just from the risk of a criminal prosecution, Roberts concluded, "[p]laintiffs face a credible threat of prosecution and should not be required to await and undergo a criminal prosecution as the sole means of seeking relief." [28] Later in the opinion, once the distinction between coordinated and independent advocacy was introduced and the statute was read to ban only coordinated advocacy, Roberts addressed the plaintiffs' complaint about the uncertainty of "exactly how much direction or coordination is necessary" to bring them within the reach of the statute. [29] Roberts then noted the generality of the plaintiffs' free speech claim against the ban on advocacy and announced that the Court would stay its hand and await the evolution of a concrete factual situation before deciding whether plaintiffs' proposed advocacy was coordinated as opposed to independent.

This line of argument reappeared near the end of the discussion of the free speech issues, after Roberts had issued a general endorsement of the statute and turned to an application of the Court's ruling to "the particular speech" that plaintiffs proposed to undertake.[30] In this context, he upheld the authority of Congress to criminalize coordinated speech when it consisted of training members of a terrorist organization—in particular, the PKK—to use peaceful methods of dispute resolution or to obtain relief from the United Nations. Yet he hesitated when the coordinated speech proposed by plaintiffs—in this instance, on behalf of both the PKK and Tamil Tigers—consisted of political advocacy. He never explained why, from a First Amendment perspective, political advocacy should be treated any differently from the training plaintiffs proposed to undertake. He merely said that plaintiffs' interest in political advocacy was "phrased at such a high level of generality that they cannot prevail in this pre-enforcement challenge."[31]

In saying that the plaintiffs' claim "cannot prevail," Roberts did not, from my perspective, mean to qualify his general endorsement of the statute and the necessary implication that the statutory ban on coordinated political advocacy is constitutional. Rather, he was simply refusing to tell the plaintiffs on what side of the constitutional line they fell—that is, whether plaintiffs' proposed advocacy was coordinated or independent. According to Roberts, plaintiffs "cannot prevail" in their constitutional attack on the ban on coordinated political advocacy because they "do not specify their expected level of coordination with the PKK or [Tamil Tigers] or suggest what their 'advocacy' would consist of."[32]

Even this limited exercise of restraint is questionable, for it contradicts the tradition, earlier recognized by Roberts and well anchored in long-established doctrine,[33] that calls for an accelerated adjudication of free speech claims. Roberts's restraint puts on the would-be speakers the burden of either initiating another injunctive proceeding for the purpose of obtaining clearance for their advocacy or running the risk of criminal prosecution and a sentence of up to fifteen years in jail for their advocacy. Under either alternative, speech loses.

## The Prism of War?

It will not be news to anyone that the Supreme Court was divided in *Humanitarian Law Project*. What might be news is that the Court was divided 6–3 and that the majority included Justices John Paul Stevens and Anthony Kennedy, often seen as friends of free speech. Neither wrote an opinion, so it is difficult to know the extent to which they subscribed to Roberts's theory. I can imagine either one of them insisting that Roberts exercise a measure of restraint and fudge the advocacy issue.

Justice Stevens retired shortly after the decision was handed down. He was succeeded by Elena Kagan, then President Obama's solicitor general, who defended the material support statute before the Court, even as it applied to political advocacy. Her theory—thoroughly rejected by Roberts—was that the material support statute regulated conduct, not speech.[34] She insisted that the word "services" primarily covered activities performed by someone for a designated organization (for example, fixing a computer) and only incidentally regulated the kind of communicative activity in which plaintiffs wanted to engage. However, as Roberts quite properly explained, the mere fact that a statute generally regulates conduct does not insulate it from a

First Amendment attack or require a less stringent standard of review when it is applied to speech.

Kagan took her bearings from *United States v. O'Brien*,[35] which upheld a congressional statute that made it a crime to burn a draft card. Roberts disagreed. He thought that the controlling precedent was *Cohen v. California*.[36] The statute that *Cohen* involved—one criminalizing breaches of the peace—generally regulated conduct, not speech. Yet the Court set aside a conviction under the statute when it was used to punish political advocacy, specifically when the statute was applied to an individual who protested the Vietnam War by wearing a jacket with "Fuck the Draft" on the back. No one knows what Elena Kagan's position might be on political advocacy now that her role has changed from advocate to associate justice, though there is no particular reason to be optimistic.

The dissenting opinion in *Humanitarian Law Project* was written by Justice Stephen Breyer, joined by Justices Ruth Bader Ginsburg and Sonia Sotomayor. Here too there is reason for disappointment. To his credit, Breyer brilliantly and forcefully rejected Roberts's distinction between independent and coordinated advocacy and, in that context, properly warned of the dangers of using the so-called legitimation rationale—for either construing a congressional ban on advocacy or defending it. What should be of concern to the Court, Breyer said, is the impact of the statute on "advocacy in *this* country directed to *our* government and *its* policies."[37] Yet the space Breyer created for such political advocacy was, in my judgment, too limited. Driven by the desire to avoid a constitutional conflict, Breyer read the statute to be applicable to political advocacy only when the speaker knows or intends that the speech will assist the designated organization in its violent activities and that assistance is significantly likely to help the organization in carrying out such activities.

Although Breyer's position is more protective of political advocacy than Roberts's and for that reason might well be preferred, it too falls short of what the First Amendment requires—incitement to imminent lawless action and a likelihood of success. Breyer said that when the requisite knowledge is present, political advocacy on behalf of a designated organization bears "a close enough relation" to violent activities to warrant criminalization.[38] He cited *Brandenburg* at this point in his argument,[39] but that strikes me as a misreading and a misappropriation of that decision, for *Brandenburg* is predicated on the distinction between incitement and general advocacy of violence and confines the censor to prohibiting incitement. A statement that extols the PKK and its use of violence may make the PKK's violence more likely, even significantly more likely, and that may be the intention of the speaker. But without a further showing, such an utterance—however detestable it may be and however close it may be to incitement—is not an incitement but rather general advocacy and thus should be treated as part of the domain of public discourse that is protected by the First Amendment.

The limited nature of Breyer's dissent did not placate Roberts. He implied that Breyer was naïve and chided him for not addressing "the real dangers at stake."[40] In the context of discussing plaintiffs' interest in being allowed to train members of the designated organization to work with the United Nations, Roberts said, "In the dissent's world, such training is all to the good."[41] He then continued, "Congress and the executive, however, have concluded that we live in a different world."[42] In this world, foreign terrorist organizations are "so tainted" that any contribution to such an organization—even political advocacy or training members of the organization to work with the United Nations—should be criminalized.[43]

Of course, Breyer is as aware of the dangers of terrorism as is

Roberts. He made a concession to free speech, and although his was more generous than Roberts's, it was not large enough to satisfy the requirements of the First Amendment. Roberts made a distinction between independent and coordinated advocacy and, in my view, allowed Congress to criminalize coordinated but not independent advocacy. Breyer rejected the distinction between independent and coordinated advocacy, but then made another distinction—this time between the peaceful and the violent activities of the designated organization. In so doing, he allowed Congress to criminalize political advocacy when the speaker knows that his advocacy will assist the organization's violent activities. Seen from this perspective, it seems fair to say that both Breyer and Roberts inhabit the same world and are driven by the same fear of terrorism that accounts for the other offenses to the Constitution that have been made over the past decade in the name of fighting terrorism. What is lacking from Roberts's and Breyer's opinions—and even more so from Elena Kagan's brief for the government—is an abiding commitment to the kind of political advocacy that is the essence of a vibrant democracy.

We have long become accustomed to sacrifices of freedom in times of war,[44] and an awareness of this tradition might temper the concerns that the *Humanitarian Law Project* decision engenders. Indeed, Roberts invoked and sought to exploit this tradition. In a coda, he quoted from the Preamble and the writings of James Madison to emphasize the need to "provide for the common defense" and to protect "against foreign danger."[45] Roberts also reached back into history and made a reference to World War II when he dismissed Breyer's willingness to assume that Congress had an interest in allowing Americans to train foreign terrorist organizations to use peaceful means of dispute resolution. Roberts said that such an assumption is as plausible as assuming Congress concluded that "assisting Japan on that front might facilitate [the United States'] war effort."[46]

This way of framing the issues in *Humanitarian Law Project* seems inapposite. Over the last decade, we have grown accustomed to thinking of the fight against terrorism as a war, and this has been as true for Obama's tenure as it was during Bush's. Although President Obama has been meticulous in avoiding the use of the phrase "War on Terror," he has repeatedly declared that we are at war with al-Qaeda. The talk of war by both President Bush and President Obama stems from the fact that the military has been deployed to achieve national objectives—to capture and, if need be, kill the fighters and leaders of al-Qaeda. Yet this military campaign against al-Qaeda does not entail the exceptional circumstances that history indicates or that we ordinarily imagine when we think of war and use it to excuse or justify the adjustment of basic liberties.

For one thing, al-Qaeda does not pose a threat to the survival of the nation in the way that Japan or our other enemies did in World War II.[47] Moreover, in contrast to other military campaigns that we have conceived of as war, there are no bounds—either geographic or temporal—to the fight against al-Qaeda. Al-Qaeda is an international organization that operates in secret. As a result, all the world might be seen as a battlefield, and the battle may go on forever.[48] Osama bin Laden is now dead, but other leaders have emerged and will continue to emerge, and local cells appear able to operate on their own.

The statute at issue in *Humanitarian Law Project* reaches al-Qaeda—it is one of about fifty terrorist organizations on the secretary of state's list. But, as I mentioned before, this statute is not confined to al-Qaeda and, in fact, extends to such organizations as the PKK and the Tamil Tigers, which makes the talk of war and the references by Roberts to World War II seem even more strained. These organizations pose no threat to the survival of the United States—the threat that, more than any other, makes war so exceptional. Isolating and starving foreign terrorist organizations like the PKK and the Tamil Tigers may protect individual Americans traveling abroad and serve foreign policy objectives such as improving our relationships with our allies, but these ends, though surely legitimate, do not have the transcendent character of the one we usually associate with a war and which might possibly justify sacrificing a constitutional liberty—the survival of the nation.

In addition, to treat any military campaign that might be undertaken by our allies against designated terrorist organizations such as the PKK or the Tamil Tigers as a war of the United States defies the bounded quality of a war, even more so than the military campaign against al-Qaeda. These organizations may have a life as long as al-Qaeda's, but even if they are annihilated, as the Tamil Tigers were, similar organizations will inevitably arise somewhere in the world. Throughout history, there has always been one group or another prepared to use violence to pursue its aims. Of course, organizations such as the PKK and the Tamil Tigers are more geographically bounded than al-Qaeda, but the ban on advocacy that the Court upheld applies to any organization in the world that the secretary of state, in his or her wisdom, is prepared to designate.

Given these considerations, it is wrong to view the material support statute and its ban on political advocacy through the prism of war or to be sanguine about the Court's willingness to sacrifice our liberty by upholding it. *Humanitarian Law Project* cannot be defended, as Roberts would have it, as a temporary concession to the felt necessities of a war against an enemy that puts the very survival of the nation at risk. The ban on political advocacy that the Court sustained will, I fear, soon become a permanent feature of ordinary life in America and may even radiate out to spheres unconnected to the fight against terrorism and in that way alter the very architecture of the doctrinal edifice that has long protected freedom of speech.

# Prologue to Chapter 9

Trevor Sutton

Although Obama's foreign policy has not been the defining el-ement of his presidency, as it was with Bush, neither has it sim-mered on the back burner. Obama, like Bush, is a war president, and his national security agenda in particular has been a reliable source of controversy. Many aspects of that agenda have drawn criticism, but a few stand out as especially contentious. In 2009, the debate over the fate of Guantánamo and the trials of key figures behind the September 11 attacks dominated headlines. In 2011, the killing of Anwar al-Aulaqi sparked a heated national conversation about drones. In 2012, the Obama administration's response to a terrorist attack on the U.S. embassy in Benghazi, Libya, spawned a litany of conspiracy theories and attack ads.

In 2013, what may be the fiercest debate of them all broke out. After Edward Snowden, a former National Security Agency contractor, disclosed that the agency had been collecting vast quantities of data related to electronic communications, the media, privacy-rights groups, and legislators of both parties raised alarms over the scope of communications surveillance undertaken by the executive branch in the name of intelligence gathering. Also subject to sudden scrutiny were the judges of the Foreign Intelligence Surveillance Court, who, the public learned, had authorized the NSA surveillance. Unusual among Obama's national security controversies, some of the sharpest criticism of his administration came from legislators who had been reliable allies, such as Senators Ron Wyden of Oregon and Mark Udall of Colorado.

This chapter, "Warrantless Wiretapping," was originally published in the fall 2012 issue of the *Yale Journal of Law and Policy*, before Edward Snowden's flight to Hong Kong and Russia captivated the country and rekindled debate over the degree of trust the public should place in clandestine agencies tasked with intelligence collection. It was also published before the public became aware that the NSA had begun a massive collection of e-mail and cellular telephone "metadata" (that is, information about the e-mail and telephone calls other than their content, such as time, destination, and length). Yet the essay is nonetheless essential reading for those seeking to understand the scandal. What "Warrantless Wiretapping" sets out clearly, and what much of the commentary on the Snowden leaks has failed to grasp, is that the Obama administration's electronic surveillance program, and the FISA court decisions that authorized them, were all but inevitable after the 2008 FISA Amendments.

Two aspects of the 2008 FISA Amendments discussed in the essay bear particular relevance to the current controversy. One is the provision that enables "blanket" authorizations for data collection, which facilitated the sweeping order issued by Judge Roger Vinson, sitting as a FISA judge, permitting the NSA to collect metadata on all phone calls within the systems of Verizon Wireless and other cellular carriers. (The disclosure of that order was among the first and most explosive of Snowden's

leaks.) The other is the provision eliminating the traditional authority of the judge to scrutinize the factual predicate of warrant
applications. This amendment diminished the FISA judge's role
to the almost clerical function of verifying that all the required
"elements" of the application were present. Had the judiciary
not been stripped of this important power in the 2008 FISA
Amendments, one can imagine that the Obama administration
would have been more restrained in its surveillance activities.

Stepping further back, "Warrantless Wiretapping" makes another important observation that has gone largely unremarked
upon in the press: that Obama has perpetuated what is essentially a Bush administration counterterrorism policy, using legal
authority passed by Congress at the urging of President Bush.
As Fiss notes in his essay, Bush ultimately concluded that the
minor inconvenience of FISA review was less onerous than the
political cost of a "principled" assertion of unitary executive
authority. Although Obama has never claimed that he has the
unilateral authority to order electronic surveillance of domestic communications for the purpose of gathering foreign intelligence, he too has taken a maximalist view of his powers under
the amended FISA statute and has, in fact, engaged in electronic
eavesdropping beyond that contemplated by Bush.

In these respects, "Warrantless Wiretapping" adds yet another
chapter to the story of how Obama, once a staunch defender of
civil liberties, came to perpetuate, and maybe even expand, the
excesses of Bush's national security strategy, albeit in a manner
that pays greater lip service to the importance of process and
coordination with the other branches of government. But, as is
often the case in Fiss's writings, executive overreach is only half
the story. The judiciary, in particular the Supreme Court, bears
its own responsibility. As Fiss observes, Obama—like Bush before him—was able to obtain far-reaching surveillance authorizations under the FISA statute only because the Supreme Court

has failed to weigh in on the constitutionality of FISA in the first place. In the case of electronic surveillance, as with executive detention and extraordinary rendition, judicial silence and abstention have given the executive virtually unlimited powers in the pursuit of its counterterror objectives.

# Chapter 9

# WARRANTLESS WIRETAPPING

In recent decades, many changes have occurred in our system of communication, some quite startling, and yet the telephone continues to be an important part of that system. It is how we have conversations with friends, family, and business associates increasingly located at a distance. Admittedly, many of the exchanges that once took place on the telephone now occur through e-mails, especially when the purpose is to convey information, issue a directive, or render an opinion. We still turn to the telephone, however, when a conversation is needed, for the transmission of the human voice permits direct, highly interactive, and spontaneous engagement with others.

Engaging in a personal conversation is not like writing in a diary. We may assume that the thoughts or sentiments expressed in the conversation remain with the person with whom we are speaking, but that assumption may well be mistaken. This is so even in a face-to-face encounter. The person with whom we are speaking may turn around and share the contents of that conversation with others—in fact, he or she may be secretly recording the conversation for that very purpose. Although such a risk is present in a conversation conducted over the phone, this mode of communication presents yet another threat to the privacy of a conversation, deriving from the fact that the conversation is being electronically transmitted. A third party may obtain access to that transmission, listen in, and record whatever is said.

In the twentieth century, as the telephone became ubiquitous and telephone conversations became more commonplace, the law increasingly sought to guard against the dangers of such interceptions by a third party (which, due to the technology initially employed to transmit telephone signals, became known as "wiretapping"). Starting in 1934, Congress prohibited private parties from ever wiretapping.[1] Although there was a question about whether government officials were covered by this law,[2] in 1967 the Supreme Court construed the Fourth Amendment to limit the authority of federal officials to eavesdrop in this way, requiring them to go before a judge and obtain a warrant authorizing the wiretap.[3]

The statutory prohibition against wiretapping by private parties remains unqualified and appears today as a fixed feature of the legal landscape. Yet the constitutional rule protecting the privacy of telephone conversations from government interceptions is now in a shambles. This turn of events is attributable in part to the reluctance of the Supreme Court headed by Warren Burger, then William Rehnquist, and now John Roberts to safeguard fully and forcefully the values protected by the Fourth Amendment. It is also attributable to the events of September 11, 2001, which generated enormous pressure to enlarge the powers of the executive in order to protect the nation, even to the point of sacrificing the right to privacy.

## Bush's Legacy

Soon after the terrorist attacks on September 11, President George W. Bush declared a "War on Terror" and gave concrete meaning to that declaration by launching a military campaign against al-Qaeda, the far-flung terrorist organization that was responsible for those attacks. He also invaded Afghanistan when that government, then controlled by the Taliban, refused to turn over Osama bin Laden and other leaders of al-Qaeda who were then harbored there.

In the context of this military campaign, President Bush, as commander in chief of the armed forces, issued a number of directives. Some of these orders reached far beyond the theater of armed conflict and had a direct and immediate impact on the quality of life in the United States. One of the most striking, issued in the fall of 2001, established the so-called Terrorist Surveillance Program, which directed the National Security Agency (NSA) to tap international telephone calls between persons in the United States and persons abroad who were suspected of having links to al-Qaeda or associated forces. The interception of these calls was not authorized by a warrant or any other form of judicial approval.

At its inception, the Terrorist Surveillance Program was hidden from public view, which, given that its purpose was to catch the unwary, is not all that surprising. On December 15, 2005, however, four years after it was instituted, the program was publicly disclosed by the *New York Times* and became the subject of a heated public controversy.[4] Although many objections were raised to the program, the principal one arose from the failure of the president to abide by the requirements of the Foreign Intelligence Surveillance Act (FISA).[5]

FISA was adopted by Congress in 1978 in the wake of the revelations of a Senate committee, headed by Senator Frank

Church, about the far-reaching and largely uncontrolled surveillance activities of American intelligence agencies. As originally enacted, the statute required the executive to obtain permission from a special court—the Foreign Intelligence Surveillance Court—before tapping the phones of agents or employees of a foreign power. The statute decreed that the membership of the court was to consist of eleven sitting federal judges specially designated for this assignment by the chief justice of the United States. Each was authorized to act alone.[6] Their identities and their proceedings were both to be kept secret. The 1978 statute defined a foreign power to include not only a foreign nation but also a "group engaged in international terrorism." The statute further provided that foreign intelligence information included information relating to "clandestine intelligence activities," "sabotage," "international terrorism," and "the conduct of the foreign affairs of the United States."[7] The act declared that the procedures that it established were to be the exclusive avenue for gathering electronic foreign intelligence.

Bush's attorney general Alberto Gonzales defended the president's refusal to abide by the procedures of the 1978 statute.[8] Gonzales claimed that the September 18, 2001, congressional resolution authorizing the use of military force against those responsible for the September 11 attacks had implicitly modified the provision of the 1978 statute that made it the exclusive procedure for intercepting the telephone calls of the agents of a foreign power. In Gonzales's view, the 2001 resolution had removed any conflict between the Terrorist Surveillance Program and the 1978 FISA statute.

Gonzales did not stop at that point. He also denied that Congress had the power to interfere with the effort of the president to discharge his duties as commander in chief. Article II of the Constitution vests the president with the authority and responsibility to act as commander in chief, and he thus has, according

to Gonzales, the authority to override the provisions of any statute that, in his judgment, unduly interfere with the discharge of
these duties. Congress cannot tell the president how to deploy
the armed forces, and similarly, Gonzales continued, Congress
cannot instruct the president in his efforts to gather intelligence
needed for the successful completion of the military campaign
against al-Qaeda and its allies.

This argument was part of a larger strategy of the administration, spearheaded by Vice President Dick Cheney and his
chief of staff, David Addington, to enlarge—or, in their view,
recover—the constitutional prerogatives of the president to act
on his own. In fact, the administration's position on the Terrorist
Surveillance Program paralleled the position it had taken on the
methods that were to be used in interrogating suspected terrorists or persons accused of having links to al-Qaeda. In signing
into law the Detainee Treatment Act of 2005, for example, Bush
took issue with the portion of the act that banned torture.[9] In his
signing statement, Bush underscored the failure of the statute to
provide a remedy to enforce the ban on torture and then went
on to declare that he would not let it interfere with the proper
discharge of his duties as commander in chief. He issued this
statement on December 30, 2005, soon after the *New York Times*
disclosed the existence of the secret wiretapping program. That
coincidence lent further prominence to the attorney general's
argument that, notwithstanding the purported conflict with the
1978 FISA statute, the order establishing the Terrorist Surveillance Program constituted a lawful exercise of the president's
power as commander in chief.

On the issue of wiretapping, it is not clear who had the better
of the argument in resolving the conflict between the president
and Congress. Article II, which enumerates the powers of the
president, declares that he is commander in chief of the armed
forces, but the Constitution also grants Congress war powers.

Article I gives Congress the authority to declare war, make general regulations governing the armed forces, and appropriate the funds for the military. In the domain of war, many of the powers of the president and Congress are shared or overlapping, and each branch can advance a claim for primacy when there is a conflict. The president speaks for the nation. Members of the Senate and the House of Representatives are more likely to feel the pull of the local constituencies that elect them, though those local ties may well enhance their accountability to electors and thus strengthen their authority to speak on behalf of the people.

In the end, the nation was saved from the difficulties inherent in resolving the conflict between the president and Congress. In January 2007, after a yearlong public debate about the Terrorist Surveillance Program, Attorney General Gonzales changed his strategy. He turned to the FISA court and got what he wanted. In a letter to the chairman and the ranking minority member of the Senate Judiciary Committee, Gonzales reported that on January 10, 2007, a judge on the FISA court had issued orders—arguably, ones that might be characterized as "blanket" orders—authorizing the wiretapping covered by the Terrorist Surveillance Program. As Gonzales put it, a FISA judge had issued "orders authorizing the Government to target for collection international communications into or out of the United States where there is probable cause to believe that one of the communicants is a member or agent of al-Qaeda." [10] Gonzales also said that, in light of this turn of events, the president had determined that there was no need to continue the Terrorist Surveillance Program, although he affirmed his belief that the program "fully complies with the law."

Factions within the administration soon grew uneasy with this newly announced willingness of the attorney general to submit to the FISA requirements. Some objected to FISA's scope, which had been construed to cover any communication routed through the United States, even telephone calls between two foreigners located abroad.[11] Others objected to the need to obtain court approval when people in the United States were parties to the conversation but when the target of the interception was a foreigner located abroad.[12] Still others were troubled by a decision by another FISA judge, who in March 2007, when considering a renewal of the original January 10 orders, took the view that applications for authorization to wiretap under FISA had to be made on a particularized or person-to-person basis.[13] On April 13, 2007, only months after Gonzales's compliant letter to the Senate Judiciary Committee, the administration gave expression to this backlash and introduced legislation that would modernize FISA—or, put otherwise, give the intelligence agencies all the power they thought they needed.[14]

Congress responded favorably to the Bush administration's overtures, first on August 5, 2007, when it passed the Protect America Act.[15] That law was conceived as a temporary measure. By its very terms it was scheduled to expire in six months, and, in fact, it expired, after a short reprieve, on February 16, 2008. But on July 10, 2008, Congress enacted a replacement statute. It was presented as an amendment of the 1978 statute and thus was appropriately named the FISA Amendments Act of 2008.[16] The 2008 act essentially allowed FISA judges to authorize wiretaps on the terms and conditions proposed by the administration. This statute was originally scheduled to expire at the end of 2012, but, unsurprisingly, it was renewed until 2017—which will be more than fifteen years after the Terrorist Surveillance Program was first instituted.[17]

## Obama and the 2008 FISA Amendments

Although the 2008 statute was sponsored by President Bush and is historically connected to the Terrorist Surveillance Program he instituted, it has been thoroughly endorsed by President Obama. Obama signed the 2012 renewal into law, but he supported the measure even before that. As a senator, Obama opposed a provision of the 2008 statute that gave immunity from civil suits to the telephone carriers that had participated in the original Terrorist Surveillance Program by giving the NSA access to their facilities. Yet once he lost that fight, he voted for the 2008 statute. His attorney general, Eric Holder, subsequently declared at his confirmation hearing in January 2009 that he would fully defend the constitutionality of the statute.[18] He was true to his word.

In July 2008, immediately after the FISA Amendments were signed into law, a lawsuit was filed challenging that measure and seeking to enjoin its enforcement. As the initial line of defense, the government—first under Bush's directive and then under Obama's—sought to block judicial review of the statute by denying that the plaintiffs had standing to challenge it. The plaintiffs consisted of a group of lawyers, journalists, and human rights researchers who have professional interests in the Middle East and who have regularly been in touch with persons in the region who might be thought to be terrorists. In fact, one of the lawyers represented Khalid Sheikh Mohammed, the alleged mastermind of the September 11 attacks, who is, as of this writing, being tried before a military commission at Guantánamo.

The plaintiffs in this injunctive suit maintained that there was a substantial risk their telephone calls would be intercepted under the authority of the 2008 statute and that, as a result, they would have to adjust their action accordingly to avoid that risk, for example, by speaking in more guarded ways or traveling to the region to have face-to-face conversations with possible witnesses or sources of information. To insist on more—namely, that the plaintiffs show that their telephone calls are in fact being intercepted or will be intercepted—would, given the clandestine nature of such surveillance, mean that virtually no one would have standing to challenge the validity of the statute. Although the target of a tap might be notified of the interception if he or she later became the subject of a criminal prosecution, such notice would hardly avoid the risk of interception to the entire group of plaintiffs, nor would it avoid the harm of which they complained—the very fear of having their telephone calls intercepted under this grant of authority. The government also pointed to provisions in the 2008 statute that gave telephone companies standing to test its validity, but the plaintiffs insisted that those provisions were not adequate to protect their distinct interests.

In late 2011, the Court of Appeals for the Second Circuit affirmed the standing of the plaintiffs.[19] But the Supreme Court would have none of it. On February 26, 2013, the Court ruled that the plaintiffs lacked standing and thus could not obtain a ruling on their claim.[20] The Court was sharply divided, 5–4. In this essay, I put the standing issue to one side and consider instead the validity of the 2008 FISA Amendments. The assumption is not that the Court will reverse itself anytime soon on the standings issue and rule on the validity of the measure. Rather, my purpose is to describe the surveillance power that was created by the 2008 statute and that is, in effect, now insulated from judicial examination.

## The Origins of the Concept of "Foreign Intelligence Gathering"

The 2008 statute is unconnected to warfare. It was enacted during an era defined by the initiation of a War on Terror, but, unlike the Terrorist Surveillance Program, it has no analytic connection to the fight against al-Qaeda or any other military operation launched in response to the events of September 11.

As an amendment of the 1978 FISA statute, the 2008 act is not linked to war but to the process governed by that statute—gathering foreign intelligence.

The concept of "foreign intelligence gathering" emerged as a distinct legal category in a rather odd manner—in the crevices of a back-and-forth between Congress and the Supreme Court on the rules that should govern wiretapping. The Supreme Court took the initiative in 1967, during the halcyon days of the Warren Court, when it ruled in *Katz v. United States*[21] that the Fourth Amendment required that government wiretapping be authorized by a judicial warrant.

In taking this step, the Supreme Court rejected an approach to the Fourth Amendment, crafted by Chief Justice William Howard Taft in the late 1920s in *Olmstead v. United States*,[22] which had placed wiretapping beyond the Fourth Amendment on the theory that it was neither a "search" nor a "seizure." For the Court in *Katz*, these two words were not to be treated as Taft imagined—narrow pigeonholes into which the Court had to fit the contested executive activity. They were part of the initial phrase of the amendment ("the right of the people to be secure in their persons, houses, papers, and effects, against unreasonable searches and seizures"), and this phrase, taken as a whole, should be understood as indicative of a purpose to protect the privacy of ordinary citizens. In the words of Justice John Harlan's concurrence, often thought of as the authoritative gloss on what the Court had decided in *Katz*, the applicability of the Fourth Amendment, now seen in part as a protection of privacy, depends on two conditions: first, a person must "have exhibited an actual (subjective) expectation of privacy and, second, . . . the expectation [must] be one that society is prepared to recognize as 'reasonable.'"[23]

As a purely technical matter—of no interest to the Court in *Katz* or, for that matter, in any of its progeny—the case before the Court did not involve wiretapping but something closer to eavesdropping. Agents of the FBI had attached a listening device to the outside of a public telephone booth. The Court fully acknowledged the limited and circumspect character of the executive's action. The FBI agents had confined their eaves-dropping to only six occasions when the accused was using the telephone booth and also had confined their eavesdropping to a short period of time (an average of three minutes). Still, the Court ruled that this action by the executive required prior judi-cial authorization—the issuance of a warrant by a detached and neutral magistrate.[24]

In insisting on a warrant, the Court was driven by an under-standing that conceived of the diffusion of powers among the various branches of government as a way of protecting free-dom. It also drew on the established rules governing intrusions into the home, long thought of as the citadel of privacy. The warrant had to identify the target of the tap with particularity. It also had to be based on an application that gave, under oath, the reasons for believing that the individual had committed, was committing, or was about to commit a crime.[25]

The Court in *Katz* carefully noted the banal character of the case under consideration. The case arose from the prosecution of an individual who was charged with participating in a gam-bling ring. The Court distinguished such a case from one in-volving issues of national security and specifically declined, in the penultimate footnote, to say whether warrants would be nec-essary in such cases. As the Court put it, "Whether safeguards other than prior authorization by a magistrate would satisfy the Fourth Amendment in a situation involving the national security is a question not presented by this case." [26]

In 1968, soon after the *Katz* decision, Congress, moved by a spirited public campaign to get tough on crime, passed the Om-nibus Crime Control and Safe Streets Act.[27] In Title III of that measure, Congress established rules governing wiretapping. It faithfully endorsed the *Katz* requirements and prescribed the procedures for obtaining warrants for wiretapping. Yet it ended with a proviso—similar to the *Katz* footnote—that declared that nothing in the measure should be read as requiring a warrant in national security cases.[28] The proviso specifically identified two situations that were exempted by the warrant requirements of the statute. One such situation arises when the president is seeking to protect against attack or other hostile acts of a foreign power, safeguard national security information against foreign intelligence activities, or obtain foreign intelligence information deemed essential to the security of the United States. The other situation covered by the proviso arises when the president is trying to protect against clear and present dangers to the structure or existence of the government.

The dialectic between the Court and Congress took yet another turn in 1972 when, in the so-called *Keith* case,[29] the Court was called upon to consider this proviso of the 1968 act. By this time, the Warren Court had begun to disintegrate, although a new institution had not fully come into being. The majority decision was written by Justice Lewis Powell, who had recently been appointed to the Court by President Richard Nixon. Another new Nixon appointee, Justice Harry Blackmun, joined his opinion, as did four who had supported *Katz*—Justices William O. Douglas, William Brennan, Thurgood Marshall, and Potter Stewart, who had written the majority opinion in *Katz*. The case arose from the radical politics engendered by widespread opposition to the Vietnam War and appeared on the Court's docket "at a time," as Justice Powell observed, "of worldwide ferment and . . . civil disorders."[30]

Three individuals were charged with participating in a conspiracy to destroy government property. One of the three was also charged with blowing up a CIA office in Ann Arbor,

Michigan. In response to a pretrial motion by this individual, the attorney general filed an affidavit in which he acknowledged that federal officials had intercepted telephone conversations in which the accused had participated. The attorney general also acknowledged that these wiretaps were not authorized by a warrant, although he went on to insist that the interception was a reasonable exercise of the president's power to protect national security and that a warrant was not required for such interceptions.

Justice Powell began his analysis by putting Title III to one side. The proviso exempted the attorney general from the general requirements of the statute in national security cases but was not a grant of authority. According to Justice Powell, the proviso left the attorney general where it found him—that is, subject to the Fourth Amendment. Yet recall that the Court had declined in *Katz* to resolve how the Fourth Amendment applies to national security cases. Justice Powell offered a partial answer to this question by drawing a distinction—arguably suggested by the proviso in Title III—between threats to national security posed by "domestic organizations," which he referred to throughout his opinion as "domestic security matters," and threats to national security posed by "foreign powers or their agents."[31] He defined domestic organizations to refer to "a group or organization (whether formally or informally constituted) composed of citizens of the United States and which has no significant connection with a foreign power, its agents or agencies."[32] He then applied the Fourth Amendment warrant requirement to "domestic security matters," as he characterized the case before him. In a manner reminiscent of *Katz*, however, he also declared that he was expressing no opinion "on the scope of the president's surveillance powers with respect to the activities of foreign powers, within or without this country."[33]

The original 1978 FISA statute sought to fill the decisional space left by the Court first in *Katz* and then narrowed in *Keith*. The statute established a procedure that required the attorney general to apply to a special court for permission or authorization to intercept telephone calls—both domestic and international—that were being transmitted through facilities located in the United States. This requirement of FISA for prior court approval should not, however, be confused with the warrant requirement that had been imposed by the Court in *Katz* and *Keith*. FISA did not require, as those two decisions had, the government to set forth reasons for believing that the target of the tap is guilty of a crime. The government need only set forth reasons for believing that the target of the surveillance is an agent or employee of a foreign power. The statute further requires the government to assure the court that there is no substantial likelihood that the interception will acquire the contents of communications to which U.S. citizens or persons admitted for permanent residence are parties. It also requires that the interception be likely to secure foreign intelligence, broadly defined by the statute as information that could (but need not) be related to criminal activity, such as sabotage or international terrorism. By the terms of the statute, foreign intelligence may also relate to alleged clandestine intelligence activities or the conduct of foreign affairs.

As a result of the 1978 statute, a dual structure emerged for wiretapping. Some taps required warrants based on probable cause; others, those specifically designed to gather foreign intelligence, did not. Remarkably, to this day—more than thirty-five years later—the Supreme Court has not ruled on the constitutionality of the FISA scheme or the dual structure it created. Yet a number of lower courts upheld the statute.[34] Those courts then faced a new quandary: could the transcript of a telephone conversation obtained through the less demanding FISA procedures be admitted into evidence in criminal prosecutions?

These courts could have held that the probable cause requirement of *Katz* and *Keith* had to be satisfied whenever the result of a wiretap was to be introduced in a criminal prosecution. They chose a more permissive rule, however, and defined that rule in terms of the purpose of the interception. As long as the primary purpose of the tap was to gather foreign intelligence, the government could follow the less demanding FISA procedures for obtaining court permission and then use the results of that interception in a criminal prosecution against the target of that tap even though that permission was not based on a showing of probable cause as understood by *Katz* and *Keith*.[35]

This ruling lessened the force of the standards that the Supreme Court had enunciated in *Katz* and *Keith*, a trend that continued with a statute passed in the immediate wake of the September 11 attacks—the USA PATRIOT Act.[36] That measure provided that the gathering of foreign intelligence had to be merely a significant, as opposed to a primary, purpose of the interception in order for the less demanding FISA procedures to govern. As a practical matter, this enabled the government to avoid the Fourth Amendment warrant requirement as understood by *Katz* and *Keith* whenever it could show a reason to believe that the target of the interception was an agent of a foreign power, that there was no significant likelihood of acquiring the contents of a communication to which an American was a party, and that foreign intelligence would be gathered by the interception. Gathering foreign intelligence could be a significant or a substantial purpose of the tap, and thus would be legitimate under the less demanding FISA procedures, even if the primary purpose of the interception was to gather evidence for a criminal prosecution.

## The Terms of the 2008 FISA Amendments

The 2008 amendments preserved the changes to FISA effectuated by the USA PATRIOT Act. The government need only show that the gathering of foreign intelligence is a significant, as opposed to a primary, purpose of the wiretap. The 2008 statute also continued the original FISA requirements for authorizing wiretaps in which the target is not a citizen but is nonetheless a person located in the United States. In these cases, the government must, in addition to the showing of significant purpose, establish a reason for believing that the target is an agent or employee of a foreign power. However, the 2008 statute introduced a further complexity in the FISA structure by establishing, as the Bush administration proposed, a special set of rules to apply when the target of the tap is located outside the United States.

Some of these persons abroad may be Americans or, in the language of the statute, "United States persons," a category defined to consist of United States citizens and persons lawfully admitted for permanent residence in the United States.[37] With respect to them, the requirements for surveillance are roughly the same as those provided by the original FISA statute as amended by the USA PATRIOT Act. The government must establish that a significant purpose of the tap is to gather foreign intelligence and that the individual is an agent or employee of a foreign power. These requirements apply regardless of whether the interception is effectuated through facilities located in the United States or through facilities located abroad.

However, in the case of non-U.S. persons—in my terms, foreigners—who are located abroad, the 2008 statute radically departs from the original FISA standards. As under the original statute, there is no need to obtain authorization of any kind from a FISA judge when the wiretap does not require access to facilities located in the United States.[38] When, however, the tap aimed at foreigners abroad requires access to facilities in the United States, permission by a FISA judge is required, but the traditional FISA standard is drastically lowered. Although the government must state that a significant purpose of the tap is to gather foreign intelligence, little more is required. The government need not have reason to suspect that the targets of the tap are agents or employees of a foreign power, only that they are foreigners and that they are located outside the United States.[39]

The 2008 statute not only lowers the standards for authorizing wiretaps aimed at specific or individual foreigners abroad, it facilitates the issuance of "blanket" authorizations for taps of such persons, as the original Terrorist Surveillance Program did.[40] Even though the entire FISA procedure is secretive, the 2008 statute relieves the government of the need to disclose to a FISA judge the identity of each individual to be targeted. It requires only that the government describe and employ procedures reasonably designed to ensure that its proposed surveillance activity will be limited to foreigners located abroad.[41] Arguably, this might permit the government to obtain authorization from a FISA judge to tap the telephone calls of an entire group of foreigners abroad (for example, "persons suspected of links with al-Qaeda" or "high-ranking officers of the Pakistani army").

All applications for warrants, even those required by *Katz* and *Keith*, are considered by a judge without notice to the target. The hope is that a judge, acting on his own, will scrutinize the factual basis of the application. This hope arguably persisted even under the original FISA scheme, though two of its features lessened the likelihood of that hope ever being realized—the judges on the FISA court are handpicked by the chief justice, and they are assured of a degree of anonymity. But the 2008 statute went further: it sought to eliminate the powers of a FISA judge to challenge the factual predicates of the government's application for authorization for a wiretap where the target is a foreigner abroad.

In 2004, Congress passed a statute establishing the Office of the Director of National Intelligence to coordinate and oversee the work of all of the intelligence-gathering agencies of the United States.[42] This statute also amended the original FISA statute to require that those applications that had to be jointly authorized by the director of the CIA and the attorney general now had to be authorized by the director of national intelligence and the attorney general.[43] The 2008 FISA Amendments continued this requirement of joint authorization by the attorney general and the director of national intelligence.[44] These officials must jointly establish a plan for governing these surveillance activities aimed at foreigners abroad, submit that plan to the FISA judge, and certify that the new FISA requirements for such targets are met.[45] In another radical departure from the original FISA scheme, the 2008 statute goes on to provide that the judge must approve the application if the certification "contains all the required elements."[46] There is no room for the judge to scrutinize, as he or she might or should have done in the past, the factual predicates of the government's FISA application. The 2008 statute also places a strict limit—thirty days—on the time the FISA judge has to consider the application.[47]

Having minimized the role of the judiciary, the 2008 statute provides for a measure of after-the-fact review of the surveillance activities of the Department of Justice and the various intelligence agencies that might be engaged in wiretapping. This review power was entrusted to a bevy of inspectors general, who on any account are administrative officials, not detached and impartial magistrates. Inspectors general are appointed by the president and are subject to removal by him. The Senate must confirm their appointment and be given thirty days' notice of their removal.[48] They were created by a 1978 statute, also a response to the disclosures of the Church committee, and are charged with reporting to Congress and the executive on the practices of the administrative agencies to which they are assigned. The 2008 FISA Amendments specifically instructed the inspector general of the Department of Justice and his or her counterpart in each of the intelligence agencies involved in the surveillance to review and report on the extent to which the surveillance targets persons ultimately determined to have been located in the country, and the extent to which the surveillance produces intelligence reports that identify Americans.[49]

## The Conflict with the Fourth Amendment

The constitutional protection of privacy is not absolute. The Fourth Amendment does not altogether deny the government access to the information that it needs to discharge its elemental duty to secure the land. Rather, it seeks to minimize or avoid the dangers inherent in surveillance by restricting the techniques and methods that the government may employ to acquire that information. It places a zone around certain domains and activities of the individual—those endowed with a "reasonable expectation of privacy"[50]—and then constructs a barrier to protect this zone. This barrier is reinforced by the understanding that each intrusion not only impairs the individual's interest in privacy and thus undermines the conditions necessary for human flourishing but may, given the particular circumstances of the intrusion and the reasons for it, threaten a multitude of other interests, including those protected by the constitutional guarantees of free speech, a fair trial, and equal treatment.

The 2008 FISA Amendments are a grant of authority. They allow the government to intercept telephone conversations and thus to interfere with an activity most certainly endowed with a reasonable expectation of privacy. The validity of the statute turns on the conditions it imposes on the exercise of this authority and whether those conditions are stringent enough to comport with the Fourth Amendment and the barriers it interposes against such intrusions of privacy. Typically, the Fourth Amendment has been used to review criminal convictions, and in that context constitutes a standard to measure, after the fact, the investigatory activity of law enforcement officials. It also has been held to establish a standard to measure prospectively legislative grants of investigative authority and the power of government officials to engage in various forms of surveillance, including wiretapping.[51]

*A. The Probable Cause Requirement.* The barrier constructed by *Katz* and *Keith* has two features. It requires court approval prior to the interception and it conditions that approval upon a showing of probable cause. FISA—as originally enacted and as amended—satisfies the first requirement of prior court approval. But it qualifies in important ways the second—the need to show probable cause.[52]

The Fourth Amendment does not elaborate on the meaning of probable cause, but, as *Katz* and *Keith* and countless other cases declared, probable cause is, as used in the Fourth Amendment, a technical term linked to criminality. It is, as Justice Ruth Bader Ginsburg recently observed, "a term in the legal argot."[53] Probable cause does not simply mean reason to believe or suspect that something is the fact, but rather reason to believe or suspect that the person whose calls are being intercepted had committed a crime, is committing a crime, or is about to commit a crime.

The burden of showing probable cause may weigh heavily on the government. The government may sometimes need to wiretap in order to acquire the information that will enable it to identify a criminal or give it reason to believe that an individual is about to commit a crime. The same could be said about intrusions into the home: they may be needed to establish probable cause. However, under the Fourth Amendment, that information must be secured by means that do not entail intercepting a conversation or intruding into a domain that is endowed with a reasonable expectation of privacy. In *Katz* and again in *Keith*, the Supreme Court stopped short of applying this understanding of probable cause to wiretapping aimed at gathering foreign intelligence and reserved that question for another day—a day that has not yet come.

The 2008 statute varies the conditions for obtaining court approval depending on the purpose of the surveillance and the citizenship and location of the target. In no instance does it require the suspicion of criminality that is the essence of probable cause. In all FISA wiretaps, the government must show that a significant purpose—not the only purpose or even the primary purpose—of the interception is to gather foreign intelligence, which, of course, may have no connection to any suspected criminal activity.[54] The statute imposes a further condition on obtaining court approval when the target of the tap is an American citizen or a person who is lawfully in the United States: the government must show that the target is an employee or agent of a foreign power.[55] If the foreign power is an international terrorist organization, it can be fairly assumed that there is reason to believe that the target is a terrorist and thus that the probable cause requirement has been satisfied. But wiretapping is allowed under FISA even if the foreign power is another nation, for example the United Kingdom or Saudi Arabia, and there is thus no reason to suspect the target of criminal activity.

There is an even more striking departure from the requirements of probable cause when the target is a foreigner abroad. In those cases, there is no need to show even that the target is an employee or an agent of a foreign power, only that he or she is a foreigner abroad. Moreover, in these cases, the FISA judge is denied the capacity, present in any probable cause hearing, of scrutinizing the factual basis of the government's application. On top of that, the 2008 amendments authorize a FISA judge to approve "blanket" wiretaps aimed at groups or categories of persons consisting of foreigners abroad—once again, sharply at variance with the constitutional concept of probable cause, which requires suspicion of criminality and thus must, of necessity, proceed on an individual or person-by-person basis.

The provisions broadening the surveillance power of the government when it is aimed at foreigners abroad may have been based on a reading of *United States v. Verdugo-Urquidez*.[56] In that case, Chief Justice William Rehnquist placed foreigners abroad into something of a constitutional free fall. He denied the protection of the Fourth Amendment—or maybe the entire Bill of Rights—to persons lacking a voluntary connection to the United States and for that reason did not govern in any way the search of a Mexican citizen's home in Mexico.[57]

Although Rehnquist's opinion was denominated the "Opinion of the Court," it needed Justice Kennedy's support to achieve that status. Justice Anthony Kennedy, then a relatively new appointee, wrote a separate opinion, in which he said that he joined the chief justice's opinion but, in fact, advanced a more cosmopolitan conception of the Constitution.[58] He brushed to one side Rehnquist's emphasis on the prefatory words of the Fourth Amendment—"the right of the people."[59] According to Kennedy, those words were nothing more than a rhetorical flourish, a way of emphasizing the importance of what was to follow rather than a means of restricting to Americans the protection of the right guaranteed. Kennedy conceded that it would be impractical to require federal officials acting abroad to be subject to the same requirements imposed on them when they are acting within the United States. For that reason, they are not, according to Kennedy, subject to the warrant requirement of the Fourth

Amendment.[60] On the other hand, he continued, federal officials are always subject to the obligation to act fairly or, in the framework of the Fourth Amendment, "reasonably." [61] Kennedy concurred in Rehnquist's outcome, but only because he felt that the federal officials had in fact acted reasonably.

Similar strains of pragmatic cosmopolitanism may be found in Justice Kennedy's opinion, this time for the majority, in the 2008 decision in *Boumediene v. Bush.*[62] In this case, Kennedy declared unconstitutional a provision of a federal statute (the Military Commissions Act of 2006) that was applied to deny access to the writ of habeas corpus to foreign nationals being detained in Guantánamo. He concluded that the statute constituted an unlawful suspension of the writ of habeas corpus. In so doing, Justice Kennedy repudiated an effort by Congress, similar to the one embodied in the 2008 FISA Amendments, to free the executive engaged in a War on Terror from constitutional constraints on its treatment of foreign nationals located abroad, though in this instance by denying them access to the writ of habeas corpus to test the legality of their detention. On the surface of his opinion, Kennedy appears to have been moved less by a regard for the rights of the prisoners than by a concern for preserving the separation of powers—the need to preserve the capacity of the judiciary to review the legality of executive detentions. Yet the consequence of his action for the rights of Guantánamo prisoners—all foreign nationals detained abroad—was manifest, and thus the *Boumediene* decision can also be read as extending the reach of the Constitution to foreigners abroad.

We need not, however, enter into the debates generated by these readings of Justice Kennedy's opinions, for even if we adopt Chief Justice Rehnquist's position in *Verdugo-Urquidez* and restrict the protection of the Fourth Amendment in the way he suggests, there is good and sufficient reason to be concerned with the surveillance authority granted the executive by the 2008 statute over telephone calls of foreigners abroad. Americans may well be parties to those calls, and the interception of those calls will interfere with their reasonable expectation of privacy. The constitutional inquiry should not be confined to assessing the impact of the government's action on the target of the interception but should consider its impact on all the parties to the conversation.

The 2008 act requires court authorization of a tap aimed at foreigners abroad only when the interception entails access to facilities located in the United States. Although sometimes a conversation between two foreigners located abroad may be routed through facilities in the United States, this is rare. Presumably, the bulk of international telephone calls routed through the United States involve at least one party who is in the United States. Some of these persons may be transitory visitors or even persons in the country illegally and thus beyond the protection of Rehnquist's interpretation of the Fourth Amendment. But more likely than not, they will be United States citizens or persons lawfully granted residence in the United States—persons who had the voluntary connection to the United States that Rehnquist demanded in *Verdugo-Urquidez*.

Accordingly, a wiretap authorized by a FISA judge that is aimed at a foreign national living abroad will, in all likelihood, give the government access to private conversations of persons unquestionably entitled to the protection of the Fourth Amendment. This is indeed true of the plaintiffs in the 2013 standing decision of the Supreme Court—journalists, lawyers, and human rights researchers whose work necessitates frequent and regular telephone calls to people in the Middle East. These individuals may not, in fact, be the target of the surveillance and, for that reason, may be characterized, as a purely technical matter, as incidental victims of the surveillance, but there can be no mistake that they are victims of the surveillance. Just as much of their personal or private information may be acquired as that of foreign nationals living abroad. They will be fearful of speaking fully and freely or may be discouraged from using the phone altogether.

The original 1978 FISA statute was mindful of this danger. It specifically required the attorney general, in seeking an authorization for an interception, to attest under oath that there "is no substantial likelihood that the surveillance would acquire the contents of any communication to which a United States person is a party." [63] The 2008 FISA Amendments significantly reduced this protection to American citizens and persons lawfully admitted to permanent residence in the United States. Those seeking authorization from the FISA court—in this instance, the attorney general and the director of national intelligence—need only attest to the fact that procedures are in place that are reasonably designed to "prevent the intentional acquisition of any communication as to which the sender and all intended recipients are known at the time of acquisition to be located in the United States." [64] The protection provided by this section of the 2008 FISA statute to the privacy interest to Americans living and working in the United States is profoundly diminished by the introduction of an intentionality requirement and the use of the word "all" (as opposed to "any").

Admittedly, in the ordinary law enforcement context, probable cause must be shown for the target but not for all the parties to the conversation. Statements by anyone who engages in a telephone conversation with the target might be used by the government in a criminal prosecution. [65] The 2008 FISA Amendments might be viewed as following a similar rule, but in truth the dangers are much greater. The target of the interception need not be an individual; it might consist of groups or categories of foreign nationals; and there is no need to establish, with respect to the target, the probable cause contemplated by *Katz* or *Keith*. The government need only give reasons for believing a target is a foreigner located abroad and that a significant purpose of the interception is to gather foreign intelligence. The threshold for interception is thereby lowered dramatically, and, as a consequence, the so-called incidental victims—U.S. citizens or lawful permanent residents of the United States speaking to a foreigner abroad—are more exposed than ever to interceptions of their private conversations.

B. *The "Special Needs" Exception.* The Fourth Amendment has an unusual grammatical structure. As Justice Kennedy's concurrence in *Verdugo-Urquidez* makes evident, the Fourth Amendment consists of two clauses. The first clause proclaims the right of the people to be protected against unreasonable searches and seizures.[66] The second, joined to the first by the word "and," sets forth the requirements for warrants.[67] Some scholars have advanced a disjunctive reading of the two clauses, arguing that in the minds of the framers the Warrant Clause sought to limit the availability of warrants, not to make their issuance decisive in determining whether an interception is, within the meaning of the first clause, reasonable.[68] The possession of a valid warrant, the argument goes, would provide an absolute defense for a government official subsequently accused of conducting an unreasonable search. By tightly prescribing the requirements of a valid warrant, the Fourth Amendment sought to limit the issuance of warrants—and, correspondingly, the availability of an absolute defense in cases seeking damages against federal officials accused of conducting unreasonable searches.

This understanding of the Warrant Clause may indeed be a plausible account of the historic origins of this provision, but even so, it does not undercut the now-ancient rule—affirmed by *Katz* and *Keith* in the context of wiretapping—requiring that if at all possible the government must seek a warrant before conducting a search, and further that the warrant should be issued only if certain requirements—including the showing of probable cause—are satisfied. Indeed, this rule may well be a fair implication from the bar on the defensive use of warrants that do not meet the specified standards. Liability rules often reflect an understanding of best practices.

In *Katz* itself, the Court acknowledged two very narrow exceptions to the warrant requirement: one for searches conducted in the course of an arrest and the other for searches conducted in "hot pursuit" of a suspected criminal.[69] The Court concluded that neither exception was applicable to the interception before it and showed no inclination to create another exception.[70] In recent decades, however, the number of cases in which an exception to the warrant requirement has been made—the most familiar involves the searches of passengers and their luggage at airports[71]—has grown. These exceptions are now grouped under the heading of "special needs"[72] and typically have been justified on the ground that the intrusion of privacy is momentary, obtaining a warrant before the search is not remotely practical, and redress of abuses of power may be obtained through an action for damages.

These conditions are clearly not satisfied by FISA wiretaps. Such surveillance is not a momentary intrusion but lasts for a considerable period of time. Under the 2008 amendments, for example, the tap can last for a year.[73] Nor can it be claimed that obtaining a warrant prior to the surveillance is a practical impossibility.[74] In contrast to airport searches, the 2008 statute requires that the government first seek judicial approval of the interception[75]—the only issue is what must be shown to obtain that approval. Moreover, given the secrecy requirements of FISA interceptions, a retroactive action for damages for abuses of executive power is not a viable alternative. Secrecy is no bar to the work of inspectors general, but they are only administrative officials and their task is to report on whether the practices of the executive comported with the statutory requirements, not with the constitutional standard of probable cause or any of its cognates. And their job is not to provide a remedy for such abuses but to report to the executive and Congress on the extent to which surveillance has targeted or led to intelligence reports mentioning persons in the United States.

Under Title III, the government is required to give all subjects of a wiretap notice of an interception after the surveillance is complete. There is no such notice requirement in FISA. In the standing case handed down by the Supreme Court in 2013, the government indicated that under the 2008 FISA Amendments, individuals would be provided notice of an interception when the government intends to use that interception as part of a criminal prosecution.[76] Justice Samuel Alito, who wrote for the majority in that case, made reference to this possibility in trying to explain why the Court's opinion denying standing to the named plaintiffs did not insulate the statute from judicial review. Although the terms and conditions of that notice remain unclear to me, let us assume that as a result of this promised notice an individual might, now and then, learn that he or she had been the subject of a FISA tap. Then that individual might be able to demonstrate in a subsequent action for damages that the surveillance was undertaken for the worst of reasons, for example, to make life difficult for a political enemy or to learn of the accused's strategy in an ongoing criminal prosecution.

But this imagined scenario hardly lives up to one of the assumptions underlying the special needs exception: namely, that a retrospective action for damages might hold the government accountable and thus avoid unreasonable infringements of privacy. The receipt of the promised notice for a FISA tap is likely to be a rare and isolated event, available only if a criminal prosecution is launched against one of the victims of the interception. In any event, such notice and the action it might prompt do not adequately guard against the principal harm of wiretapping—the fear of being heard by others. This fear might limit conversations, or discourage them altogether, which would be a tremendous loss for the individual and impair the democratic character of society, even though it is not likely to be a sufficient basis for an action for damages.

   *C. Extraordinary Crimes and the Problem of Overbreadth.* In an era that began with the terrorist attacks of September 11, 2001, the temptation is great to develop a special rule for surveillance activities aimed at preventing further terrorist attacks. This rule would free the government from the Fourth Amendment warrant requirement in such cases and might be justified in terms of the magnitude or severity of the harm to be avoided. No warrants are required, under this theory, for the investigation of extraordinary crimes.

   Such a rule might be understood as an expansion of the special needs exception, which is premised on the disjunctive reading of the two clauses of the Fourth Amendment that makes reasonableness the touchstone of legality. The test is not whether the surveillance is authorized by a warrant based on probable cause but whether the government's action is unreasonable. From this perspective, it would be difficult to fault the government for instituting a wiretap without first obtaining a warrant when the purpose of the surveillance is to prevent terrorism.

   In a recent case, *United States v. Jones,*[77] Justice Alito suggested yet another way of conceptualizing this special rule for terrorism, though the result would be the same—no warrant would be required. For Alito, the Fourth Amendment does not protect privacy but only a reasonable expectation of privacy, and the severity of the harm to be avoided would enter into the judgment as to whether there was a violation of that expectation.[78] When investigating extraordinary offenses, such as those involving terrorism, there may be, under Alito's theory, no intrusion of a reasonable expectation of privacy, and thus no warrant would be required.[79]

In the *Jones* case, the police had installed a Global Positioning System (GPS) tracking device in the undercarriage of a suspect's car without first obtaining an adequate warrant. The device was used to track the vehicle's movement over the next twenty-eight days.[80] Justice Scalia wrote the opinion for the Court and in it he applied a methodology reminiscent of Chief Justice Taft's decision in *Olmstead*. Scalia first said that the car was an "effect" within the meaning of the Fourth Amendment, and then concluded that the act of installing the GPS device constituted a trespass and thus was a "search" or "seizure" within the meaning of that amendment.[81] Justice Alito wrote a special concurrence in which he disassociated himself from Justice Scalia's mode of analysis. Condemning the police practice within the framework of *Katz*, Alito maintained that the police had violated a reasonable expectation of privacy and thus were required to obtain an appropriate warrant authorizing the surveillance.[82]

In insisting on such a warrant, Justice Alito emphasized the length of the surveillance—twenty-eight days.[83] He thought that relatively short-term monitoring of a person's movement on a public street might be in accord with "expectations of privacy that our society has recognized as reasonable."[84] In restating this conclusion, however, Alito also made the nature of the offense relevant for determining whether there was interference with a reasonable expectation of privacy and thus whether a warrant was necessary. As he put it, "the use of longer term GPS monitoring in investigations of most offenses impinges on expectations of privacy."[85] In saying this, and speaking of "most offenses," Justice Alito appears to contemplate a special rule for exceptional or extraordinary offenses. Mindful of the novelty of this approach, however, and perhaps in an effort to satisfy the other justices who joined his opinion—Justices

Breyer, Ginsburg, and Kagan—he ended his opinion with a disclaimer, so evocative of the national security disclaimer in *Katz* and the foreign intelligence gathering disclaimer in *Keith*: "We also need not consider whether prolonged GPS monitoring in the context of investigations involving extraordinary offenses would similarly intrude on a constitutionally protected sphere of privacy." [86]

The defendant in *Jones* was charged with drug trafficking—surely not an extraordinary offense. Terrorist activities on the scale of the 9/11 attack or any other acts of international terrorism may have that quality of extraordinariness to which Justice Alito referred. My inclination, however, is to resist the temptation to allow an exception to the warrant requirement for so-called extraordinary crimes, regardless of how the exception is formulated.

For one thing, I fear that an exception to the warrant requirement for extraordinary crimes would be susceptible to great abuse. The government can always claim that it is seeking to prevent an extraordinary crime and then defend that claim on the basis of knowledge that it alone has. Even more, I fear the jurisprudential consequences of such an approach. It would impair the authority and near-sacred quality of the Constitution, which, in addition to establishing the structure of government, defines the highest ideals of the nation. It would also put judges into the business of making exceptions to a standard rule that is not easily cabined and that is at odds with their obligation to say what the law is. Pragmatic considerations often enter into judicial judgments, but never in a way that permits disregard for a clearly established constitutional rule.

However, even if Justice Alito has his way and an exception to the Fourth Amendment warrant requirement were allowed for extraordinary offenses, it is hard to see how it might save the 2008 statute, or even the FISA scheme in general. These statutes, in contrast—say, to President Bush's Terrorist Surveillance Program—are in no way limited to surveillance that is aimed at al-Qaeda or associated forces, or even international terrorism in general. As originally enacted, the 1978 FISA statute defined a foreign power to include a group engaged in international terrorism and then defined foreign intelligence in a way to include information about international terrorism. Yet the statute is not confined to terrorism. In 2004, FISA was amended to include suspected terrorists who acted on their own,[87] but that only broadened the reach of the statute.

In utilizing the powers granted by the 2008 statute, the attorney general may be guided by an understanding of the historical context in which the statute was enacted—the statute was passed during an era defined by the War on Terror and, in essence, sought to give legislative authorization for President Bush's Terrorist Surveillance Program. Under these circumstances, the attorney general might well decide to use the 2008 grant of authority only for the purpose of preventing international terrorism or pursuing those who have engaged in such terrorist activities. But we can never be sure of that. The FISA regime—as originally enacted and amended in 2008—reaches more broadly and thus exacts a toll on our freedom. The very existence of the statute gives rise to the fear that international telephone calls will be tapped without the kind of judicial scrutiny and authorization required by the Fourth Amendment.

In the context of the First Amendment and its guarantee of freedom of speech, we have learned to judge statutes on their face—on the basis of all their possible applications. Under the so-called overbreadth doctrine, the Court will strike down statutes that arguably may have some constitutionally permissible applications if there are a substantial number of applications that impinge on activities that are concededly constitutionally protected.[88] The Court will declare the statute invalid on its face as a way of enlarging the freedom of citizens to participate in those activities that are constitutionally protected. Legislators remain free to prohibit the activities that may be constitutionally unprotected, although they must do so in a way that narrowly targets those activities and thus economizes on the sacrifice of First Amendment freedoms.

A similar doctrine needs to be recognized in the Fourth Amendment context.[89] In the First Amendment context, the overbreadth doctrine was announced as a protection against the chilling effect of a criminal statute. The 2008 act, as well as the original FISA statute, is a grant of authority to the executive, not a criminal statute addressed to the citizenry, and yet such a grant of authority may have the effect of discouraging—or chilling—the exercise of personal liberty, in this instance the liberty to engage in private telephone conversations. Thus, even if Justice Alito's theory is embraced—even if there are some offenses that are so extraordinary that we may allow the government to investigate them without a warrant—the statute that permits or authorizes such investigative activity must fall when it reaches such a broad category of investigative activity as "foreign intelligence gathering." The legislators must go back to the drawing board and come up with a statute confined to investigations related to international terrorism. Then and only then will the Supreme Court have reason to decide whether international terrorism is the kind of extraordinary offense that Justice Alito contemplated and whether an investigation of such an offense justifies an abandonment of the traditional warrant requirement of the Fourth Amendment.

One branch of the principle requiring separation of powers warns against unilateral exercises of executive power. From this perspective, the 2008 statute, compared to President Bush's Terrorist Surveillance Program, might be seen as a step forward, or maybe a half step. In it, the role of the judiciary is minimized, but Congress nonetheless authorized what Bush had decreed. From the perspective of the Fourth Amendment and the values it seeks to protect, however, the 2008 statute is a step backward because its authorization of warrantless wiretapping is in no way confined to terrorism or to the investigation of any other extraordinary offense. Like much of what has happened during the post–September 11 era, such as the use of military commissions and prolonged, indefinite imprisonment without a trial, the 2008 statute has transformed the exception into the rule. At the moment, the authority to engage in warrantless wiretapping is confined to the process of gathering foreign intelligence, broadly construed. If left unchecked, it will provide the foundation for a similar authority in other realms and thus become, I fear, a new point of departure.

# Prologue to Chapter 10

Trevor Sutton

Most of the essays in this volume examine national security policies that originated during the Bush administration and were subsequently extended by President Obama. Although critics of these policies can justifiably blame Obama for prolonging them, it is important to recognize that Obama's choices were to a significant degree constrained by his predecessor's actions. Obama may have failed to close Guantánamo, but it was Bush who established the Guantánamo prison in the first place. Obama may have failed to try Khalid Sheikh Mohammed and other accused terrorists in federal court, but it was Bush who propagated the belief that some individuals are too dangerous to be tried by Article III judges and juries. Obama may have failed to investigate and prosecute practices such as "enhanced interrogation" and waterboarding, but it was under Bush that those practices actually occurred.

The topic of the following essay is different. It concerns an area of government activity for which Bush laid some legal foundation but which Obama transformed into a major component—maybe the central component—of his counterter-rorism strategy: the use of targeted killings to eliminate terrorist threats outside a theater of armed combat, typically by drone attack. Bush lifted the twenty-five-year-old ban on assassination in the wake of the September 11 attacks, but for the remainder of his term that power was exercised sparingly (so far as we know). For all the justified criticism that accompanied the Bush adminis-tration's prosecution of the War on Terror, it was chiefly a mil-itary campaign, and not one conducted by the CIA. Moreover, away from hot battlefields, al-Qaeda members were less likely to be killed outright than to be apprehended for interrogation and prolonged detention.

Obama, by contrast, has by some estimates authorized the targeted killing of thousands of individuals, mostly in areas too impractical or politically sensitive to deploy troops, such as Yemen, Somalia, and the tribal areas of Pakistan. The killings have been extensively documented by NGOs and foreign gov-ernments, and were widely reported on by both American and international media. So widespread and routine have the kill-ings become that in April 2013 the *New York Times* referred to a captured son-in-law of Osama bin Laden as having joined "one of the most select groups of the Obama era: high-level terror-ist suspects who have been located by the American counterter-rorism juggernaut, and who have not been killed." Despite all this scrutiny, however, the Obama administration has never ex-pressly acknowledged the existence of its targeted-killings pro-gram (although it has confirmed some individual strikes).

This chapter, "The Targeted Killing of Alleged Terrorists," focuses on the most famous target of Obama's assassination pro-gram other than Osama bin Laden: Anwar al-Aulaqi, the fire-brand cleric killed in a drone strike in Yemen on September 30, 2011. Much of al-Aulaqi's infamy came because he was an Ameri-can citizen, not because he was an influential member of al-Qaeda or because the government had compelling evidence of his involvement in a terrorist attack. For some, this distinction made al-Aulaqi's killing—along with the killing of his teenage son several weeks later—distressing in a way that other targeted killings had not been.

Fiss's focus on al-Aulaqi does not derive from al-Aulaqi's American citizenship. To the contrary, "The Targeted Killing of Alleged Terrorists" is adamant that, under the Due Process Clause, a person's eligibility for assassination should not turn on an accident of birth. Instead, the essay's main concern is two legal challenges filed by relatives in United States courts: one before the al-Aulaqis' deaths, the other after. In Fiss's view, both of these challenges marked a failed opportunity for the judiciary to weigh in on a vital matter of constitutional significance. Not unlike the judicial response to the various legal challenges to extraordinary rendition (discussed in chapter 7, "Torture and Extraordinary Rendition"), the judges in both suits eschewed substantive analysis and dismissed the case on the basis of standing concerns and deference to the political branches.

The model of judicial review presented in the following pages is rooted in Fiss's understanding of the role of the Constitution in American society. But it also has a more direct inspiration: the jurisprudence of Aharon Barak, discussed at length in chapter 5, "Law Is Everywhere." One of Barak's most controversial—and most celebrated—decisions placed limits on the use of targeted killings by Israeli armed forces. For Fiss, Barak's insertion of the Israeli judiciary into a sensitive matter of national security demonstrates that fundamental values and public safety can be reconciled. If such a reconciliation is possible in a country like Israel, where the threat of terrorism is an everyday fact, then it should be no less possible in the United States.

# Chapter 10

# THE TARGETED KILLING OF ALLEGED TERRORISTS

Torture is not an integral part of war, but killing is. A nation at war seeks to kill enemy soldiers as a way of either defending its own soldiers or of vanquishing the enemy. When possible, simple humanity requires the military to capture rather than kill enemy soldiers. That option may not be available, however, or it may be achievable only by a maneuver that puts the lives of the nation's own troops in jeopardy.

Although the War on Terror announced by President Bush was only an exercise in political rhetoric and devoid of any legal content, the armed pursuit of al-Qaeda during his administration and that of his successor can properly be considered a war—an unusual war because al-Qaeda is a far-flung terrorist organization that operates in secret, but still a war. As such, the United States is entitled to kill individuals fighting on behalf of al-Qaeda who cannot be captured. This has been American policy from the very beginning—since the fall of 2001—but it received dramatic expression on May 2, 2011, when Osama bin Laden, the self-declared leader of al-Qaeda, was killed by a team of Navy SEALs who penetrated his compound in Pakistan in the middle of the night.

This killing provoked a measure of controversy, but none of it questioned the bedrock principle governing wars—the right to kill enemy soldiers. Some objected to the president's failure to honor one principle that governed even traditional warfare— capture if you can. Others were provoked by the president's boast that "justice was done." Killing bin Laden may have been the only option and thus allowed, but these critics posited that justice—true justice—required a trial and judgment by a court of law. Objections were also raised on behalf of Pakistan, sometimes by Pakistani officials, on the ground that the attack was beyond the theater of armed conflict and constituted an invasion of its sovereign territory. Pakistan had long been viewed as an ally of the United States in the fight against al-Qaeda, and as a result Pakistan's claim of sovereignty was muted by the suggestion that the mission to capture or kill bin Laden had the implicit approval of that country—in other words, Pakistan would have approved the mission if asked, but it was just too risky to ask.

In the months following the killing of Osama bin Laden, the news media—perhaps on the basis of leaks from the White House—reported that the United States had plans to target an alleged terrorist named Anwar al-Aulaqi. In contrast to the killing of Osama bin Laden, these reports provoked sharp and prolonged controversy. This controversy did not relate to the issue of sovereignty. At the time, al-Aulaqi was in Yemen, also an ally of the United States in the fight against terrorism, but, unlike Pakistan, Yemen was not especially jealous about the bounds of its territory. Some objected to the fact that al-Aulaqi was outside an active theater of armed conflict. But the principal objection to targeting al-Aulaqi—differentiating it from the case of bin Laden—was that al-Aulaqi was an American citizen and had no ostensible connection to al-Qaeda.

The press reported that al-Aulaqi had instigated a number of terrorist attacks against the United States—killings by a military officer in Fort Hood, the failed attempt of a passenger on a KLM flight to detonate a bomb as his plane approached Detroit, and the attempt, once again foiled, to send bombs to the United States hidden in printer cartridges. The connection between these acts and al-Qaeda—the organization responsible for the 9/11 attacks and the one with which we are at war—was not at all clear. Al-Aulaqi was the reputed head of a group known as al-Qaeda in the Arabian Peninsula. Aside from the name, however, the links between this organization and the one headed by Osama bin Laden seemed, at least to some in the press, speculative. At the time of the 9/11 attacks, al-Aulaqi was an imam in the United States and used his pulpit to denounce those attacks. In the absence of demonstrated ties between al-Aulaqi, or his organization, and al-Qaeda, targeting him might bring the United States to the threshold of expanding the war against al-Qaeda to any terrorist group that borrowed al-Qaeda's name and wrapped itself in the mantle of Islam.

On August 30, 2010, Nasser al-Aulaqi, Anwar's father, a resident of the United States, filed a suit in the federal district court in Washington, D.C., to prevent the administration from going forward with the alleged plan to kill his son. The defendants were the president, the secretary of defense, and the director of the CIA. They did not admit or deny the existence of a plan to target Anwar al-Aulaqi but challenged the court's jurisdiction to adjudicate the merits of the suit. In essence, the defendants argued that even if there was such a plan it was not the role of the court to prevent its implementation. On December 7, 2010, the suit was dismissed by the federal judge, John Bates, on this very theory.[1] Nine months later, on September 30, 2011, while he was driving on a road in Yemen, Anwar al-Aulaqi was killed in a drone attack launched by the CIA from a base in Saudi Arabia.

He was with another American citizen, an associate who was the editor of the English-language online magazine of al-Qaeda in the Arabian Peninsula. The associate was also killed in the attack.

At first blush, the defendants' challenge to the jurisdiction of the district court had great appeal, at least in the popular mind. Would the military need to get the prior approval of a court each time it targeted an enemy soldier? Such an arrangement would make the conduct of war a practical impossibility and, at the same time, place an extraordinary strain on the judiciary, requiring it to make judgments far beyond its competence. This reaction to the al-Aulaqi suit, however, misconceived the function of the suit. It was not seeking judicial review of an executive decision to target Anwar al-Aulaqi but—much as Aharon Barak and the Israeli Supreme Court had done in 2005[2]—to have the court formulate and announce the legal standards that should govern the practice of targeting alleged terrorists such as al-Aulaqi. The plaintiff assumed that the standards announced by the court would render the alleged plan to target his son unlawful, and thus lend his son a measure of protection. The motivation behind the suit should not, however, obscure the distinction between the articulation of the governing standards and the consequences that might follow from the proper implementation of those standards. The chief responsibility of the district court was to articulate the standards.

## The Legal Standards

What should the standards be for targeting suspected terrorists? What might be their source? As an exercise of its treaty-making power, the United States is a party to the United Nations Charter and bound by it. The Charter requires each nation to respect, as a general matter, the territorial sovereignty of other nations.

Article 2 of the Charter postulates that the United Nations is based on the "sovereign equality of its Members," and further declares that all members shall refrain from the "use of force against the territorial integrity or political independence of any state." Article 2 is no bar to enforcement action authorized by the Security Council. Nor would Article 2 bar the targeted killing by the United States of terrorists within the territory of another state if that state gives, either formally or implicitly, permission to the United States to enter the country for that purpose. The claim of sovereignty also seems hollow if the state is unable—in some gross and systematic way—to suppress terrorist threats aimed at other states. The sovereignty protected by the UN Charter cannot be claimed by a "failed state."

A more difficult situation arises, however, where there is no consent and the state is able to suppress the threat but is unwilling to do so. In those cases, the United States might view the state as complicit in the terrorist threat. The United States could then invoke the right of self-defense protected by Article 51 of the UN Charter to justify its invasion of the territory of another state for the purpose of suppressing or eradicating the terrorist threat. The United States relied on such a theory to justify the invasion of Afghanistan in the fall of 2001, when the Afghan government, then controlled by the Taliban, refused to surrender Osama bin Laden and other leaders of al-Qaeda. The right of self-defense protected under Article 51 does not require an attack on the United States to have already occurred, as it did on 9/11. It permits preemptive strikes. The sovereignty of a state hosting a terrorist organization can be violated when that organization threatens the United States and an attack is imminent. Article 51 has generally been construed to allow preemptive but not preventive attacks, and the dividing line between the two is the imminence of the threat.[3]

The Constitution declares treaties to be the supreme law of

the land, and thus subjects the executive to the requirements of the UN Charter. However, the most enduring constraint on the targeting policy of the executive, and the one most central to our constitutional tradition, arises not from the duty to honor treaties but from the Due Process Clause of the Fifth Amendment. It denies the government the authority to deprive any person of his life, or his liberty, or even his property, without due process of law. At its most basic level, this provision bans summary executions and requires the government to file charges against anyone it seeks to kill and then swiftly place that individual on trial in a court of law. Such a trial serves instrumental ends—to make certain that the individual has engaged in or is about to engage in a crime against the United States. It also seeks to achieve a measure of fairness by placing the burden on the government to substantiate the charges and by providing the accused with an opportunity to defend himself.

Although the Due Process Clause makes trial the basic norm of the constitutional order and prohibits U.S. officials from depriving any individual of his life without first convicting him of a crime punishable by death, an exception has to be made for the killing that is an integral part of war. The Constitution acknowledges the authority of the United States to engage in a war, and, as I said, the capacity to fight a war necessarily entails the power to kill enemy soldiers on the battlefield. The authority to target suspected terrorists derives from this power, though it may entail, as the killing of Osama bin Laden indicates, a looser or more global conception of the battlefield

The Constitution locates the power to declare the nation at war in Congress, and thus a preliminary condition to targeting a terrorist is that Congress has declared war against the terrorist's organization. In the case of al-Qaeda, the necessary congressional declaration can be found in the September 18, 2001, resolution authorizing the use of military force against those individuals or organizations responsible for the 9/11 attacks. Although this resolution can be read as authorizing military operations against al-Qaeda and those who harbored the organization, the resolution does not reach other terrorist organizations unless they are tied to al-Qaeda and thus properly considered a co-belligerent—for example, an organization that seeks to shield and protect al-Qaeda and that, as a general matter, operates under its direction. The United States might, as President Obama repeatedly declared, be at war with al-Qaeda and "associated forces," but this should not be understood to mean that the United States is at war with every terrorist organization in the world, not even with those that happen to use al-Qaeda's name but may have no further ties to the organization.

It is the responsibility of the executive to direct whatever war may be declared. In discharging this responsibility, the executive has the authority to target enemy combatants. This authority should be seen as an exception to the basic requirement of due process—trial in a court of law—and should be construed accordingly. This means, above all, that the executive may not target civilians, provided we understand that appearances should not be confused with reality. An individual may present himself as a civilian—as is usually the case with terrorists—but may be treated as an enemy combatant if it is determined that he is, in fact, the leader of a terrorist organization with which the United States is at war, or someone directly engaged in violent activity on behalf of such an organization, or quite possibly someone who provides significant support for the organization's violent activities. Given the stakes, this determination should be made with a high degree of certainty.

Even if it is determined that the individual to be targeted falls into one of these categories and thus may be treated as an enemy combatant, the decision of the executive to target this individual should be constrained by two further rules that govern combat and that, in the counterterrorism context, might properly be seen as rooted in due process. One requires the executive to capture the alleged terrorist if it can. The other requires the government to desist from the attack if it would entail the killing or harming of civilians and if this harm would be disproportionate to the military gains to be achieved by the attack. In either situation, the lethal attack cannot be justified as a matter of military necessity or of the executive's war-making power. As a result, the ordinary processes of the law must be followed.

Although these various constraints on the executive in the exercise of its war-making power have counterparts in the laws of war or international human rights law, I view them as part of constitutional due process. My claim is not that the Due Process Clause incorporates these bodies of law but that the Due Process Clause and the values it seeks to protect—trial in a court of law—contemplate the same checks on the U.S. government in the pursuit of terrorists. In that respect, the rules governing the targeting of terrorists can be seen as analogous to the least-restrictive-alternative test that has long governed the First Amendment and its protection of free speech.

Despite the wording of the First Amendment—"Congress shall make no law . . . abridging the freedom of speech"—the Supreme Court has allowed statutes or executive action that furthers government objectives, such as guarding national security, maintaining public order, or protecting children from explicit sexual images. The Court has required, however, that the purpose of such a statute or executive action be compelling and, furthermore, that the means chosen to pursue that end be the least restrictive alternative or, put differently, that the means be narrowly tailored to achieve the government's objective.[4] In this way, the Court has required the government to minimize the sacrifice of free speech values. Similarly, though the government may be allowed, even under the Due Process Clause, to engage in targeted killings of suspected terrorists as a legitimate exercise of its war-making power, it must use that power sparingly and avoid the sacrifice of the central due process value—trial in a court of law—before taking the life of some individual.

In a speech at Northwestern Law School on March 5, 2012, five months after the killing of Anwar al-Aulaqi, Attorney General Eric Holder endorsed a number of principles usually associated with traditional warfare.[5] As he put it, the government can target an individual only when "capture is not feasible." Invoking the rule of proportionality, he said that the harm to civilians— so-called collateral damage—must not be "excessive in relation to the anticipated military advantage." He also acknowledged, under the rubric of honoring "the principle of distinction," that civilians cannot be lawfully targeted. According to Holder, only "combatants, civilians directly participating in hostilities, and military objectives" can be intentionally targeted. Holder further acknowledged that the person targeted must have been deemed to pose an "imminent threat of violent attack against the United States." Such an imminence requirement may be implicit in the principle mandating "capture if you can" and, quite possibly, a reading of Article 51 of the United Nations Charter that permits preemptive but not preventive strikes in self-defense.

In a speech delivered at the National Defense University on May 23, 2013—more than a year after Holder's speech— President Obama expressed uneasiness with the proportionality rule and seemed unprepared to accept any killing of civilians as collateral damage, whether or not it is proportional.[6] This strikes me as a wise amendment of the policy Holder announced, if that is what was intended. The collateral damage acceptable in traditional warfare may be unacceptable when a suspected terrorist, such as Anwar al-Aulaqi, is targeted. In that situation, there will be an inescapable element of doubt as to the conditions allowing the United States to take such action. Even if there is no doubt as to whether the target is a leader of a terrorist organization, there may be doubt as to whether capture is feasible, or whether the lethal attack might be deferred until a later date when the killing of civilians would be avoided, or whether the terrorist organization is a co-belligerent of al-Qaeda, or whether the nation in which the suspected terrorist is located has relinquished its claim to sovereignty. These uncertainties seem inevitable and are significantly greater than those associated with the killings that invariably take place in a combat zone or an active theater of armed conflict. As a consequence, the advantage to be gained by killing a suspected terrorist is, as a matter of morality and legality, too slender to shoulder the ensured killing of civilians, under the theory that such killings would be nothing more than collateral damage.

The global nature of the war against a terrorist organization such as al-Qaeda may present additional reasons for departing from the rule of traditional warfare that would allow, subject to the proportionality requirement, the killing (though not the targeting) of civilians. It is one thing to apply the traditional rule in a combat zone or hot battlefield and another to apply it, as the global War on Terror invites, to any community in the world in which a suspected terrorist might reside.[7] The combat zone is by necessity geographically limited, and the people who live in it are abundantly conscious of the dangers they face. The War on Terror has no geographic bounds; it embraces every community in the world in which a leader or an operative of al-Qaeda can be found. Unleashing a lethal power so vast has profound and disturbing implications for those to be targeted, but allowing civilians to be killed on the theory that they are collateral damage would create a new harm. It would strain the relationship among the members of these communities. Individuals would fear that they might be killed because a terrorist lives within their midst, and in time this fear would erode the human bonds that are the essence of civilization. The sovereignty of each nation protected by the UN Charter might provide a bulwark against such fears. Yet, as the case of Yemen indicates, ordinary citizens can never be sure of the deals that their national leaders might make with the sponsor of the War on Terror.

For these reasons, a rule might well be adopted prohibiting lethal attacks against suspected terrorists if such attacks would entail the killing of persons who are clearly and unambiguously civilians. Such a rule might have prohibited the drone strike targeting Anwar al-Aulaqi, who at the moment of the attack was riding with a colleague who had not, at least according to news reports, forfeited his status as a civilian. Or imagine that Anwar al-Aulaqi had a three-year-old daughter and she was riding in the car with him at the time of the attack. The United States might have been entitled to kill Anwar al-Aulaqi under the theory that he was an enemy combatant or the leader of an organization that is a co-belligerent of al-Qaeda, but no such theory could be advanced to justify the killing of his daughter. The fact that she was not a target would not modulate either the inhumanity of killing her or its offense to the Constitution.

The targeted killing of Anwar al-Aulaqi raised the further question as to whether American citizens enjoy a special immunity from being targeted. The relevance of American citizenship in the formulation and application of counterterrorism policies over the past decade has been a controverted issue on which neither President Bush nor President Obama took consistent or well-reasoned positions. The jurisdiction of the military commissions established by Bush through an executive order issued in the fall of 2001 was confined to foreign nationals. The pattern was continued in the Military Commissions Act of 2006 and the Military Commissions Act of 2009. On the other hand, the policy of prolonged, indefinite imprisonment without trial instituted by President Bush and continued by President Obama reached both citizens and foreign nationals, though in 2011, rather belatedly, President Obama announced that this policy would not be applied to United States citizens.[8] To take another example, Bush's original executive order authorizing the NSA to engage in warrantless wiretapping as part of the War on Terror made no distinction between citizens and foreign nationals. The FISA Amendments of 2008 (renewed in 2012) limited such surveillance to situations where the target of the interception is a foreign national located abroad (although the other parties to the telephone conversation may be United States citizens located in the United States). With respect to all three of these policies, it is difficult to know whether the distinction drawn by the president or Congress between citizens and noncitizens was based on politics, understood in the crudest way, or on some unarticulated theory governing the reach of the Constitution—or both.

The position of the Bush administration on the scope of its policy of targeted killing is unclear. There are no reports that the Bush administration had targeted an American citizen, although in one instance an American citizen—Kamal Derwish—was killed as the result of a drone attack aimed at another person—a foreign national—who was in the car in which Derwish was riding. The Obama administration killed a number of American citizens through the use of drones (some were bystanders), but as we know, at least one—Anwar al-Aulaqi—was the target of such an attack. The targeting of American citizens has been strongly criticized in political quarters, but it is difficult to formulate a constitutional theory that would allow the president to target foreign nationals but not American citizens. By its very terms, the Due Process Clause protects persons, not citizens, and as such provides no additional protection to citizens. The power to target alleged terrorists flows from the theory that the government is entitled to kill enemy soldiers on the battlefield and, as we discovered in many wars, United States citizens have

taken up arms against the United States and in those circumstances have been lawfully subjected to lethal force used by the
United States.

In his Northwestern Law School speech, Holder expressed
some equivocation on the relevance of citizenship. He began his
analysis by noting that "some of the threats we face come from
a small number of United States citizens who have decided to
commit violent attacks against their own country from abroad,"
and concluded, "it is clear that United States citizenship alone
does not make such individuals immune from being targeted."
Then the attorney general switched course. He insisted that
"the government must take into account all relevant constitutional considerations with respect to United States citizens," and
ended his analysis on a note that misrepresented the Due Process Clause when he suggested that it protects only citizens. In
that context, he said: "Of these, the most relevant is the Fifth
Amendment's Due Process Clause, which says that the government may not deprive a citizen of his or her life without due
process of law." In response to stormy congressional hearings
that were triggered by the targeted killing of al-Aulaqi, Holder
wrote a two-sentence letter to Senator Rand Paul declaring that
the president lacked "the authority . . . to kill an American citizen not engaged in combat on American soil." He offered no
constitutional theory that would limit the administration's targeting policy in its war against al-Qaeda in this way. No one not
engaged in combat (or its terrorist equivalent) can be killed, on
or off American soil.

The attorney general was not clear in identifying the source
of the rules he announced governing targeted killings. At one
point he declared, "The Constitution's guarantee of due process
is ironclad, and it is essential." Moreover, he never denied that
the principles protecting civilians or requiring proportionality,

or even the imminence requirement, are rooted in the Due Process Clause. At other times, however, he referred to the principles of distinction and proportionality as requirements of "the law of war"; he even spoke of a "principle of humanity" as the source of yet another rule he mentioned—to use weapons in targeted killings that "will not inflict unnecessary suffering." This language suggests that the rules governing the targeted killing of alleged terrorists announced by the attorney general were inspired by the laws of war or by international human rights law. Let us assume, however, that the attorney general was in fact grounding the rules he announced in constitutional due process. Let us also assume that the rules he announced and to which he bound himself are roughly the same as a fair-minded judge might have announced in the al-Aulaqi suit. I would maintain, nevertheless, that there is a special value to having these rules announced by a court, and that the dismissal of the al-Aulaqi suit was improper.

The attorney general is, of course, entitled to interpret the Constitution. Indeed, I would say that he, like every government official, has an obligation to do so. The Constitution is the basic law of the nation that defines the duties and prerogatives of every official acting on behalf of the United States. Yet the interpretation of the Constitution by a judge has an authority and force that transcends that of the attorney general or any other official in the executive or legislative branch. This authority derives not from the personal qualities of the individuals involved—Eric Holder vs. John Bates—but from the rules that govern the exercise of their power. Although Holder's speech, like the opinion Bates could or should have rendered, made appeal to public reason, the judge, unlike the attorney general, is insulated from control by any political agency; he is required to listen to all aggrieved parties; and he must conduct his proceedings in an open court.[9] These are important differences, and because of them the judge's interpretation of the Due Process Clause and the announcement of the standards governing the targeted killings of alleged terrorists would have the authority of the law. They will govern even when there is a change of administration, and they command a measure of respect not due to the standards put forward by the attorney general in his Northwestern speech.

## Procedures for Assessing Compliance

Although, as I maintain, the essential function of the judiciary in the al-Aulaqi case was to formulate and announce the constitutional principles that are to govern the executive's targeting policy, a controversy is likely to erupt over the application of those principles even after they are announced. As a result, a question will arise as to the role of the judiciary in policing the executive's judgment in the implementation of those principles, most notably in the determination that the individual targeted is not a civilian but a terrorist who could properly be treated as an enemy combatant.

In the closing passages of his Northwestern speech, Holder acknowledged the need for "robust oversight" of the executive in the implementation of its targeting policy. It turns out, however, that the oversight he contemplated was to be provided by Congress, not the judiciary, and there was nothing especially robust about it. He was referring to a scheme whereby "the Executive Branch regularly informs the appropriate members of Congress about [its] counterterrorism activities." Under this scheme, we would have one political actor (the attorney general) reporting to another (Congress), with no requirement that the institution performing the oversight publicly announce its decision or justify that decision on the basis of principle. In that respect, the oversight system Holder contemplated compounds the political character of the standards he announced.

Following the Northwestern speech, the president issued guidelines to ensure that the policies Holder announced were, in fact, followed. Internal review processes were established to monitor compliance. They were to be implemented by officers in the executive branch. An arrangement was also made to notify the appropriate congressional committees—not just individual members of Congress—after a drone strike had occurred. Notifying the committee, as opposed to select members of Congress, might have the effect of making that strike part of the official business of Congress and thus subject to further debate and consideration. None of these measures, however, constitutes an adequate substitute for the constraint that might be brought to bear on the executive by a court of law reviewing the implementation of the targeted-killing program.

Obama implicitly recognized this lacuna when, in his speech at the National Defense University in May 2013, he toyed with the idea—which went nowhere—of "bringing a third branch of government into the process." [10] In that context, he mentioned the possibility of establishing a "special court" that would review plans to target suspected terrorists. Yet all the features that would make such a tribunal "special"—using a cadre of hand-picked judges, ensuring that the court operated in secret, and having the court act after it heard from only one side (the government's)—would deprive that tribunal from speaking with the authority that rightly belongs to the judiciary. A court needs to review the executive's implementation of the standards governing targeted killing, but it should not be a "special court."

The need for judicial oversight in reviewing executive determinations generated by the War on Terror was recognized by the Supreme Court in its 2004 decision in *Hamdi v. Rumsfeld*. The Court held that the executive's determination that an individual captured in Afghanistan and imprisoned in a naval brig in the United States as an enemy combatant was entitled, as a matter of due process, to an evidentiary hearing on his claim that he had not taken up arms against the United States. Justice Clarence Thomas deferred to the executive's judgment and maintained that no review of the executive's determination as to the status of the individual would be appropriate. However, all the other justices took a contrary view and refused to make the decision of the executive the last word. Justice Antonin Scalia, joined by Justice John Paul Stevens, required a criminal trial. They insisted that the prisoner could not be denied his constitutional right to freedom without first having been found guilty by a federal court for having committed a crime against the United States.

Justice Sandra Day O'Connor, for her part, expressed the view that although due process required that an evidentiary hearing be held before an impartial decision maker to assess the prisoner's claim of freedom, that hearing could be held before a properly constituted military tribunal—an idea that might seem to lend credence to Obama's call for a "special court." We should not, however, assume that O'Connor spoke for a majority on this issue. Her opinion was styled as the opinion of the Court, but it is not clear that it had the support of five justices. Justice David Souter, in an opinion joined by Justice Ruth Bader Ginsburg, indicated his willingness to join O'Connor's opinion, but only with the understanding that a military tribunal was no substitute for the federal habeas court for purposes of holding the evidentiary hearing to which the prisoner was entitled. Moreover, two of the justices who joined O'Connor's opinion without reservation— Justices Anthony Kennedy and Stephen Breyer—subsequently revealed their disagreement with O'Connor's view about the acceptability of using military tribunals to determine a prisoner's status when, in 2008, the Court handed down its decision in *Boumediene v. Bush*. In an opinion written by Kennedy and endorsed by Breyer, *Boumediene* held that those individuals imprisoned in Guantánamo as enemy combatants were entitled to have a federal court, acting on a writ of habeas corpus, to hear their claim that they had not raised arms against the United States.[11] In the end, it appears that only Justice O'Connor and Chief Justice William Rehnquist endorsed the idea put forth in *Hamdi* of substituting military tribunals for the federal habeas court. All the others who signed on to O'Connor's opinion understood the importance of having a federal habeas court assess the prisoner's claim to personal freedom and believed that this was the essence of due process.

Of course, targeted killing does not involve imprisonment, and thus the writ of habeas corpus does not come into play. Still, the denial of freedom—long the province of habeas corpus—in a targeted killing is more complete and devastating than even prolonged imprisonment. More procedure should be required, not less, when the taking of a life hangs in the balance. It would be ironic to have the judiciary review the legality of the executive's decision to imprison an individual captured in a theater of armed conflict, as Yaser Hamdi was, but not its decision to kill an individual off the battlefield, as was true of Anwar al-Aulaqi. Accordingly, the judiciary must be allowed to review the executive's determination that the conditions that would permit the individual to be targeted were indeed fulfilled. Justice Scalia, presumably followed by Justice Stevens, conditioned the right of an alleged enemy combatant being held by the United States to demand a full-blown criminal trial in federal court on the fact that the prisoner was an American citizen. The citizenship of the prisoner was emphasized in O'Connor's opinion in *Hamdi*, but she did not explicitly state that the procedures outlined in her decision for reviewing an executive determination would be unavailable to noncitizens, nor should they be. The need for the judiciary to review a decision of the executive arises whenever the executive deprives an individual—any individual—of his liberty or his life.[12]

In determining the precise role of the judiciary in reviewing the determination of the executive to target an alleged terrorist, a distinction should be drawn between retrospective and prospective inquiries. A retrospective inquiry might arise after an individual has been killed and some relatives or friends maintain that the killing violated the Constitution because, for example, the target was a civilian, not a terrorist, or that he could have been captured, or that civilian bystanders were killed, or that the harm caused by the targeting was grossly disproportionate to the military gain. The opportunity for such a retrospective inquiry into the legality of targeting Anwar al-Aulaqi arose when his father, Nasser al-Aulaqi, brought a second lawsuit, this one in 2012, after Anwar was killed. In the second suit, Nasser sought damages for the wrongful killing of Anwar and also for the killing of Abdulrahman al-Aulaqi, Anwar's sixteen-year-old son and Nasser's grandson. Abdulrahman was killed in a separate drone attack approximately two weeks after the one that killed his father, Anwar. Abdulrahman was not the target of the attack, only collateral damage, which only strengthened the claim that he was deprived of his life without due process of law.

Claims for damages such as Nasser's must be adjudicated by a federal court in the exercise of its federal question jurisdiction and the applicable rules, which, under *Bivens v. Six Unknown Named Agents*,[13] authorize damages for a violation of constitutional rights. In such a suit, the executive is likely to defend on the ground that the right was not clearly established at the time of the contested action.[14] In a number of lawsuits seeking damages for torture, the executive successfully sought dismissal of the suit on the ground that the litigation risked disclosure of state secrets or that it presented special factors requiring an exception to the *Bivens* rule.[15] The executive is likely to invoke these doctrines as a defense to a suit seeking damages for the consequences of its targeted-killing policy. Admittedly, in such a proceeding, the facts and circumstances of the killings must be laid bare, and for that reason may be inconvenient for the executive. Yet it must be remembered that such a proceeding is an essential means of determining the legality of the executive's action and thus for holding the executive accountable to the law.

The burden on the executive is greatly increased if the challenge to its authority to target an alleged terrorist can be brought prospectively—as in the initial suit brought by Nasser—before the killing takes place, and on the basis of a claim or fear that the person in question is on a "kill list." In his Northwestern speech, Attorney General Holder focused his attention on such a prospective suit and complained of the risk that such a suit would create. It would require, according to Holder, "the President to delay action until some theoretical stage of planning when the precise time, place, and manner of attack [would] become clear." Holder protested that "such a requirement would create an unacceptably high risk that our efforts would fail and that Americans would be killed."

Arguably, Aharon Barak was moved by such pragmatic considerations in writing for the Israeli Supreme Court. Although he announced the standards for the targeted killing of terrorists and was warmly celebrated around the world for doing so, he made a distinction between prospective and retrospective inquiries into the military's compliance with the standards, and required only a retrospective hearing.[16] We may want to take our bearings from his decision and relieve the executive from obtaining, to use the attorney general's characterization, "prior approval" or "permission" from a federal court for the targeted killing of a suspected terrorist. Even so, this would not relieve the court of the burden—bravely discharged by Barak—of articulating the constitutional standards for targeting alleged terrorists or for requiring that such targeting be subject to a retrospective inquiry. The announcement of standards would tell the executive—Holder and his successors—what the Constitution requires, and that might be a sufficient guide to the executive in formulating and implementing its targeting policy. The executive professed obedience to the law and has political reasons to be true to its word. Moreover, the prospect of a retroactive inquiry into the executive's action will itself provide further incentives for the executive to respect the law and to keep its action within the bounds of the law.

## The Court's Decision

Although the original al-Aulaqi suit was of the prospective variety, Judge Bates did not draw a distinction between retrospective and prospective suits and the unique practical burdens of the latter. He dismissed the suit in its entirety and denied even the possibility of ever laying down the constitutional standards for the targeted killing of alleged terrorists. In part, this determination was based on the political question doctrine, although we can readily see the error in his reliance on that doctrine. The judge was not being asked to second-guess matters that lay properly within the province of the political branches. He could assume that the pragmatic judgments of the executive are correct and then proceed to establish the normative framework for its action—to define the constitutional standards within which the executive can engage in targeted killings of suspected terrorists. Although these standards may constrain the executive and deny the executive the authority to engage in operations that it deems would have a tangible national security benefit, the standards announced will do so only on the basis of the constitutional values that the judiciary is entrusted to interpret and protect.

Bates's use of the political question doctrine to dismiss Nasser's suit was not forced by Supreme Court case law. Historically, the Supreme Court confined the political question doctrine to those cases where there is some specific constitutional provision that reserves the question presented to the political branches. The suit to set the standards for targeted killings of suspected terrorists does not fall within the scope of that rule. The Constitution may reserve to Congress the power to declare war, but as the 2004 decision in *Hamdi v. Rumsfeld* and the 2008 decision in *Boumediene v. Bush* make abundantly clear, the war against al-Qaeda—an ongoing military campaign against an international terrorist organization—is subject to constitutional constraints, and the judiciary has the power to construe and implement those constraints.

Recently, the Supreme Court created another category of cases deemed to present political questions. This category consists of those cases in which no constitutional standards are readily ascertainable. It was on this basis that the Court dismissed a suit to formulate the standards to govern political gerrymandering in 2004.[17] The original al-Aulaqi suit is of a different matter altogether. Admittedly, the judiciary has thus far declined to give specific content to due process when the government kills, or assassinates, or targets alleged terrorists. But as revealed by the work of other tribunals, including the Israeli Supreme Court, and, ironically, by the attorney general's Northwestern speech, the promulgation of such standards is well within the reach of the judiciary, though the standards actually promulgated may vary in some particulars from the ones described or proposed in this chapter. In truth, the question before Judge Bates was analogous to the questions before the Court in *Hamdi v. Rumsfeld*. In *Hamdi*, the Court had first to decide whether a person detained by the military as an enemy combatant was entitled, as a matter of due process, to an evidentiary hearing on his status and, second, what the rules should be in such a hearing.

In addition to relying on the political question doctrine, Judge Bates dismissed the original al-Aulaqi suit on the ground that the plaintiff—Nasser al-Aulaqi, the father of the alleged target— lacked the standing required by Article III of the Constitution. I have some sympathy with this ruling insofar as Nasser purported to act as the next friend or representative of Anwar. There is no reason to doubt the attachment of Nasser to Anwar, but it is not clear to me that Anwar would have initiated this suit even if he could have done so without putting his life at risk—for example, by sending an electronic message to the lawyers representing Nasser saying that he joined the suit.[18] As Judge Bates noted, Anwar al-Aulaqi had repeatedly denounced the United States in the most demonic terms, and he would have undermined his political credibility if he were now to turn to the judiciary of the United States to provide protection for him.

On the other hand, as Judge Bates understood, Nasser was not just representing Anwar. He was also seeking to protect his own interest—that of a father—to prevent Anwar from being killed. The interest of a parent in the life of his child has all the requisite specificity and intensity that could possibly be required of a "case" or "controversy" under Article III. This interest is sufficient to ensure a full, adversary presentation of the facts and the law and to make certain that the judicial power is not wasted on idle or academic controversies. It also has the particularized and differentiated character required by the Supreme Court in recent years to make certain that the Court is acting as a court.[19]

Admittedly, the government might have denied the existence of a plan to kill Anwar, which would have rendered the alleged threat too speculative or uncertain to justify the issuance of an injunction or a declaratory judgment. However, dismissing the suit on that ground would be quite different than dismissing it for lack of Article III standing. One dismissal is based on the nature of the remedy sought and the other on the constitutional limits of the judiciary. In any event, it should be emphasized that the government deliberately refrained from putting forward such a defense to the original al-Aulaqi suit, and that, as history indicates, such a defense would have been an untruth. As it turns out, the lethal attack on Anwar al-Aulaqi on September 30, 2011, was part of a larger program of targeted killings. Best estimates indicate that between 2002 and 2013 there have been more than four hundred drone strikes, principally in Pakistan and Yemen, and that they have killed at least three thousand people.[20]

The suit before Judge Bates was most unusual. On the basis of a fear that his son was on a kill list and was soon to be targeted by the government, Nasser al-Aulaqi asked the judge to formulate the legal standards to govern such horrific action. The unusual character of this suit only reflected the unusual nature of the executive's action. First Bush and now Obama have committed our nation to a war that knows no limits—geographically and perhaps even temporally—and one in which the combatants often appear as ordinary civilians. In so doing, they have adopted policies that confound the traditional division between civilian and military activities, and whose lawfulness cannot be ascertained on the basis of preexisting doctrines and constitutional tests. But the novelty of the challenges presented is not an excuse for judicial passivity. Now that the executive has adjusted the prerogatives of war to a new environment, so must the courts.

# NOTES

## Chapter 1: In the Shadow of War

This chapter is based on "In the Shadow of War," *University of Miami Law Review* 58 (2003): 449–70.

1. UN Charter art. 51.

2. S.C. Res. 1368, UN SCOR, 56th Sess., 4370th mtg., UN Doc. S/RES/1368 (2001).

3. S.C. Res. 678, UN SCOR, 45th Sess., 2963d mtg., UN Doc. S/RES/678 (1990).

4. S.C. Res. 687, UN SCOR, 46th Sess., 2981st mtg., UN Doc. S/RES/687 (1991).

5. S.C. Res. 1441, UN SCOR, 57th Sess., 4644th mtg., UN Doc. S/RES/1441 (2002).

6. See Neta C. Crawford, "The Best Defense: The Problem with Bush's Preemptive War Doctrine," *Boston Review*, February–March 2003, 20.

7. See Elaine Scarry, "Resolving to Resist," *Boston Review*, February–March 2004, 6.

8. See David Cole, *Enemy Aliens: Double Standards and Constitutional Freedoms in the War on Terrorism* (New York: The New Press, 2003).

9. Al Odah v. United States, 321 F.3d 1134 (D.C. Cir. 2003).

10. See R. on the Application of Abbasi & Anor. v. Sec'y of State for Foreign & Commonwealth Affairs, (2002) EWCA Civ. 1598, para. 64 (UK Sup. Ct. Judicature [C.A.], November 6, 2002), www.bailii.org/ew/cases/EWCA/Civ/2002/1598 .html.

11. Hamdi v. Rumsfeld, 316 F.3d 450 (4th Cir. 2003).

12. Hamdi v. Rumsfeld, 296 F.3d 278 (4th Cir. 2002).

13. *Hamdi*, 316 F.3d at 459.

14. Geneva Convention Relative to the Treatment of Prisoners of War, August 12,

1949, 6 U.S.T. 3316, 75 U.N.T.S. 135; Geneva Convention Relative to the Protection of Civilian Persons in Time of War, August 12, 1949, 6 U.S.T. 3516, 75 U.N.T.S. 287.

15. "Fact Sheet: Status of Detainees at Guantanamo," news release, February 7, 2002, 2001-2009.state.gov/p/sca/rls/fs/7910.htm.

16. Padilla *ex rel.* Newman v. Bush, 233 F. Supp. 2d 564 (S.D.N.Y. 2002), *opinion adhered to on reconsideration sub nom.* Padilla ex rel. Newman v. Rumsfeld, 243 F. Supp. 2d 42 (S.D.N.Y. 2003).

17. Padilla *ex rel.* Newman v. Rumsfeld, 243 F. Supp. 2d 42 (S.D.N.Y. 2003).

18. Padilla v. Rumsfeld, 352 F.3d 695 (2d Cir. 2003).

19. United States v. Lindh, 212 F. Supp. 2d 541 (E.D. Va. 2002).

20. Johnson v. Eisentrager, 339 U.S. 763, 793 (1950) (Black, J., dissenting) (citing *Ex parte* Quirin, 317 U.S. 1, 30–31 [1942]).

21. Plea Agreement, United States v. Lindh, 212 F. Supp 2d 541 (E.D. Va. 2002) (No. 02-37A), www.justice.gov/ag/plea-agreement.

22. Geneva Convention Relative to the Treatment of Prisoners of War, August 12, 1949, art. 4, 6 U.S.T. 3316, 75 U.N.T.S. 135. The pertinent provisions of Article 4 are:

> A. Prisoners of war, in the sense of the present Convention, are persons belonging to one of the following categories, who have fallen into the power of the enemy:
>
> (1) Members of the armed forces of a Party to the conflict as well as members of militias or volunteer corps forming part of such armed forces.
>
> (2) Members of other militias and members of other volunteer corps, including those of organized resistance movements, belonging to a Party to the conflict and operating in or outside their own territory, even if this territory is occupied, provided that such militias or volunteer corps, including such organized resistance movements, fulfill the following conditions:
>
> > (a) that of being commanded by a person responsible for his subordinates;
> >
> > (b) that of having a fixed distinctive sign recognizable at a distance;
> >
> > (c) that of carrying arms openly;
> >
> > (d) that of conducting their operations in accordance with the laws and customs of war.
>
> (3) Members of regular armed forces who profess allegiance to a government or an authority not recognized by the Detaining Power.

23. *Lindh*, 212 F. Supp. 2d at 557n35 ("Thus, all armed forces or militias, regular and irregular, must meet the four criteria if their members are to receive combatant immunity").

24. Ibid., 556–57.

25. 308 F.3d 198 (3d Cir. 2002), *cert. denied*, 538 U.S. 1056 (2003).

26. Detroit Free Press v. Ashcroft, 303 F.3d 681 (6th Cir. 2002).

27. 540 U.S. 1003, 124 S. Ct. 534 (2003) (Nos. 03-334, 03-343) (*Al Odah*); 540 U.S.

1099, 124 S. Ct. 981 (2004) (No. 03-6696) (*Hamdi*); 540 U.S. 1173, 124 S. Ct. 1353 (2004) (No. 03-1027) (*Padilla*).

28. "DoD Announces Detainee Allowed Access to Lawyer," news release, December 2, 2003, www.defense.gov/Releases/Release.aspx?ReleaseID=5831.

29. "Padilla Allowed Access to Lawyer," news release, February 11, 2004, www .defense.gov/Releases/Release.aspx?ReleaseID=7070.

30. Gherebi v. Bush, 352 F.3d 1278 (9th Cir. 2003), *vacated*, 542 U.S. 952 (2004).

31. "Excerpts from Marshall News Conference," *Los Angeles Times*, June 29, 1991, A23.

# Chapter 2: The War on Terror and the Rule of Law

This chapter is based on the H.L.A. Hart Lecture in Jurisprudence and Moral Philosophy, which was delivered on May 10, 2005. It was later published as "The War against Terrorism and the Rule of Law," *Oxford Journal of Legal Studies* 26 (2006): 235–356.

1. Rumsfeld v. Padilla, 542 U.S. 426 (2004).

2. Hamdi v. Rumsfeld, 542 U.S. 507 (2004).

3. Rasul v. Bush, 542 U.S. 466 (2004).

4. Padilla *ex rel.* Newman v. Rumsfeld, 243 F. Supp. 2d 42, 49–50 (S.D.N.Y. 2003).

5. Padilla *ex rel.* Newman v. Bush, 233 F. Supp. 2d 564, 605 (S.D.N.Y. 2002), *opinion adhered to on reconsideration sub nom.* Padilla ex rel. Newman v. Rumsfeld, 243 F. Supp. 2d 42 (S.D.N.Y. 2003).

6. Padilla v. Rumsfeld, 352 F.3d 695, 699 (2d Cir. 2003).

7. Padilla v. Hanft, 432 F.3d 582, 585 (4th Cir. 2005). On January 4, 2006, the Supreme Court granted the government's application to transfer Padilla from military to civilian custody to face criminal charges, adding that it "will consider [Padilla's] pending petition for certiorari in due course." Hanft v. Padilla, 546 U.S. 1084 (2006). In response to the petition for certiorari, the government insisted that the transfer of Padilla to civilian authority rendered moot the question of whether he can be detained as an enemy combatant. On April 3, 2006, the Court denied Padilla's petition.

8. Non-Detention Act of 1971, 18 U.S.C. § 4001(a) (2000).

9. *Padilla*, 352 F.3d at 711.

10. Authorization for the Use of Military Force, Pub. L. No. 107-40, 115 Stat. 224 (2001). In its decision in September 2005, rejecting Padilla's bid for freedom, the Fourth Circuit relied on the same reasoning.

11. *Hamdi*, 542 US at 553 (Souter, J., concurring).

12. Justice Scalia's and Justice Stevens's opinions come close to endorsing the principle of freedom but fall short of doing so by restricting their rule to American citizens and providing that American citizens cannot be held as enemy combatants. Ibid., 554 (Scalia, J., dissenting).

13. Ibid., 536.

14. In *Hamdi*, Justice O'Connor says, "Certainly, we agree that indefinite detention for the purposes of interrogation is not authorized." Ibid., 521. This sentence does not fit into the overall structure of the opinion, which is to impose procedural limitations on the government. But Ronald Dworkin read it as imposing a substantive limitation, also rooted in due process, on the capacity of the government to detain enemy combatants who, like Hamdi, are American citizens. According to Dworkin, American citizens can be held only to prevent them from returning to fight against the United States, and not for coercive interrogation. Ronald Dworkin, "What the Court Really Said," *New York Review of Books*, August 12, 2004, at 26, 29, available at www.nybooks.com/articles/17293.

15. *Hamdi*, 542 US at 533.

16. Ibid., 539.

17. Ibid., 553 (Souter, J., concurring).

18. Ibid., 533, 537.

19. Ibid., 535.

20. Ibid., 538. Justice O'Connor did not rely on *Ex Parte* Quirin for that proposition, and with good reason. *Quirin* involved seven German soldiers who were captured within the United States, which they had entered for purposes of sabotage. One of them claimed to be an American citizen. The Supreme Court allowed all seven prisoners to be tried by military tribunal, but in contrast to *Hamdi*, in *Quirin* it was undisputed that the prisoners were German soldiers and thus enemy combatants. *Ex Parte* Quirin, 317 US 1 (1942).

21. Ibid., 554 (Souter, J., concurring).

22. 424 U.S. 319 (1976).

23. Owen Fiss, *The Law As It Could Be* (New York: NYU Press, 2003).

24. Goldberg v. Kelly, 397 U.S. 254 (1970).

25. 452 U.S. 18 (1981); see also M.L.B. v. S.L.J., 519 U.S. 102 (1996).

26. See Perry v. Sindermann, 408 U.S. 593 (1972); Bd. of Regents v. Roth, 408 U.S. 564 (1972).

27. After the Supreme Court's ruling, lawyers for Yaser Hamdi and the government began negotiations. On October 11, 2004, Hamdi was released from custody and transferred to Saudi Arabia. The release agreement requires Hamdi to renounce any claim to United States citizenship and to obey travel restrictions preventing him from travel to the United States, Afghanistan, Iraq, Israel, Pakistan, Syria, and the West Bank and Gaza Strip.

28. *Rasul*, 542 U.S. at 481.

29. Johan Steyn, "Guantánamo Bay: The Legal Black Hole," *International and Comparative Law Quarterly* 53, no. 1 (2004): 1–15.

30. Al Odah v. United States, 321 F.3d 1134, 1141 (D.C. Cir. 2003), *rev'd sub nom.* Rasul v. Bush, 542 U.S. 466 (2004).

31. Khalid v. Bush, 355 F. Supp. 2d 311, 323 (D.D.C. 2005), *vacated sub nom.* Boumediene v. Bush, 476 F.3d 981 (D.C. Cir. 2007), *rev'd*, 553 U.S. 723 (2008).

32. Ibid., 322.

33. In re Guantánamo Detainee Cases, 355 F. Supp. 2d 443 (D.D.C. 2005).,

34. These claims might be made under the Alien Torts Claims Act, 28 U.S.C. § 1350 (2000), on the theory that torture violates various treaties or international norms prohibiting torture. The act, dating from the earliest days of the Republic, grants the district courts original jurisdiction of civil actions by aliens for torts committed in violation of the law of nations or a treaty of the United States. On December 30, 2005, a federal statute was passed, providing: "No individual in the custody or under the physical control of the United States Government, regardless of nationality or physical location, shall be subject to cruel, inhuman, or degrading treatment or punishment." Department of Defense, Emergency Supplemental Appropriations to Address Hurricanes in the Gulf of Mexico, and Pandemic Influenza Act, 2006, Pub. L. No. 109–148, 119 Stat. 2739 (2006). The means of enforcing this prohibition were not specified in the statute, and on signing the legislation, the president stated that he did not view the statute either to give rise to a private cause of action or to be enforceable through habeas corpus. The president further insisted that he will construe the statute in a manner consistent with his authority as commander in chief and the constitutional limitations on the judicial power. "Statement on Signing the Department of Defense, Emergency Supplemental Appropriations to Address Hurricanes in the Gulf of Mexico, and Pandemic Influenza Act, 2006," *Weekly Compilation of Presidential Documents*, December 30, 2005, 1918. The new statute defines "cruel, inhuman, or degrading treatment or punishment" as consisting of those punishments prohibited by the Fifth, Eighth, and Fourteenth Amendments of the Constitution. The statute further provides that the United States Reservations, Declarations and Understandings to the United Nations Convention Against Torture and Other Forms of Cruel, Inhuman or Degrading Treatment or Punishment shall be determinative of which punishments proscribed by those constitutional provisions are within the reach of the statute.

35. 494 U.S. 259 (1990).

36. Ibid., 273 ("The United States frequently employs armed forces outside this country—over 200 times in our history—for the protection of American citizens or national security. Congressional Research Service, Instances of Use of United States Armed Forces Abroad, 1798–1989 [E. Collier ed. 1989]. Application of the Fourth Amendment to those circumstances could significantly disrupt the ability of the political branches to respond to foreign situations involving our national interest.")

37. Ibid., 284 (Brennan, J., dissenting).

38. Ibid., 285 (Brennan, J., dissenting).

39. See generally Reid v. Covert, 354 U.S. 1 (1957).

40. Downs v. Bidwell, 182 U.S. 244 (1901) (Harlan, J., dissenting). See generally

Owen Fiss, "The Troubled Beginnings of the Modern State, 1888–1910," in *The Oliver Wendell Holmes Devise, History of the Supreme Court*, vol. 8, ed. Stanley Katz (New York: Macmillan, 1993), 225–56.

41. *Verdugo-Urquidez*, 494 U.S. at 275.

42. But see Thomas Nagel, "The Problem of Global Justice," *Philosophy and Public Affairs* 33 (2005): 113, 121 (discussing "the political conception of justice, which asserts that "justice is something we owe through our shared institutions only to those with whom we stand in a strong political relation").

43. See Gerald L. Neuman, *Strangers to the Constitution: Immigrants, Borders, and Fundamental Law* (Princeton, NJ: Princeton University Press, 1996), 54–56 (discussing *The Federalist*'s argument that aliens have no constitutional rights as they are not parties to the Constitution).

44. *Verdugo-Urquidez*, 494 U.S. at 275 (Kennedy, J., concurring).

45. Ibid., 276 (Kennedy, J., concurring).

46. Ibid., 278 (Kennedy, J., concurring).

47. Ibid.,277 (Kennedy, J., concurring).

48. Rasul v. Bush, 542 U.S. at 487 (Kennedy, J., concurring).

49. Ibid., 488 (Kennedy, J., concurring).

50. Ibid.

## Chapter 3: The Perils of Minimalism

This chapter is based on the first annual Cegla Lecture on Legal Theory, delivered at Tel Aviv University on October 24, 2007. It was later published under the same title in *Theoretical Inquiries in Law* 9 (2008), 643–64.

1. See, e.g., HCJ 769/02 Pub. Comm. against Torture in Israel v. Gov't of Israel [December 11, 2006].

2. United States v. Verdugo-Urquidez, 494 U.S. 259 (1990).

3. *Verdugo-Urquidez*, 494 U.S. at 277-78 (Kennedy, J., concurring).

4. See, e.g., Cass Sunstein, *Radicals in Robes* (New York: Basic Books, 2005); Cass Sunstein, *One Case at a Time: Judicial Minimalism on the Supreme Court* (Cambridge, MA: Harvard University Press, 2001); Cass Sunstein, "Minimalism Versus Perfectionism in Constitutional Theory: Second-Order Perfectionism," *Fordham Law Review* 75 (2007): 2867–83; Cass Sunstein, "Testing Minimalism: A Reply," *Michigan Law Review* 104 (2005): 129–35; Michael C. Dorf, "Legal Indeterminacy and Institutional Design," *New York University Law Review* 78 (2003), 875–981.

5. The federal habeas statute provides that "writs of habeas corpus may be granted by the Supreme Court, any justice thereof, the district courts and any circuit judge within their respective jurisdictions." 28 U.S.C. § 2241(a) (2000).

6. 542 U.S. 466 (2004).

7. Al Odah v. United States, 321 F.3d 1134, 1141 (D.C. Cir. 2003).

8. Memorandum from Paul Wolfowitz, Deputy Secretary of Defense, to the Secretary of the Navy, July 7, 2004, available at www.defenselink.mil/news/Jul2004 /d20040707review.pdf.

9. 542 U.S. 507 (2004).

10. Detainee Treatment Act of 2005, Pub. L. No. 109-148, div. A, tit. X, § 1005(e)(1), 119 Stat. 2680, 2742 (the specific provision quoted in the text was codified at 28 U.S.C. § 2241(e)(1) [2000], and was subsequently amended in 2006).

11. 548 U.S. 557 (2006).

12. Detainee Treatment Act, div. A, tit. X, § 1005(h)(1) (codified at 10 U.S.C.A. § 801 note [2000]).

13. Ibid., § 1005(h)(2) (codified at 10 U.S.C.A. § 801 note [2000]).

14. *Hamdan*, 548 U.S. at 612–13.

15. 10 U.S.C. § 821 (amended 2006).

16. Ibid., § 836(b) (amended 2006).

17. *Hamdan*, 548 U.S. at 612.

18. Geneva Convention Relative to the Treatment of Prisoners of War, August 12, 1949, art. 3, 6 U.S.T. 3316, 75 U.N.T.S. 135.

19. See, e.g., Oona Hathaway, "*Hamdan v. Rumsfeld*: Domestic Enforcement of International Law," in *International Law Stories*, ed. John Noyes, Mark Janis, and Laura Dickinson (New York: Foundation Press, 2007): 229, 253; David Scheffer, "*Hamdan v. Rumsfeld*: The Supreme Court Affirms International Law," *Jurist*, June 30, 2006, jurist.org/forum/2006/06/hamdan-v-rumsfeld-supreme-court.php.

20. Military Commissions Act of 2006, Pub. L. No. 109-336, § 7(b), 120 Stat. 2600, 2636. The act also extended the geographic scope of the bar against habeas petitions by prisoners so that the bar applies to all non-U.S. citizens that the government determines to be illegal enemy combatants, regardless of where the government is holding them. Ibid., § 7(a).

21. For example, the Military Commissions Act requires judges to exclude evidence if its prejudicial value substantially outweighs its probative value. The act also requires that prosecutors give notice of and an opportunity to rebut hearsay evidence before they are permitted to use it. C.f. Military Commissions Act § 949a(b)(2), with United States Department of Defense, Military Commission Order No. 1, March 21, 2002, available at www.defenselink.mil/news/Mar2002/d20020321ord.pdf.

22. Boumediene v. Bush, 476 F.3d 981 (D.C. Cir. 2007).

23. Ibid., 987.

24. Ibid., 992.

25. Linda Greenhouse, "The Mystery of Guantánamo Bay," *Berkeley Journal of International Law* 27, no. 1 (2009): 1–21.

26. *Hamdan*, 548 U.S. at 636 (2006) (Breyer, J., concurring).

27. See Stephen Breyer, *Active Liberty* (New York: Knopf, 2005).

28. Sunstein, *One Case at a Time*.

29. *Hamdan*, 548 U.S. at 636 (Breyer, J., concurring).

30. See Neil S. Siegel, "A Theory in Search of a Court, and Itself: Judicial Minimalism at the Supreme Court Bar," *Michigan Law Review* 103 (2005): 1951, 1963–64.

31. Rasul v. Bush, 542 U.S. 466, 486 (2004) (Kennedy, J., concurring).

32. Hamdan v. Rumsfeld, 415 F.3d 33 (D.C. Cir. 2005), *rev'd*, 548 U.S. 557 (2006).

33. 274 U.S. 357, 372–80 (1927) (Brandeis, J., concurring).

# Chapter 4: Aberrations No More

This chapter is based on the William H. Leary Lecture at the University of Utah's S. J. Quinney College of Law, delivered on October 26, 2010. It was later published under the same title in the *Utah Law Review* 2010 (2010): 1085–99.

1. Jane Mayer, "Outsourcing Torture: The Secret History of America's 'Extraordinary Rendition' Program," *New Yorker*, February 14, 2005, 106, 106–23, www.new yorker.com/archive/2005/02/14/050214fa_fact6.

2. Padilla *ex rel.* Newman v. Bush, 233 F. Supp. 2d 564, 572, 605–9 (S.D.N.Y. 2002). For further developments in this case, see chapter 2, "The War on Terror and the Rule of Law."

3. Military Order of November 13, 2001: Detention, Treatment, and Trial of Certain Non-Citizens in the War Against Terrorism, 3 C.F.R. § 918 (2002), reprinted in 10 U.S.C. § 801 (Supp. IV 2004).

4. *Ex parte* Quirin, 317 U.S. 1 (1942). For background on the case, see Louis Fisher, "Military Tribunals: The *Quirin* Precedent," Congressional Research Service, RL 31340, March 26, 2002.

5. Military Order of November 13, 2001, sec. 4.

6. U.S. Department of Justice, "Legal Authorities Supporting the Activities of the National Security Agency Described by the President," January 19, 2006, 1–3, www .justice.gov/opa/whitepaperonnsalegalauthorities.pdf.

7. Katz v. United States, 389 U.S. 347, 358 n. 23 (1967).

8. United States v. U.S. Dist. Court (*Keith*), 407 U.S. 297, 317–21 (1972).

9. Foreign Intelligence Surveillance Act of 1978, Pub. L. No. 95-511, 92 Stat. 1783.

10. Detainee Treatment Act of 2005, Pub. L. No. 109-148, 119 Stat. 2680 (codified at 42 U.S.C. § 2000dd [2006]).

11. "Presidential Statement on Signing the Department of Defense, Emergency Supplemental Appropriations to Address Hurricanes in the Gulf of Mexico, and Pandemic Influenza Act 2006," *Weekly Compilation of Presidential Documents*, December 30, 2005, 1918, available at www.presidency.ucsb.edu/ws/index.php?%20pid=65259 (declaring that "[t]he Executive branch shall construe" the prohibition "in a manner consistent with the constitutional authority of the President . . . to supervise the unitary executive branch and as Commander in Chief and consistent with the constitu-

tional limitations on the judicial power" in order to "protect[] the American people from further terrorist attacks").

12. See U.S. Constitution, art. I., § 8, cl. 11–15.

13. Detainee Treatment Act of 2005 § 1005(e)(1).

14. Military Commissions Act of 2006, Pub. L. No. 109-366, § 7, 120 Stat. 2600.

15. The courts have since rejected the military commissions' jurisdiction over material support for terrorism as an international law crime. Hamdan v. United States (Hamdan II), 696 F.3d 1238, 1250 (D.C. Cir. 2012). June 14, 2014 en banc decision.

16. See Alberto Gonzales, "Prepared Statement of Hon. Alberto R. Gonzales, Attorney General of the United States," February 6, 2006, www.justice.gov/archive/ag/speeches/2006/ag_speech_060206.html.

17. Letter from Alberto Gonzales, Attorney General, to Senators Patrick Leahy and Arlen Specter, Chairmen of the Committee on the Judiciary, January 17, 2007, available at graphics8.nytimes.com/packages/pdf/politics/20060117gonzales_Letter.pdf.

18. Protect America Act of 2007, Pub. L. No. 110-55. 121 Stat. 552.

19. FISA Amendments Act of 2008, Pub. L. No. 110-261, 122 Stat. 2436.

20. Hamdi v. Rumsfeld, 542 U.S. 507, 509 (2004).

21. Ibid., 324–39.

22. Rumsfeld v. Padilla, 542 U.S. 426 (2004).

23. Padilla v. Hanft, 389 F. Supp. 2d 678, 692 (D.S.C. 2005).

24. Padilla v. Hanft, 423 F.3d 386, 389 (4th Cir. 2005).

25. Padilla v. Hanft, 547 U.S. 1062 (2006).

26. Rasul v. Bush, 542 U.S. 466, 483–85 (2004).

27. Detainee Treatment Act of 2005, Pub. L. No. 109-148, § 1005, 119 Stat. 2680, 2740–44 (codified at 42 U.S.C. § 2000dd [2006]).

28. Hamdan v. Rumsfeld, 548 U.S. 557, 572–84 (2006).

29. Military Commissions Act of 2006, Pub. L. No. 109-366, § 7(b), 120 Stat. 2600, 2636.

30. Rasul v. Myers, 512 F.3d 644, 665 (D.C. Cir. 2008).

31. 553 U.S. 723 (2008).

32. Ibid., 764–66.

33. Ibid., 796–98.

34. Ibid., 753–71.

35. Ibid., 766.

36. 424 U.S. 319 (1976).

37. Exec. Order No. 13,491, 74 Fed. Reg. 4,893 (January 22, 2009).

38. Exec. Order No. 13,492, 74 Fed. Reg. 4,897 (January 22, 2009).

39. Exec. Order No. 13,491, 74 Fed. Reg. at 4,894.

40. Carrie Johnson, "Prosecutor to Probe CIA Interrogations," *Washington Post*, August 25, 2009, www.washingtonpost.com/wp-dyn/content/article/2009/08/24/AR2009082401743.html.

41. Mark Mazzetti, "Obama Releases Interrogation Memos, Says C.I.A. Opera-tives Won't Be Prosecuted," *New York Times*, April 16, 2009, thecaucus.blogs.ny times.com/2009/04/16/secret-interrogation-memos-to-be-released/?ref=politics. See also chapter 7, "Torture and Extraordinary Rendition."

42. Mohamed v. Jeppesen Dataplan, Inc., 614 F.3d 1070 (9th Cir. 2010) (en banc).

43. Arar v. Ashcroft, 585 F.3d 559, 574–78 (2nd Cir. 2009) (en banc).

44. Benjamin Weiser and Colin Moynihan, "Guilty Plea in Times Square Bomb Plot," *New York Times*, June 25, 2010, www.nytimes.com/2010/06/22/nyregion /22terror.html.

45. Charlie Savage, "Nigerian Indicted in Terrorist Plot," *New York Times*, Janu-ary 7, 2010, A14; U.S. Department of Justice, "Umar Farouk Abdulmutallab Indicted for Attempted Bombing of Flight 253 on Christmas Day," news release, January 6, 2010, www.justice.gov/opa/pr/2010/January/10-nsd-004.html.

46. See, e.g., *Oversight of the Department of Justice: Hearing Before the S. Comm. on the Judiciary*, 111th Cong. (2009) (statement of Attorney General Eric Holder); see also Charlie Savage, "Holder Defends Decision to Use U.S. Court for 9/11 Trial," *New York Times*, November 19, 2009, A18.

47. Military Commissions Act of 2006, Pub. L. No. 109-366, § 3(a)(1), 120 Stat. 2600.

48. National Defense Authorization Act for Fiscal Year 2010, Pub. L. No. 111-84, § 1802, 123 Stat. 2190, 2574 (2009).

49. See notes 18 and 19, above.

50. Johan Steyn, "Guantánamo Bay: The Legal Black Hole," *International and Comparative Law Quarterly* 53, no. 1 (2004): 1–15.

51. Al Maqaleh v. Gates, 604 F. Supp. 2d 205, 231–32 (D.D.C. 2009).

52. Al Maqaleh v. Gates, 605 F.3d 84, 99 (D.C. Cir. 2010).

53. Al Maqaleh v. Hagel, 738 F. 3d 312 (D.C. Cir. 2013).

54. Clapper v. Amnesty Int'l U.S.A., 133 S. Ct. 1138 (2013). See generally chapter 9.

## Chapter 5: Law Is Everywhere

This chapter is based on "Law Is Everywhere," *Yale Law Journal* 117 (2007): 256–78.

1. Aharon Barak, "Constitutional Law Without a Constitution: The Role of the Judiciary," in *The Role of Courts in Society*, ed. Shimon Shetreet (Dordrecht, Nether-lands: Martinus Nijhoff Publishers, 1988): 448–67.

2. CA 6821/93, 1908/94, 3363/94 United Mizrachi Bank v. Migdal Coop. Vffl. 49(4) 221 [1995] (Isr.), translated in *Israeli Law Review* 31 (1997): 777–94.

3. See Yuval Yoaz, "Friedmann Seeks New Version of Intifada Law, Bypassing Court," *Haaretz*, June 5, 2007, www.haaretz.com/hasen/spages/867274.html.

4. HCJ 5100/94 Pub. Comm. against Torture in Isr. v. State of Israel [Septem-

ber 6, 1999](Isr.) slip op., available at elyon1.court.gov.il/files_eng/94/000/051/a09 /94051000.a09.pdf.

5. HCJ 769/02 Pub. Comm. against Torture in Isr. v. Gov't of Israel [December 11, 2006] (Isr.) slip op. para. 22 (quoting HCJ 7957/04 Mara'abe v. Prime Minister [2005] para. 29), available at elyon1.court.gov.il/files_eng/02/690/007/a34/02007690.a34 .pdf.

6. HCJ 2056/04 Beit Sourik VOL Council v. Gov't of Israel [June 30, 2004] (Isr.) slip op., available at elyon1.court.gov.il/files_eng/04/560/020/a28/04020560.a28 .pdf.

7. HCJ 769/02 Pub. Comm. against Torture in Isr. v. Gov't of Israel [December 11,2006] (Isr.) slip op., available at elyon1.court.gov.il/Files_ENG/02/690/007 /A34/02007690.A34.pdf.

8. See Aharon Barak, *The Judge in a Democracy* (Princeton, NJ: Princeton University Press, 2006), 256–57.

9. HCJ 769/02 Pub. Comm. against Torture in Isr. v. Gov't of Isr. [December 11, 2006] (Isr.) slip op. para. 40, available at elyon1.court.gov.il/files_eng/02/690/007 /a34/02007690.a34.pdf.

10. Korematsu v. United States, 323 U.S. 214 (1944).

11. See, e.g., Parents Involved in Cmty. Sch. v. Seattle Sch. Dist. No. 1,551 U.S. 701 835 (2007) (Breyer, J., dissenting); Nixon v. Shrink Mo. Gov't PAC, 528 US. 377, 401–2 (2000) (Breyer, J., concurring); Dist. of Colum. v. Heller, 554 U.S. 570 (2008) (Breyer, J., dissenting).

12. See, e.g., Barak, *Judge in a Democracy*, 309.

## Chapter 6: Imprisonment Without Trial

This chapter is based on "Imprisonment Without Trial," *Tulsa Law Review* 47 (2011): 347–62.

1. U.S. Constitution, art. 1, § 9, cl. 2 ("The Privilege of the Writ of Habeas Corpus shall not be suspended, unless when in Cases of Rebellion or Invasion the public Safety may require it.").

2. Geneva Convention Relative to the Treatment of Prisoners of War art. 118, August 12, 1949, 6 U.S.T. 3316, 75 U.N.T.S. 135.

3. See ibid., art. 87 ("Prisoners of war may not be sentenced by the military authorities and courts of the Detaining Power to any penalties except those provided for in respect of members of the armed forces of the said Power who have committed the same acts.").

4. Military Order of Nov. 13, 2001, 66 Fed. Reg. 57833 (November 16, 2001); see also Memorandum from President George W. Bush to Vice President Richard B. Cheney et al., "Humane Treatment of al-Qaeda and Taliban Detainees," February 7,

2002, reprinted in *The Torture Papers: The Road to Abu Ghraib*, ed. Karen J. Greenberg and Joshua L. Dratel (New York: Cambridge University Press, 2005), 134.

5. United States v. Lindh, 212 F. Supp. 2d 541, 552-58 (E.D. Va. 2002).

6. Geneva Convention Relative to the Treatment of Prisoners of War art. 3.

7. President Barack Obama, "Remarks by the President on National Security," May 21, 2009, www.whitehouse.gov/the-press-office/remarks-president-national -security-5-21-09.

8. Ibid.

9. Harold Hongju Koh, Legal Advisor, U.S. Department of State, "The Obama Administration and International Law," March 25, 2010, at III.B.1.b, www.state.gov /s/l/releases/remarks/139119.htm. See also Alissa J. Rubin, "U.S. Backs Trial for Four Detainees in Afghanistan," *New York Times*, July 18, 2010, A6 (describing the process of transferring responsibility for prisoners held in Afghanistan) ("One potential problem that has yet to be confronted is that an Afghan court could acquit a detainee whom the American review board deems a continuing threat. Then whose law will prevail? 'Anybody not found guilty can be released, but we have an intense interest in not releasing people that pose a risk to the people of Afghanistan and to us,' said Capt. Gregory Belanger, director of legal operations for Task Force 435.").

10. Geneva Convention Relative to the Treatment of Prisoners of War, art. 2 ("Although one of the Powers in conflict may not be a party to the present Convention, the Powers who are parties thereto shall remain bound by it in their mutual relations. They shall furthermore be bound by the Convention in relation to the said Power, if the latter accepts and applies the provisions thereof.").

11. See, e.g., Obama, "Remarks by the President on National Security" ("Now let me be clear: We are indeed at war with al-Qaeda and its affiliates. We do need to update our institutions to deal with this threat."); President Barack Obama, "Remarks by the President on Strengthening Intelligence and Aviation Security," January 7, 2010, www.whitehouse.gov/the-press-office/remarks-president-strengthening-in telligence-and-aviation-security ("We are at war. We are at war against al-Qaeda, a far-reaching network of violence and hatred that attacked us on 9/11, that killed nearly 3,000 innocent people, and that is plotting to strike us again.").

12. *Guantanamo Review Task Force, Final Report* (January 22, 2010), 23, www.jus tice.gov/ag/guantanamo-review-final-report.pdf.

13. Obama, "Remarks by the President on National Security."

14. Ibid.

15. Exec. Order No. 13,491, 74 Fed. Reg. 4893 (January 22, 2009).

16. See, e.g., United States v. Moussaoui, 365 F.3d 292 (2004) (balancing national security interests against constitutional rights in the production of evidence).

17. See, e.g., U.S. Department of Justice, "Statement of Attorney General John Ashcroft Regarding the Padilla Case," news release, February 20, 2004. See also Letter from Paul Wolfowitz, Deputy Secretary of Defense, to James Comey, Deputy Attorney General, May 28, 2004.

18. U.S. Deparment of Justice, "Jose Padilla Charged with Conspiracy to Murder Individuals, Providing Material Support to Terrorists," news release, November 22, 2005, www.justice.gov/archive/opa/pr/2005/November/05_crm_624.html.

19. *Oversight of the Department of Justice: Hearing Before the S. Comm. on the Judiciary*, 111th Cong. 1 (2009) (statement of Attorney General Eric Holder) ("And one of the things that this Administration has consistently said—in fact, Congress has passed legislation that would not allow for the release into this country of anybody who was deemed dangerous. And so that if—if there were the possibility that a trial was not successful, that would not mean that that person would be released into our country. That would—that is not a possibility. But again, I want to emphasize that I am confident that we will be successful in the trial of these matters.").

20. Obama, "Remarks by the President on National Security."

21. Ibid.

22. Peter Baker, "Obama Says Current Law Will Support Detentions," *New York Times*, September 24, 2009, A23.

23. Authorization for the Use of Military Force, Pub. L. No. 107-40, 115 Stat. 224 (2001).

24. Harold Hongju Koh, "The Obama Administration and International Law," March 25, 2010, www.state.gov/s/l/releases/remarks/139119.htm.

25. Exec. Order No. 13,567, 76 Fed. Reg. 13277 (March 7, 2011), www.fas.org/irp/offdocs/eo/eo-13567.htm.

26. David Cole, "Out of the Shadows: Preventive Detention, Suspected Terrorists, and War," *California Law Review* 97 (2009): 693 750.

27. Charlie Savage, "Embracing Bush Argument, Obama Upholds a Policy on Detainees in Afghanistan," *New York Times*, February 22, 2009, A6. See also chapter 4, "Aberrations No More."

28. U.S. Department of Justice, "Umar Farouk Abdulmutallab Indicted for Attempted Bombing of Flight 253 on Christmas Day," news release, January 6, 2010, www.justice.gov/opa/pr/2010/January/10-nsd-004.html; Charlie Savage, "Nigerian Indicted in Terrorist Plot," *New York Times*, January 7, 2010, A14.

29. U.S. Attorney, Southern District of New York, "Accused Al Shabaab Leader Charged with Providing Material Support to al Shabaab and al-Qaeda in the Arabian Peninsula," news release, July 5, 2011, www.justice.gov/usao/nys/pressreleases/July11/warsameindictmentpr.pdf; Charlie Savage and Eric Schmitt, "U.S. to Prosecute a Somali Suspect in Civilian Court," *New York Times*, July 6, 2011, A1.

30. Respondents' Memorandum Regarding the Government's Detention Authority Relative to Detainees Held at Guantanamo Bay at 1, *In re* Guantanamo Bay Detainee Litigation, No. 08-442 (D.D.C. March 13, 2009).

31. See Andy Newman and Colin Moynihan, "Faisal Shahzad Arraigned on Terror Charges," *New York Times*, May 18, 2010, cityroom.blogs.nytimes.com/2010/05/18/faisal-shahzad-to-be-arraigned.

32. "Presidential Statement on Signing the National Defense Authorization Act for

Fiscal Year 2012, 2011," *Daily Compilation of Presidential Documents*, December 31, 2011, 1, 2. The National Defense Authorization Act for Fiscal Year 2012 codified and affirmed the policy of imprisonment without trial, but in doing so, it declared that the act was not applicable to American citizens or lawful resident aliens of the United States. See the National Defense Authorization Act for Fiscal Year 2012, Pub. Law. No. 112-81, § 1021(e), 125 Stat. 1298, 1562 (2011) ("Nothing in this section shall be construed to affect existing law or authorities relating to the detention of United States citizens, lawful resident aliens of the United States, or any other persons who are captured or arrested in the United States.").

33. See U.S. Department of Justice, "Al-Marri Indicted for Proving Material Support to al-Qaeda," news release, February 27, 2009, www.justice.gov/opa/pr/2009/February/09-ag-177.html; John Schwartz, "Admitted al-Qaeda Agent Receives Prison Sentence," *New York Times*, October 30, 2009, A22.

34. Non-Detention Act, Pub. L. No. 92-128, 85 Stat. 347 (1971) (current version codified at 18 U.S.C. § 4001(a)) ("No citizen shall be imprisoned or otherwise detained by the United States except pursuant to an Act of Congress.").

35. Hamdi v. Rumsfeld, 542 U.S. 507 (2004).

36. Boumediene v. Bush, 553 U.S. 723, 766 (2008).

37. Al Maqaleh v. Gates, 605 F.3d 84 (D.C. Cir. 2010). Al Maqaleh v. Hagel, 738 F.3d 312 (D.C. Cir. 2013).

## Chapter 7: Torture and Extraordinary Rendition

This chapter is based on "The Example of America" (2009), *Faculty Scholarship Series*, Paper 1308, available at digitalcommons.law.yale.edu/fss_papers/1308.

1. Convention against Torture and Other Cruel, Inhuman, or Degrading Treatment or Punishment, December 10, 1984, 1465 U.N.T.S. 85.

2. The principal implementing statute is the Foreign Affairs Reform and Restructuring Act of 1998, Pub. L. No. 105-277, § 2242, 112 Stat. 2681-822 (codified at 8 U.S.C. § 1231 [2012]). Other implementing statutes consist of the Foreign Relations Authorization Act, Fiscal Years 1994 and 1995, Pub. L. 103-236, 108 Stat. 382 (codified at 18 U.S.C. §§ 2340, 2340A [2012]); and the Torture Victims Relief Act of 1998, Pub. L. 105-320, 112 Stat. 3017 (codified at 22 U.S.C. 2152 [2012]).

3. For a general overview of the Constitution's prohibitions against torture, see Seth F. Kreimer, "Too Close to the Rack and the Screw: Constitutional Constraints on Torture in the War on Terror," *University of Pennsylvania Journal of Constitutional Law* 6 (2003): 278–325.

4. Rochin v. California, 342 U.S. 165, 172 (1952).

5. Pierce v. Soc'y of Sisters, 268 U.S. 510 (1925); Meyer v. Nebraska, 262 U.S. 390 (1923).

6. Lawrence v. Texas, 539 U.S. 558 (2003).

7. See President George W. Bush, "Statement on United Nations International Day in Support of Victims of Torture," *Public Papers of the President*, June 26, 2004, 1141.

8. For an overview of the origins of this phrase, see Mark Danner, "US Torture: Voices from the Black Sites," *New York Review of Books*, April 9, 2009. Danner cites the widespread use of this language and specifically quotes Cofer Black, former head of the CIA's Counterterrorism Center. See *Joint Investigation into September 11th: Hearing Before the J.H.S. Intelligence Comm.*, 109th Cong. (2002) (statement of Cofer Black, former director, CIA Counterterrorism Center).

9. Memorandum from Jay S. Bybee, Assistant Attorney General, U.S. Department of Justice, to Alberto Gonzales, Counsel to the President, Executive Office of the President, August 1, 2002, available at www.washingtonpost.com/wp-srv/nation /documents/dojinterrogationmemo20020801.pdf.

10. Ibid., 1.

11. 18 U.S.C. § 2340.

12. Memorandum from William Haynes, Gen. Counsel, U.S. Department of Defense, to Donald Rumsfeld, Secretary of Defense, November 27, 2002, available at dspace.wrlc.org/doc/bitstream/2041/70971/00512_021127_001display.pdf.

13. Ibid.

14. Ibid.

15. Memorandum from Donald Rumsfeld, Secretary of Defense, to Gen. James T. Hill, Commander, U.S.S. Command, April 16, 2003, available at dspace.wrlc.org /doc/bitstream/2041/71014/00721display.pdf (noting in Tab A that techniques "A-Q," authorized in the memo, are authorized by the Army Field Manual 34-52, but that "[f]urther implementation guidance with respect to techniques R-X will need to be developed by the appropriate authority").

16. According to a letter sent to a federal judge by an Acting U.S. Attorney, the CIA destroyed ninety-two interrogation tapes. See Letter from Lev L. Dassin, Acting U.S. Attorney, S.D.N.Y., to Alvin K. Hellerstein, Judge, S.D.N.Y., March 2, 2009, available at www.aclu.org/pdfs/safefree/lettertohellerstein_ciainterrogationtapes.pdf.

17. See Danner, "US Torture," chap. 7, n8.

18. "Nightline: Inside the CIA; Inside the Secret Prisons," ABC television broadcast, December 10, 2007.

19. *Confirmation Hearing of Michael Mukasey Before the S. Comm. on the Judiciary*, 110th Cong. (2007).

20. Memorandum from Daniel Levin, Acting Assistant Attorney General, to James B. Comey, Deputy Attorney General, December 30, 2004, available at www .aclu.org/files/torturefoia/released/082409/olcremand/2004olc96.pdf.

21. Detainee Treatment Act of 2005, Pub. L. No. 109-148 (2005).

22. President George W. Bush, "President's Statement on Signing of H.R. 2863," December 30, 2005, available at www.presidency.ucsb.edu/ws/index.php?pid =65259.

23. Jane Mayer, *The Dark Side: The Inside Story of How the War on Terror Turned into a War on American Ideals* (New York: Doubleday, 2008); see also Parliamentary Assembly of the Council of Europe, Alleged Secret Detentions and Unlawful Interstate Transfers of Detainees Involving Council of Europe Member States, Res. No. 1507 (2006) (estimating that "hundreds of persons" had been "entrapped" in a U.S. system of secret detentions and extraordinary rendition).

24. Mayer, *Dark Side*, 121.

25. Farmer v. Brennan, 511 U.S. 825, 833 (1994).

26. Arar v. Ashcroft, 585 F.3d 559 (2d. Cir. 2009).

27. 18 U.S.C. § 2340A.

28. Boumediene v. Bush, 553 U.S. 723 (2008).

29. Dorr v. United States, 195 U.S. 138 (1904); *accord* Balzac v. Porto Rico, 258 U.S. 298 (1922).

30. *Dorr*, 195 U.S. at 149.

31. Ibid., 148.

32. Declaratory Judgment Act, 28 U.S.C. §2201 (2006).

33. Bivens v. Six Unknown Fed. Narcotics Agents, 403 U.S. 388 (1971).

34. Fed R. Civ. P. 54(c) (stating that every judgment "should grant the relief to which each party is entitled").

35. United States v. Reynolds, 345 U.S. 1 (1953).

36. See El-Masri v. United States, 479 F.3d 296 (4th Cir. 2007).

37. 479 F.3d at 305.

38. Mohamed v. Jeppesen Dataplan, Inc., 614 F.3d 1070 (9th Cir. 2010).

39. Ibid., 1083. In 2012, the European Court of Human Rights ruled in favor of the victim of a rendition to torture who was the plaintiff in the case dismissed by the Fourth Circuit decision discussed in the text at footnotes 36 and 37. El-Masri v. The Former Yugoslav Republic of Macedonia, App No. 39639/09, Eur. Ct. H.R. ¶45 (2012). This decision not only reflects the independence of the European Court, but even more significantly for our purposes it indicates that El-Masri did not need the information possessed by the U.S. government to prevail.

40. See Aharon Barak, *The Judge in a Democracy* (Princeton, NJ: Princeton University Press, 2006), 246–47.

41. See Exec. Order No. 13,491, 74 Fed. Reg. 16 (January 27, 2009); Exec. Order No. 13,492, 74 Fed. Reg. 16 (January 27, 2009); Exec. Order No. 13,493, 74 Fed. Reg. 16 (January 27, 2009).

42. President Barack Obama, "Press Conference at the White House," February 9, 2009, available at www.nytimes.com/2009/02/09/us/politics/09text-obama.html.

43. President Barack Obama, "Address to Joint Session of Congress," February 24, 2009, www.whitehouse.gov/the_press_office/remarks-of-president-barack-obama -address-to-joint-session-of-congress.

44. *Confirmation Hearing of Eric Holder, S. Comm. on the Judiciary*, 111th Cong.

2009 (including the statements of Eric Holder and several members of the Senate declaring that waterboarding and other "shameful" techniques are torture).

45. "Panetta: No 'Extraordinary Rendition,'" CBS News, February 5, 2009, www .cbsnews.com/news/panetta-no-extraordinary-rendition/.

46. See John Schwartz, "Obama Backs Off a Reversal on State Secrets," *New York Times*, February 9, 2009, A12.

47. Obama, "Press Conference at the White House."

48. "Panetta, 'No Extraordinary Rendition.'"

49. See *Nunca Más: The Report of the Argentine National Commission on the Disappeared*, ed. Ernesto Sabato with an introduction by Ronald Dworkin (New York: Farrar, Straus and Giroux, 1986).

# Chapter 8: Criminalizing Political Advocacy

This chapter is based on the Arlin M. and Neysa Adams Lecture in Constitutional Law at Temple University Beasley School of Law, which was delivered on March 1, 2011. It was later published as "The World We Live In," *Temple Law Review* 83, no. 2 (2011): 295–308.

1. For these developments, see chapter 9, "Warrantless Wiretapping."

2. 561 U.S. 1 (2010).

3. See generally Owen Fiss, "Aberrations No More," *Utah Law Review* 4 (2011): 1085–99.

4. 18 U.S.C. §§ 2339A, 2339B (2006). The lineage of these statutes is outlined in *Humanitarian Law Project*, 561 U.S. at 7 (2010).

5. 8 U.S.C. § 1189 (2006).

6. 18 U.S.C. § 2339B(a)(1).

7. Ibid., § 2339A(b)(1).

8. *Humanitarian Law Project*, 561 U.S. at 23–24 (2010).

9. See, e.g., Jon Lee Anderson, "Death of the Tiger," *New Yorker*, January 17, 2011, 41.

10. *Humanitarian Law Project*, 561 U.S. at 16–18.

11. Ibid., 33–39.

12. Ibid., 25–26.

13. Harry Kalven Jr., *A Worthy Tradition: Freedom of Speech in America*, ed. Jamie Kalven (New York: Harper & Row, 1988), 120.

14. 395 U.S. 444 (1969).

15. *Confirmation Hearing on the Nomination of John G. Roberts, Jr. to Be Chief Justice of the United States: Hearing Before the S. Comm. on the Judiciary*, 109th Cong. 144–45 (2005) (statement of Senator Arlen Specter, chairman, Senate Committee on the Judiciary) (asking Judge Roberts whether *Roe v. Wade* qualified as a "super-duper precedent in light . . . of 38 occasions to overrule it").

16. *Brandenburg*, 395 U.S. at 447.

17. See Kalven, chap. 8, n13, 119–236.

18. 376 U.S. 254 (1964).

19. *Sullivan*, 376 U.S. at 270–71.

20. *Humanitarian Law Project*, 561 U.S. at 39.

21. See generally Lloyd Corp., Ltd. v. Tanner, 407 U.S. 551 (1972) (holding that protesters dispersing handbills within a shopping center did not have First Amendment right to do so when alternative means—the sidewalks outside—were available).

22. *Humanitarian Law Project*, 561 U.S. at 38.

23. Ibid., 28.

24. Ibid., 36.

25. Ibid., 37 (internal quotation marks omitted).

26. Ibid. (internal quotation marks omitted).

27. Ibid., 15.

28. Ibid. (internal quotation marks omitted).

29. Ibid., 24.

30. Ibid., 36.

31. Ibid., 37–38.

32. Ibid., 37.

33. Dombrowski v. Pfister, 380 U.S. 479, 489 (1965). See also Owen Fiss, "Dombrowski," *Yale Law Journal* 86 (1977): 1103–64.

34. *Humanitarian Law Project*, 561 U.S. at 26–27.

35. 391 U.S. 367 (1968).

36. 403 U.S. 15 (1971).

37. *Humanitarian Law Project*, 561 U.S. at 42 (Breyer, J., dissenting).

38. Ibid., 2740.

39. The citation was introduced by the signal "*Cf.*" *Humanitarian Law Project*, 561 U.S. at 57. This signal expresses an equivocation likely to be missed by the ordinary reader of the *United States Reports*. The *Bluebook* says that "*cf.*" supports a "proposition different from the main proposition but sufficiently analogous to lend support." The *Bluebook* continues that "[l]iterally, '*cf.*' means 'compare.'" *The Bluebook: A Uniform System of Citation*, 19th ed. (Cambridge, MA: Harvard Law Review Association, 2010), R. 1.2(a), 55.

40. *Humanitarian Law Project*, 561 U.S. 38 (majority opinion).

41. Ibid.

42. Ibid.

43. Ibid.

44. See generally Geoffrey R. Stone, *Perilous Times: Free Speech in Wartime* (New York: W.W. Norton, 2004); Harry Kalven Jr., "Foreword: Even When a Nation Is at War," *Harvard Law Review* 85 (1971): 3–37.

45. *Humanitarian Law Project*, 561 U.S. at 40.

46. Ibid., 38.

47. See Bruce Ackerman, *Before the Next Attack: Preserving Civil Liberties in an Age of Terrorism* (New Haven, CT: Yale University Press, 2006), 171 (providing chart defining types of conflicts).

48. See chapter 6, "Imprisonment Without Trial."

## Chapter 9: Warrantless Wiretapping

This chapter is based on Owen Fiss, "Even in a Time of Terror," *Yale Law & Policy Review* 1 (2012): 1–31.

1. Communications Act of 1934, Pub. L. No. 73-416, § 605, 48 Stat. 1064, 1103–4 (codified as amended at 47 U.S.C. § 605 [2012]).

2. Compare Nardone v. United States, 302 U.S. 379, 381–83 (1937) with *To Authorize Wire Tapping: Hearings on H.R. 2266 and H.R. 3099 Before Subcomm. No. 1 of the H. Comm. on the Judiciary*, 77th Cong. 17–18 (1941).

3. Katz v. United States, 389 U.S. 347 (1967).

4. James Risen and Eric Lichtblau, "Bush Lets U.S. Spy on Callers Without Courts," *New York Times*, December 16, 2005, www.nytimes.com/2005/12/16/pol itics/16program.html (correction appended).

5. Foreign Intelligence Surveillance Act of 1978, Pub. L. No. 95-511, 92 Stat. 1783 (codified as amended in scattered sections of 8, 18, and 50 U.S.C. [2012]).

6. Provision was also made for review of the decisions of individual judges by a specially designated three-judge appellate court. Given the secretive nature of the FISA proceedings, this right of review is available only to the government. *Id.*§ 1803(b).

7. Ibid., § 1801(e).

8. See *Wartime Executive Power and the National Security Agency's Surveillance Authority: Hearing Before the S. Comm. on the Judiciary*, 109th Cong. 10–15 (2006), www.gpo .gov/fdsys/search/pagedetails.action?granuleId=CHRG-109shrg27443&package Id=CHRG-109shrg27443.

9. President George W. Bush, "Statement on Signing the Department of Defense, Emergency Supplemental Appropriations to Address Hurricanes in the Gulf of Mexico, and Pandemic Influenza Act, 2006," December 30, 2005, available at www.presi dency.ucsb.edu/ws/index.php?%20pid=65259.

10. 153 Cong. Rec. 1380–81 (2007).

11. "Your World with Neil Cavuto," Fox News television broadcast, July 31, 2007, transcript available at www.foxnews.com/story/2007/08/01/house-minority-lead er-john-boehner-on-dow-jonesnews-corp/ (quoting John Boehner's understanding that, according to a judge, FISA "prohibit[ed] the ability of our intelligence services and our counterintelligence people from listening in to two terrorists in other parts of the world where the communication could come through the United States"); see also Mark Hosenball, "An 'Intel Gap': What We're Missing," *Newsweek*, August 6,

2007, 9 ("[I]ntel-collection officials concluded that FISA court authorizations should be obtained to eavesdrop not just on messages where at least one party is inside the country, but also for eavesdropping on messages between two parties overseas that pass through U.S. communications gear.").

12. Greg Miller, "New Limits Put on Overseas Surveillance," *Los Angeles Times*, August 2, 2007, articles.latimes.com/2007/aug/02/nation/na-spying2 (quoting officials confirming that FISA affected cases " 'where one end is foreign and you don't know where the other is'—meaning warrants would be required even when it was unclear whether communications were crossing the United States or involved a person in the United States").

13. Joby Warrick and Walter Pincus, "How the Fight for Vast New Spying Powers Was Won," *Washington Post*, August 12, 2007, www.washingtonpost.com/wp-dyn/content/article/2007/08/11/AR2007081101349.html ("The decisions had the immediate practical effect of forcing the NSA to laboriously ask judges on the Foreign Intelligence Surveillance Court each time it wanted to capture such foreign communications from a wire or fiber on U.S. soil.").

14. See U.S. Department of Justice, "Fact Sheet: Title IV of the Fiscal Year 2008, Intelligence Authorization Act, Matters Related to the Foreign Intelligence Surveillance Act," news release, April 13, 2007, www.justice.gov/opa/pr/2007/April/07_nsd_247.html.

15. Protect America Act of 2007, Pub. L. No. 110-155, 121 Stat. 552 (codified at 50 U.S.C. §§ 1801, 1803, 1805 [2012]).

16. FISA Amendments Act of 2008, Pub. L. No. 110-261, 122 Stat. 2436 (codified at 50 U.S.C. § 1881a [2012]).

17. FISA Amendments Act Reauthorization Act of 2012, Pub. L. No. 112-238, 126 Stat. 1631 (codified in scattered section of 18 and 50 U.S.C.).

18. *Nomination of Eric H. Holder, Jr., Nominee to Be Attorney General of the United States: Hearing Before the S. Comm. on the Judiciary*, 111th Cong. 104 (2009).

19. Amnesty Int'l USA v. Clapper, 638 F.3d 118 (2d Cir. 2011).

20. Clapper v. Amnesty Intl. USA, 133 S. Ct. 1138 (2013).

21. 389 U.S. 347 (1967).

22. 277 U.S. 438 (1928).

23. 389 U.S. at 361 (Harlan, J., concurring).

24. Ibid., 358 (majority opinion).

25. Ibid., 356–57.

26. Ibid., 358n23.

27. Omnibus Crime Control and Safe Streets Act of 1968, Pub. L. No. 90-351, 82 Stat. 197 (codified in scattered sections of 5, 18, and 42 U.S.C. [2012]).

28. Ibid., § 2511.

29. United States v. U.S. District Court (Keith), 407 U.S. 297 (1972).

30. Ibid., 319.

31. Ibid., 321–22.

32. Ibid., 309n8.

33. Ibid., 308.

34. See, e.g., United States v. Duggan, 743 F.2d 59 (2d Cir. 1984); United States v. Nicholson, 955 F. Supp. 588 (E.D. Va. 1997).

35. See, e.g., United States v. Pelton, 835 F.2d 1067, 1075–76 (4th Cir. 1987).

36. Uniting and Strengthening America by Providing Appropriate Tools Required to Intercept and Obstruct Terrorism (USA PATRIOT Act) of 2001, Pub. L. No. 107-56, 115 Stat. 272 (codified in scattered sections of 8, 12, 15, 18, 20, 31, 42, 47, 49, and 50 U.S.C. [2012]).

37. See FISA Amendments Act of 2008, 122 Stat. at 2437).

38. 50 U.S.C. § 1802(a)(1) (2012).

39. Ibid., § 1881a(a)–(g).

40. See William C. Banks, "Programmatic Surveillance and FISA: Of Needles in Haystacks," *Texas Law Review* 18 (2010): 1633, 1635 ("The [2008 statute] codified a procedure to permit broad, programmatic surveillance focused on patterns of suspicious activities and not on a specific individual or the contents of their communications through changes in FISA that overcame the case-specific orientation of the original statute.").

41. 50 U.S.C. § 1881a(a)–(g).

42. Intelligence Reform and Terrorism Protection Act of 2004, Pub. L. No. 108-458, 118 Stat. 3638 (codified in scattered sections of 42 and 50 U.S.C. [2012]).

43. Ibid., § 1071(e).

44. 50 U.S.C. § 1881a(a).

45. Ibid., § 1881a(a)–(g).

46. Ibid., § 1881a(i)(3).

47. Ibid., § 1881a(i)(1)(B).

48. Inspector General Act of 1978, 5 U.S.C.A. App. 3 (2010).

49. 50 U.S.C. § 1881a(l)(2).

50. Katz v. United States, 389 U.S. 347, 360 (1967) (Harlan, J., concurring).

51. For example, in *Berger v. New York*, 388 U.S. 41 (1967), the Supreme Court overturned a bribery conviction based on evidence obtained without a warrant that met the Fourth Amendment standards of particularity. The Court also declared unconstitutional on its face the New York statute that established the scheme governing electronic surveillance under which the warrant was issued for failing to include a sufficient particularity requirement.

52. Some have suggested that FISA's qualification of the probable cause requirement does not go far enough, and that further qualification or even elimination of that requirement would improve the statute (or replacement legislation). See, e.g., Stephanie Cooper Blum, "What Really Is at Stake with the FISA Amendments Act of 2008 and Ideas for Future Surveillance Reform," *Boston University Public Interest Law Journal* 18 (2009): 269, 291–94, 308–12.

53. Ashcroft v. al-Kidd, 131 S. Ct. 2074, 2088, n. 3 (2011) (Ginsburg, J., concur-

ring in the judgment). In response to Justice Ginsburg's observation, Justice Antonin Scalia indicated that he had a looser conception of probable cause, one that required "individualized suspicion," but not tied to criminality. The case involved the arrest and imprisonment of an individual as a material witness. Scalia said: "No usage of the word is more common and idiomatic than a statement such as 'I have a suspicion he knows something about the crime,' or even, 'I have a suspicion she is throwing me a birthday party.'" Ibid., 2082n2. Scalia did not offer any evidence, as might be expected from an Originalist, indicating that this contemporary or idiomatic usage was intended by the framers of the Fourth Amendment. In any event, Justice Scalia's understanding of probable cause should not be read as an authoritative gloss on the Fourth Amendment. Speaking for a majority, he held that when an individual is arrested and imprisoned as a material witness and the arrest warrant is based on a showing of probable cause, the motivation of the government in obtaining the warrant is irrelevant. The lawyers representing the individual arrested conceded that the warrant was valid and they did not object to the validity of the statute under which it was issued. For that reason, Justice Scalia did not rule on the validity under the Fourth Amendment of the warrant or of the statute authorizing it. This limitation on Scalia's opinion was emphasized by Justice Kennedy in a concurrence, which was joined by Justice Ginsburg as well as Justices Breyer and Sotomayor. Justice Kagan did not participate in the case.

54. See note 6, above, and accompanying text.

55. Ibid., § 703 (codified at 50 U.S.C. § 1881b).

56. 494 U.S. 259 (1990).

57. Ibid., 274–75.

58. Ibid., 275 (Kennedy, J., concurring).

59. Ibid., 276–77.

60. Ibid., 277–78.

61. Ibid.

62. 553 U.S. 723 (2008).

63. Foreign Intelligence Surveillance Act § 102.

64. FISA Amendments Act of 2008 § 702 (g)(2).

65. See, e.g., United States v. Perillo, 333 F. Supp. 914, 919-21 (D. Del. 1971) (citing Alderman v. United States, 394 U.S. 165, 175 n.10 [1969]) (deeming constitutional the government's use of conversations between the target of surveillance and a third party in a subsequent criminal prosecution of the third party, where the surveillance was conducted pursuant to a warrant applying only to the target of surveillance and the government had made no prior probable cause showing regarding the third party); see also United States v. Kahn, 415 U.S. 143, 157 (1974) (holding that the government's interception of incriminating telephone calls by the wife of a target of surveillance, and the subsequent use of those calls in a criminal prosecution against the wife, did not violate the Fourth Amendment even though the government had not established probable cause regarding the wife before beginning surveillance).

66. U.S. Constitution, Fourth Amendment ("The right of the people to be secure in their persons, houses, papers, and effects, against unreasonable searches and seizures, shall not be violated. . . .").

67. Ibid. ("[A]nd no Warrants shall issue, but upon probable cause, supported by Oath or affirmation, and particularly describing the place to be searched, and the persons or things to be seized.").

68. See, e.g., Akhil Reed Amar, *The Constitution and Criminal Procedure: First Principles* (New Haven, CT: Yale University Press, 1998), 31–45; Akhil Reed Amar, "Fourth Amendment First Principles," *Harvard Law Review* 107 (1994): 757, 762, 774. But see Carol S. Steiker, "Second Thoughts about First Principles," *Harvard Law Review* 107 (1994): 820–57.

69. 389 U.S. 347, 357–58 (1967).

70. Ibid.

71. See, e.g., United States v. Edwards, 498 F.2d 496, 499–500 (2d Cir. 1974).

72. Justice Blackmun introduced the phrase in New Jersey v. T.L.O., 469 U.S. 325, 351 (1985) (Blackmun, J., concurring in the judgment). See also MacWade v. Kelly, 460 F.3d 260, 268 (2d Cir. 2006) (acknowledging that *United States v. Edwards* exemplifies what later came to be known as the "special-needs exception").

73. 50 U.S.C. 1881a(a) (2012).

74. Although the attorney general and the director of national intelligence must ordinarily wait for a judicial order before authorizing surveillance, the 2008 FISA amendments permit the institution of a wiretap without a judicial order where the attorney general and the director determine that "exigent circumstances" exist. Id. § 1881a(c)(2); see also id. § 1881a(a) (granting the attorney general and the director the ability to authorize surveillance). In such cases, the attorney general and the director must submit a certification for the interception within seven days of its commencement, if such a certification is not already pending. Ibid., § 1881a(g)(1)(B).

75. Ibid., § 1881a(g)(1)(A).

76. Transcript of Oral Argument at 4, Clapper v. Amnesty Int'l USA, 133 S. Ct. 1138 (2013), www.supremecourt.gov/oral_arguments/argument_transcripts/11-1025.pdf (remarks of Solicitor Gen. Donald Verrilli, Jr.) ("Your Honor, under the statute, there are two clear examples of situations in which the individuals would have standing. The first is if an aggrieved person, someone who is a party to a communication, gets notice that the government intends to introduce information in a proceeding against them "); see also ibid., 12–13. As it turned out, however, the notice promised by the solicitor general has seldom been furnished. See Charlie Savage, "Justice Dept. Defends Its Conduct on Evidence," *New York Times*, February 14, 2014, www.nytimes.com/2014/02/15/us/justice-dept-defends-its-conduct-on-evidence.html; Adam Liptak, "A Secret Surveillance Program Proves Challengeable in Theory Only," *New York Times*, October 29, 2013, www.nytimes.com/2013/07/16/us/double-secret-surveillance.html.

77. 132 S. Ct. 945 (2012).

78. Ibid., 957–64 (Alito, J., concurring in the judgment).

79. Ibid.

80. Ibid., 948 (majority opinion).

81. Ibid., 949–53.

82. Ibid., 958, 964 (Alito, J., concurring in the judgment).

83. Ibid., 964.

84. Ibid.

85. Ibid.

86. Ibid.

87. Intelligence Reform and Terrorism Prevention Act of 2004, Pub. L. No. 108-458, § 6001(a), 118 Stat. 3638, 3742 (codified as amended at 50 U.S.C. § 1801(b)(1)(C) [2012]).

88. See Dombrowski v. Pfister, 380 U.S. 479 (1965).

89. As discussed earlier, see note 55, above. The Supreme Court in *Berger v. New York*, 388 U.S. 41 (1967), declared unconstitutional a New York statute establishing a process to obtain warrants allowing eavesdropping. The Court declared the statute invalid on its face and spoke of its "broad sweep," ibid., 54, but did not formally invoke the First Amendment overbreadth doctrine.

# Chapter 10: The Targeted Killing of Alleged Terrorists

1. Al-Aulaqi v. Obama, 727 F.Supp.2d 1, 17 (2010).

2. HCJ 769/02 Pub. Comm. Against Torture in Isr. v. Gov't of Isr. (PCATI) (December 11, 2005), available at elyon1.court.gov.il/files_eng/02/690/007/a34/02007690.a34.pdf.

3. See chapter 1, "In the Shadow of War."

4. See Owen Fiss, "Silence on the Street Corner," *Liberalism Divided: Freedom of Speech and the Many Uses of State Power* (Boulder, CO: Westview Press, 1996): 47, 51.

5. Eric Holder, Attorney General, "Speech at Northwestern University School of Law," March 5, 2012, www.justice.gov/iso/opa/ag/speeches/2012/ag-speech-1203051.html.

6. President Barack Obama remarks that "no civilians will be killed or injured—the highest standard we can set." Note that the president used the words "killed or injured" rather than "targeted."

7. Although Aharon Barak (see note 2, above, paragraphs 41–46) would allow the killing of civilians provided such killings were proportional to the gain to be achieved by the targeted killing, he fashioned this rule for a geographically limited area, specifically the Occupied Palestinian Territories.

8. Barack Obama, "Presidential Statement on Signing the National Defense Authorization Act for Fiscal Year 2012, 2011," *Daily Compilation of Presidential Documents*, December 31, 2011, 1, 2 (Obama stated, "I want to clarify that my Administration will

not authorize the indefinite military detention without trial of American citizens"). The National Defense Authorization Act for Fiscal Year 2012 codified and affirmed the policy of imprisonment without trial, but declared that the act was not applicable to American citizens or lawful resident aliens of the United States. See the National Defense Authorization Act for Fiscal Year 2012, Pub. Law. No. 112-81, § 1021(e), 125 Stat. 1298, 1562 (2011). See chapter 6, "Imprisonment Without Trial."

9. Owen Fiss, "Between Supremacy and Exclusivity," *Syracuse Law Review* 57 (2007): 187–208.

10. Obama acknowledged that such an arrangement would raise "serious constitutional issues about presidential and judicial authority."

11. In reaching that judgment, Justice Kennedy specifically pointed to the inadequacies of the procedures of the military tribunals set up in Guantánamo to determine the status of prisoners. Kennedy's willingness to extend the writ of habeas corpus to the Guantánamo prisoners might not constitute an outright rejection of O'Connor's proposal but only a rejection of the way in which the Department of Defense implemented that proposal. Boumediene v. Bush, 553 U.S. 723, 787–92 (2008).

12. See chapter 2, "The War on Terror and the Rule of Law."

13. 403 U.S. 388 (1971).

14. Ashcroft v. al-Kidd, 131 S. Ct. 2074 (2011).

15. See chapter 7, "Torture and Extraordinary Rendition."

16. See note 2, above, paragraph 59.

17. Vieth v. Jubelirer, 541 U.S. 267 (2004).

18. In addressing the standing issue, Judge Bates considered the possibility of Anwar al-Aulaqi's "presenting himself to the United States Embassy in Yemen and expressing the desire to vindicate his constitutional rights in U.S. courts." Bates appreciated that al-Aulaqi might be extremely hesitant to do so for fear that he would be endangering his life. At that point, Bates added that under these circumstances both international and domestic law would "prohibit using lethal force or other violence against him" and cited *Tennessee v. Garner*, 471 U.S. 1 (1985) as support for that proposition. *Garner* arose under the Fourth Amendment and in that context indicated that domestic law enforcement officers may use deadly force to prevent the escape of a suspected felon only if the officers have reason to believe that the suspect poses a threat of serious physical harm to themselves or others. Professor Jack Goldsmith pounced on this passage in Judge Bates's opinion and declared it a minor victory for al-Aulaqi's lawyers. He read Bates to suggest that there are constitutional limits on the president's targeting practices and that some of these limits arise from the Fourth Amendment. See Jack Goldsmith, "What ACLU and CCR Won in al-Aulaqi," *Lawfare*, December 7, 2010, www.lawfareblog.com/2010/12/what-aclu-and-ccr-won -in-al-aulaqi; Jack Goldsmith, *Power and Constraint: The Accountable Presidency After 9/11* (New York: W.W. Norton, 2012): 198. As indicated by Holder's Northwestern speech in March 2012 and Obama's National Defense University speech in May 2013, the administration fully acknowledges the constraints of the Constitution on their

action, but treats the Fifth Amendment, not the Fourth, as the most relevant source of these constraints. What is disputed is the content of those constraints and who has the authority to formulate them.

19. Lujan v. Defenders of Wildlife, 504 U.S. 555 (1992).

20. See e.g., "Get the Data: Drone Wars," *Bureau of Investigative Journalism*, www.thebureauinvestigates.com/category/projects/drones/drones-graphs/ (accessed October 14, 2013); "Drone Wars Pakistan: Analysis," Year of the Drone Project: New America Foundation, natsec.newamerica.net/drones/pakistan/analysis (accessed October 14, 2013); "Air and Drone Wars Yemen: Analysis," Year of the Drone Project: New America Foundation, natsec.newamerica.net/drones/yemen /analysis (accessed October 14, 2013); Bill Roggio and Bob Barry, "Charting the Data for US Air Strikes in Yemen, 2002–2013," *Long War Journal*, www.longwarjour nal.org/multimedia/Yemen/code/Yemen-strike.php (accessed October 14, 2013); and Bill Roggio and Alexander Mayer, "Charting the Data for US Airstrikes in Pakistan, 2004–2013," *Long War Journal*, www.longwarjournal.org/pakistan-strikes.php (accessed October 14, 2013). See also "Numbers," Living Under Drones: Stanford/ NYU Project, www.livingunderdrones.org/numbers/ (accessed October 14, 2013) (analyzing the various drone strike data aggregators and their methodologies).

# INDEX

Abdulmutallab, Umar Farouk, 162, 163
Abu Ghraib, 58, 67, 174
Addington, David, 229
Afghanistan, 24, 180
    detention facilities in, 117, 119, 122,
        152 (*see also* Bagram Air Field
        detainees)
Afghanistan, war in, 4, 38, 45–46, 67,
        73, 117, 148–49, 151–53, 159–60,
        227, 266
    Bush administration and, 7–10, 12,
        15, 20, 24, 31
    Charter of the United Nations and, 8
    legality of, 8, 9–10
    Obama administration and, 104,
        151, 171
    prisoners of war and, 12–13, 119
    Third Geneva Convention and,
        149–50
    unlawful combatants in, 21–22
al-Aulaqi, Anwar, 221, 260–61,
        311–12n18
    alleged terrorist activities of, 264
    congressional hearings sparked by
        killing of, 274
    court's decision in suit of, 282–85
    targeted killing of, 263–85
    U.S. citizenship of, 261, 263, 272–73

al-Aulaqi, Nasser
    standing to file suit, 284–85
    suits filed by, 263–85, 311–12n18
Alien and Sedition Acts, 197
Alien Torts Claims Act, 291n34
Alito, Samuel, 96, 252, 255–57
    *Hamdan v. Rumsfeld* and, 96
    *Katz v. United States* and, 254
    *United States v. Jones* and, 253–55
al-Marri, Ali Saleh Kahlah, 164
*Al Odah v. United States*, 12–15, 17, 20,
        21, 30–31
al-Qaeda, ix, 73, 77, 129, 149, 201–2,
        227, 229–30, 260, 266
    Bush administration and, 7–8, 12–13,
        15, 19, 22, 24, 39, 41
    detention of members, 153–61, 162,
        260
    as enemy combatants, 21–23, 153,
        155
    imprisonment without trial and,
        153–61, 162
    Obama administration and, 104–7,
        109, 111, 113
    principle of freedom and, 153–61
    war against, 39, 41, 118–19, 153–55,
        159–60, 262–63, 267–68, 271 (*see
        also* War on Terror)

314      INDEX

al-Qaeda in the Arabian Peninsula,
264, 265
American Society of International Law,
152, 159
Amman, Jordan, terrorist attacks in, 104
Arar, Maher, case, 180–95
Army Field Manual, 118, 175, 176, 193
Ashcroft, John, 29–30, 112–13
assassination, ban on, 260
See also targeted killing
Authorization for the Use of Military
Force (AUMF), 46, 159–60,
164–65

Bagram Air Field detainees, 117, 119,
122, 123, 162, 163, 166, 189
Barak, Aharon, xiii–xiv, xvii, 7, 126,
128–39, 261, 265, 281–82, 310n7
approach to conflicting values,
132–33, 138
early life of, 128
fundamental values and, 135–36
human dignity and, 130–33, 138–39
inquiries into substantive rationality,
137–38
The Judge in a Democracy, 126
limits on deference due to the
military, 133–34
"proportionality test" and, 135–36
question of necessary torture and, 132
retirement of, 126, 128
rulings on terrorism, 133
on security fence, 133, 138
on targeted killing, 133, 136–37
Basic Laws (Israel), 130–39
Bates, John, 264, 275, 282–83, 283–84,
311–12n18
Begin, Menachem, 128
Benghazi, Libya, terrorist attack on U.S.
embassy in, 221
bifurcated exclusionary rule, 144, 157
Bill of Rights, 8–9, 14, 19–20, 41, 44,
62–64, 105, 116, 130
Detainee Treatment Act of 2005
and, 111

habeas corpus and, 145, 165
torture and, 178, 183
warrantless wiretapping and, 246
See also U.S. Constitution; specific
amendments
bin Laden, Osama, ix, 81, 104–5, 148,
154, 219, 227, 262–63, 266, 267
Bivens v. Six Unknown Named Agents,
170, 184–85, 186, 188, 192, 195,
280–81
Blackmun, Harry, 64, 236
"black sites," 118, 193
Boumediene v. Bush, xi, xii, xv, 4–5,
70–71, 116–17, 121–22, 165–67,
247, 278–79, 311n11
Brandeis, Louis, 98, 207
Brandenburg v. Ohio, xiv–xv, 197–98,
208, 209, 217
Brennan, William, xvi, 60–61, 62,
64–66, 236
Breyer, Stephen, 137–38
Boumediene v. Bush and, 279
Hamdan v. Rumsfeld and, 86, 90, 93,
96–97
Hamdi v. Rumsfeld and, 46–48, 278
Holder v. Humanitarian Law Project
and, 216–18
as minimalist, 69
Rasul v. Bush and, 95, 96–97
United States v. Jones and, 255
Brown v. Mississippi, 169
Burger Court, xii, 170, 226
Bush, George W., 99, 103, 221
2001 executive order authorizing
use of military commissions, 107,
112, 120
declaration of opposition to torture,
174
declaration of War on Terror, 227,
285
imprisonment without trial and,
164
Obama's repudiation of, 99–100
policies on torture, 174–79
See also Bush administration

Bush administration, xi–xiii, 3–4,
33–37, 67, 104–17, 125, 149–50,
159, 178–79, 181, 202, 227, 259, 285
CIS interrogation and detention
policy under, 171
Combatant Status Review Tribunals
and, 111
constitutional rights and, 15–16
Detainee Treatment Act of 2005 and,
110–11, 178–79, 229
detention policy of, 33–35, 37–38,
46–47, 74–76, 105–6, 111–12,
161–62, 171, 272–73
enemy combatants and, 77
establishment of military
commissions, 107–8
FISA and, 227–31
Guantánamo detainees and, 77–89
interrogation policy and, 171
Iraq War and, 10–11
Military Commissions Act of 2006
and, 88, 111–12
Obama administration's continuation
of Bush-era policies, 100–102,
103, 117–24, 143–44, 163, 194
targeted killing policy of, 273–74
Terrorist Surveillance Program and,
256–58
USA PATRIOT Act and, 12
violations of constitutional tradition
by, 104–17, 124, 147
warrantless wiretapping and, 122,
201, 227–31
Bybee, Jay, 174, 176, 177–78

cellular telephone communications.
See electronic communications;
telephone communications
censorship, of violent political
advocacy, 202–20
Charter of the United Nations, 7–8, 9,
265–67
Article 2, 266
Article 51, 266, 270
Iraq War and, 10–11

NATO's humanitarian intervention
in Kosovo and, 10–11
territorial sovereignty and, 272
Cheney, Dick, 177, 229
Church, Frank, 227–28
Christmas Day bomber, 264
CIA, 180, 189, 193, 236, 260
de facto granting of immunity to, 119
FISA Amendments Act of 2008 and,
242
interrogation and detention policy
under, 171, 176–77
secret prisons abroad, 118
state secrets doctrine and, 189–90,
191, 194
use of torture by, 171, 194
citizens. See U.S. citizens
Cohen v. California, 216
Cole, David, 160, 198
Combatant Status Review Tribunals,
79, 80–82, 89, 111, 114, 115
constitutionalism, 37
constitutional rights, 4, 12–15, 51–52,
129, 135, 196
of citizens, 15–16, 22, 23–24, 106–7,
180, 272–73, 279–80
complicity of government branches
in violating, 110–17
curtailed at times of war, 197–99,
200–220, 218
curtailed under Obama, 100–101,
103, 117–24
of enemy combatants, 15–16, 18–20,
22–25, 52–68, 120–21
extraterritorial reach of, 3, 13, 58–66,
246–50
federal judiciary and, 3–4, 110–17, 170
of Guantánamo detainees, 73–75,
107, 182–83, 278–79
of noncitizens, 22, 53–68, 74–75, 107,
112, 115–16, 180, 182, 272–73
cosmopolitanism, 60–61, 62, 63, 73–74,
94, 246–47
counsel, right to, 47–48, 80
courts-martial, 83–88

damages, suits for, 184–86, 188–92, 195,
280–81
declarations of war, 267–68
declaratory judgments, 184, 186–90
Defense Intelligence Agency, 23, 40
democracy, xvii
as a deliberative process, 77, 91, 93
and First Amendment, 210–11
and human dignity, 131–32
vs. majoritarianism, 77, 91
minimalism and, 70, 90–91
and political advocacy, 218
presidential system, 90–91, 134–35
statutory interpretations and, 76
U.S. Constitution and, 77
deportation program, 29–30
Derwish, Kamal, 273
Detainee Treatment Act of 2005, xii,
80–82, 89, 110–11, 113, 115, 118,
135, 178–79, 182–83, 184, 229
detention facilities. *See* Bagram Air
Field detainees; Guantánamo
Bay Naval Base, prison at;
Guantánamo detainees)
detention policy, 12–15, 23–24, 33–35,
196
of Bush administration, 37–38,
46–47, 74–76, 105–6, 111–12,
272–73
enemy combatants and, 18–19
legality of, 38–68
of Obama administration, 161–67,
272–73, 310–11n8
U.S. Congress and, 76
*Detroit Free Press v. Ashcroft*, 5
dignity principle, 173, 180, 182, 188, 195
doctrine of enumerated powers, 61–62
domestic terrorist organizations, First
Amendment and, 208
Douglas, William O., 236
Doumar, Robert J., 16–17
drone strikes, x, xv, 221, 260–61, 273–74
due process, 38, 98, 161, 173
citizens and, 3, 15–16, 23–24, 39–40,
113–14

enemy combatants and, 4, 45–52,
52–68, 284–85
Guantánamo detainees and, 77–89,
96, 278–79
military commissions and, 94
noncitizens and, 3, 13, 40, 53–68
targeted killing and, 267–70, 273–75,
280
U.S. Constitution and, 274–75, 276
Warren Court era and, 108
*See also* Due Process Clause
Due Process Clause, 77–89, 165, 169,
173, 261, 267–70, 273–74. *See also*
due process
Dworkin, Ronald, 34, 290n14

Egypt, 105, 128, 180
Eighth Amendment, 63, 105, 111, 192
ban on "Cruel and Unusual
Punishments," 168–69
prohibition of torture in, 168–69,
172–73, 178, 180, 182–83, 188,
291n34
electronic communications, surveillance
of, 101, 221–58
Ellis, T.S., III, 26–29
enemy combatants, 15, 20, 47
al-Qaeda as, 153, 155
burden of proof of innocence,
135
Bush administration and, 77
citizens as, 80, 106, 262–85
classification of, 67–68
constitutional rights of, 15–16,
18–20, 22–23, 52–68, 105–6
designation as, 47–50, 67–68, 78–80
detention of, 18–19
distinguishing from civilians,
136–37
due process and, 4, 45–68, 284–85
federal judiciary and, 4
habeas corpus and, 52–68, 77, 106,
111–12, 115–17, 165–67
imprisonment of, 33–35, 38–68, 148,
159–60

lawful vs. unlawful, 20–24 (*see also* unlawful enemy combatants)
legal status of, 18–20
military commissions and, 107–8
noncitizens as, 112
proof in support of designation as, 47–50, 67–68
Taliban as, 149–50, 153
targeted killing of, 262–85
*See also* unlawful enemy combatants
enumerated powers, doctrine of, 61–62
Espionage Act of 1917, 197
evidence
discovery and admission of, 161
rules of, 79–80, 84, 120
secret, 108, 157–58 (*see also* state secrets doctrine)
*See also* evidentiary hearings
evidentiary hearings, 18–20, 23, 33–34, 50, 52, 67–68, 79–80, 106–7, 113–14, 278, 284–85
evidentiary rules, military commissions and, 120
exclusionary rule, 157
executive branch, 3, 33–34, 67, 90
authority to carry out targeted killings, 281
deference to in times of war, 17–19, 75, 105–6, 134–35, 170–71, 177–78, 185, 192, 228–30
federal judiciary and, 4, 276–82
*Hamdan v. Rumsfeld* and, 86–87
intelligence gathering and, 221–22
legislative branch and, 90–91, 177–78
military commissions and, 96
oversight of, 4, 276–82
power of, 177–79, 228–30 (*see also* separation of powers)
prerogative of, 228–30, 285
prohibition of torture and, 177–78
responsibility to direct wars, 268–69
rule of law and, 177
targeted killing policy and, 268–85
unilateral exercises of power by, 257–58

war and, 17–19, 75, 105–6, 134–35, 170–71, 177–78, 185, 192, 228–30, 268–69
*See also* Bush administration; Obama administration
*Ex Parte Milligan*, xi, 125
*Ex Parte Quirin*, xi, 125, 290n20
extrajudicial killings, x, 262–85
extraordinary rendition, xiv, 105, 118–19, 123, 135, 169–70, 193–94, 302n39
definition of, 179
interrogation and, 179–80
to Syria, 181–82, 183
*See also* targeted killing

federal judiciary, 3–4, 12–13, 16, 17, 19
constitutional rights and, 160–61, 170 (*see also specific rights*)
FISA Amendments Act of 2008 and, 242–43
jurisdiction of, 19–20
marginalization of role of, 170–71
prerogative of, 285
responsibility to safeguard the Constitution, xi–xii, xv–xvi, 12–13, 16–17, 19, 29–30, 50, 68, 71, 76–77, 89–94, 98, 100, 113, 137, 170–71, 178, 192, 223–24, 257–58, 261, 275–76
retrenchment on injunctive relief, 170–71
role in ending torture, 169–70
Federal Register, 203
Federal Rules of Civil Procedure, Rule 54(c), 187
Fifth Amendment, 38, 63, 105, 111, 147, 192
Due Process Clause of, 41, 48, 52, 74, 81, 84, 132, 165, 173, 267–70, 273–75
prohibition of torture in, 178, 180, 182, 183, 188, 291n34
First Amendment, 51, 197–99, 256–57, 269
democracy and, 210–11

First Amendment (*cont.*)
domestic terrorist organizations
and, 208
*Holder v. Humanitarian Law Project*
and, 202–20
political advocacy and, 207–15
FISA Amendments Act of 2008, 113,
122–23, 135, 222–23, 231–39,
240–44, 247–50, 252, 256–58, 273,
309n74
Fiss, Owen, x, xi, 4, 6, 35, 70, 100, 125,
143–44, 170–71, 223, 261
The Law As It Could Be, 126–27
Fleischer, Ari, 101–2
Foreign Intelligence Surveillance Act
(FISA), xv, 112–13, 122, 135, 201,
222–24
adoption of in 1978, 227–28
Bush administration and, 227–31
dual structure for wiretapping and,
238–39
probable cause and, 307n52
USA PATRIOT Act and, 240
U.S. Congress and, 109
U.S. Supreme Court and, 238–39
warrantless wiretapping and, 229–31,
249–51, 255–58, 305–6n11, 305n6
Foreign Intelligence Surveillance
Court, xv, 222, 228, 230–31,
240–41, 245–46, 248–49
foreign terrorist organizations, xiv–xv,
202–20
Fort Hood, killings at, 264
Fourteenth Amendment
Due Process Clause of, 169
prohibition of torture in, 291n34
Fourth Amendment, 59–64, 74–75,
108–9, 132, 201, 247–48, 258
extraordinary crimes and the
problem of overbreadth and,
253–58
FISA Amendments Act of 2008,
243–44
privacy and, 253–54
probable cause, 244–50

"special needs" exception and,
250–53
*United States v. Verdugo-Urquidez*
and, 63–66
warrant requirement and, x, xv, 226,
234, 237, 239, 243–58, 307–8n53,
307n51
Fourth Geneva Convention, 20, 21, 26,
29, 86
Article 3, 84–85, 86
Article 4, 288n22
Article 75 of Protocol 1, 85
Protocol 1, 85
requirement of humane treatment
in, 176
United States' refusal to ratify, 85
freedom of speech, x, xiv–xv, xvii, 207,
256–57, 269
curtailed at times of war, 196–99,
201–20
*Holder v. Humanitarian Law Project*
and, 207–15
U.S. Supreme Court, 197–99, 207–15

Gaza, 129
Geneva Conventions, 84, 88, 96
Article 3, 86, 88
imprisonment without trial and,
148–53
*See also specific conventions*
Ginsburg, Ruth Bader
*Hamdan v. Rumsfeld* and, 86, 96–97
*Hamdi v. Rumsfeld* and, 46, 48, 80,
278
*Holder v. Humanitarian Law Project*
and, 216
as minimalist, 69
on probable cause, 307–8n53
on probable cause, 244
*Rasul v. Bush* and, 95, 96–97
*United States v. Jones* and, 255
Giuliani, Rudolph, 198
globalization, 63
Global Positioning System (GPS),
254–55

Goldsmith, Jack, 311–12n18
Gonzales, Alberto, 228–29, 230–31
government action, substantive
    rationality and, 137–38
grant of authority, FISA Amendments
    Act of 2008, 243–44
Guantánamo Bay Naval Station, prison
    at, x, 12–15, 21, 30, 34–35, 38, 53,
    56, 70–73, 155–56, 221
    constitutional rights of prisoners
        held in, 73–75
    Court of Appeals and, 88–89
    extraterritoriality of, 13–14
    habeas corpus and, 121–22
    interrogation techniques allowed at,
        175–76
    jurisdiction of, 31
    legal status of, 4
    Obama's executive order to close,
        156, 193
    Obama's promise to close, 99,
        121–22, 143, 259
    opening of, 89–90
    prisoners in, 73, 76
    territoriality of, 20, 54–58, 66–67,
        88 89, 183
    U.S. sovereignty over, 14, 20, 183
Guantánamo detainees, 119, 155–56
    Bush administration and, 77–89
    civilian courts and, 156
    congressional opposition to transfer
        of, 156–57
    constitutional rights of, 76, 77–89,
        92, 93, 107, 182–83, 278–79 (see
        also specific rights)
    due process and, 77–89, 96, 278–79
    habeas corpus and, 80–81, 89–90,
        95–97, 107, 114–17, 121–22,
        156, 166, 182–83, 247, 278–79,
        311n11
    hunger strike by, 143, 144–45
    imprisonment without trial and,
        143 44, 162–63
    interrogation of, 174–76
    legal status of, 77–89

military commissions and, 108, 121,
    156
obligation to repatriate, 151
as unlawful enemy combatants, 175–76
See also Guantánamo Bay Naval
    Station, prison at

habeas corpus, x, 4, 12–15, 18–20,
    22–24, 33, 35, 38–68, 45–52, 77,
    166–67, 293n20
    Bagram Air Field detainees and, 122,
        123, 166
    citizens and, 15–16, 39–44, 106–7,
        113–14
    constitutional basis of, 77–78
    denial of, 110
    enemy combatants and, 52–68, 77,
        106, 111–12, 115–17, 122, 165–67
    evidentiary hearings and, 106
    federal judiciary and, 160–61
    Guantánamo detainees and, 80–81,
        89–90, 95, 96, 97, 107, 114–16,
        121–22, 156, 166, 182–83, 278–79,
        311n11
    Hamdan v. Rumsfeld and, 81–82
    imprisonment without trial and,
        165–67
    Military Commissions Act of 2006
        and, 111–12, 120
    military necessity to prevent exercise
        of, 66–67
    noncitizens and, 12–15, 40, 53–68,
        70–71, 78, 107, 122, 165–66
    Padilla and, 41–44
    statutory basis of, 77–78
    Suspension Clause, 166
    suspension of, 77–78, 88, 147, 165–66
    unlawful enemy combatants and,
        115–17, 122
    U.S. Congress and, 247
Hamas, 129, 132, 204
Hamdan, Salim Ahmed, 81
Hamdan v. Rumsfeld, xi, 71
    Alito and, 96
    Breyer and, 86, 90, 93, 96–97

*Hamdan v. Rumsfeld* (*cont.*)
    Court of Appeals and, 88
    executive branch and, 86–87
    Ginsburg and, 86, 96–97
    habeas corpus and, 81–82
    Kennedy and, 85–86, 96
    minimalism and, 82–83, 86
    Souter and, 96–97
    Stevens and, xiii, 82–89, 96
    U.S. Congress and, 87–88
    U.S. Senate and, 87–88
    U.S. Supreme Court and, xii, xiii,
        81–89, 90, 93, 95, 97, 98
Hamdi, Yaser Esam, 15–17, 18–20, 21,
        38, 39–40, 67–68, 279, 290n14
    constitutional rights of, 45–52
    due process and, 45–52
    father of, 15, 47, 49
    release to Saudi Arabia, 290n27
*Hamdi v. Rumsfeld*, x–xii, xv, 4–5,
        15–21, 29, 30–31, 33–35, 38, 70,
        71, 79–80, 98, 113–14, 135, 164–65,
        277–79, 283–84, 290n14, 290n20,
        290n27
    Breyer and, 278
    Ginsburg and, 80, 278
    Kennedy and, 278
    O'Connor and, 79–80, 113–14, 135,
        164–65, 278–79, 290n14, 290n20
    Rehnquist and, 279
    Scalia and, 278–79
    Souter and, 80, 278
    Stevens and, 278–79
    Thomas and, 278
Harlan, John, 65, 234
Haynes, William, 174–75
Hezbollah, 129, 132, 204
Holder, Eric, 122–23, 158–59, 193, 194,
        232, 275–78, 282
    principle of distinction and, 270
    proportionality rule and, 270, 274–75
    speech at Northwestern Law School,
        270, 274–77, 281, 283
    on targeted killing of U.S. citizens,
        274–78

*Holder v. Humanitarian Law Project*,
        xiv–xv, 201–22
    Breyer and, 216–18
    First Amendment and, 202–20
    free speech tradition and, 207–15
    Ginsburg and, 216
    Kagan and, 218
    Roberts and, 198, 204–7, 209–19
    Sotomayor and, 216
    Stevens and, 215–16
    U.S. Congress and, 205–6, 217
Holmes, Oliver Wendell, 207
Hoover, Herbert, 169
human dignity, 130–33, 138–39
    *See also* dignity principle
humanitarian intervention, 11
human rights tradition, 130, 133
Hussein, Saddam, 11, 21, 31

immigration proceedings, 5
immunity, state secrets doctrine and,
        189–90
imprisonment, 20, 37–38
    after acquittal, 158–59
    of citizens, 163–64
    constitutionality of, 12–15
    indefinite, 106, 148, 154, 156–59,
        290n14
    legality of, 12–15
    of noncitizens, 163–64
    Obama's detention policy, 159–67
    oversight system, 159–61
    principle of freedom and, 163
    rule of law and, 163
    of unlawful enemy combatants,
        158–60
    without trial, xiii, xiv, 110, 119, 123,
        143–44, 146–67, 272–73, 310–11n8
    *See also* habeas corpus
*In Re Yamashita*, xi, 125
*Insular Cases*, 170
intelligence gathering, 221–22, 227–58,
        233–39, 305–6n11
    *See also* FISA Amendments Act
        of 2008; Foreign Intelligence

Surveillance Act (FISA);
    wiretapping
international law, 7–8, 22
    authoritative character of, 7–8
    Iraq War and, 31
    vs. law of the nation-state, 9
    torture and, 169, 172
interrogation, 21–22, 105, 110, 116,
    118, 157
    Army Field Manual and, 118, 175,
        193
    by CIA, 176
    coercion and, 108
    defined as torture, 176
    enhanced, 176, 259
    extraordinary rendition and, 179–80
    Guantánamo detainees and, 174–76
    in Israel, 131–32
    torture and, 168–69, 172–76
Iraq
    disarmament obligations after
        Persian Gulf War, 10
    invasion of, 5, 7–8, 10–11
    Persian Gulf War and, 10
    UNSC resolutions against, 10
    See also Iraq War
Iraq War, x, 4, 5, 7, 21, 58, 67, 105
    Charter of the United Nations and,
        8, 10–11
    international law and, 31
    legality of, 8, 9–10
    troop withdrawal from Iraq, 117
Israel, xiii–xiv, 125–26
    constitutional law in, 130
    cosmopolitanism and, 73–74
    interrogation in, 131–32
    jurisprudence in, 126, 133
    legislature of (Knesset), 130–31
    military in, 132–34, 261
    national security in, 136
    parliamentary system of, 130–31, 135
    principle of legislative supremacy
        in, 130–31
    prohibition of torture in, 131–32
    security fence in, 133, 138

Supreme Court of, xiii–xiv, 126, 128,
    265, 281–82, 283
targeted killing and, 133
terrorism and, 128–39

Jacoby, Lowell E., 23, 40
Japanese Americans, internment during
    World War II, 45, 137, 164
The Judge in a Democracy (Barak), 126
judicial minimalism. See minimalism

Kagan, Elena, 215
    Holder v. Humanitarian Law Project
        and, 218
    United States v. Jones and, 255
Kalven, Harry, 207
Katz v. United States, 234–39, 241,
    244–45, 249–51, 254–55
Keith case, 236–39, 241, 244–45, 249–50,
    255
Kennedy, Anthony, 71, 74–75, 307–8n53
    Boumediene v. Bush and, 116–17, 122,
        166, 247, 279, 311n11
    Hamdan v. Rumsfeld and, 85–86, 96
    Hamdi v. Rumsfeld and, 46–48, 278
    as minimalist, 69
    Rasul v. Bush and, 66–67, 95
    United States v. Verdugo-Urquidez
        and, 64–67, 246–47, 250
killing
    of enemy combatants, 273–74
    as integral part of war, 262
    targeted, 260, 262–85
Korematsu case, 137
Kosovo, humanitarian intervention
    in, 11
Ku Klux Klan, 208
Kurdistan Workers Party (PKK), 202,
    204–5, 209, 212–13, 214, 217,
    219–20
Kurds, 203–4, 213–14, 217

Lassiter v. Dept. of Soc. Servs. of
    Durham County, 51
The Law As It Could Be (Fiss), 126–27

lawful combatants
    categories of, 26–27
    status of, 20–24, 26–29
Lindh, John Walker, case, 24–29, 107,
    149–50, 164

Madison, James, 218
Marshall, Thurgood, 32, 64, 236
material witnesses, 38
*Matthews v. Eldridge*, 50–51, 117
Mayer, Jane, 180
McCain, John, 110–11, 118, 179, 184
metadata, collection of, 222
military commissions, xiii, 21–22, 82,
    93, 95–96, 98, 100, 107–8, 110, 123,
    232, 295n15
    authority for the establishment of,
        83, 85–91
    due process and, 94
    enemy combatants and, 107–8
    evidentiary rules and, 120
    executive branch and, 96
    Guantánamo detainees and, 101, 108,
        121, 156
    *Hamdan v. Rumsfeld* and, 81–89
    institutionalization of, 120–21
    jurisdiction of, 108, 272–73
    noncitizens and, 112, 121
    Obama administration and,
        119–21
    procedural issues, 84–86
    rules of evidence in, 84
    structural aspects of, 85–86
    transformation from necessity to
        convenience, 108
    trial of Khalid Sheikh Mohammed,
        101
    unconstitutionality of, 96–97
    U.S. Congress and, 87
    U.S. Department of Defense and,
        108
    in World War II, 108
    *See also* Military Commissions Act
        of 2006; Military Commissions
        Act of 2009; military tribunals

Military Commissions Act of 2006, 70,
    87–90, 111–13, 121, 135, 247, 272,
    293n20, 293n21
    Court of Appeals and, 88
    habeas corpus and, 111–12, 120
    legality of, 88
    Obama administration and, 120
    torture and, 112
    U.S. Congress and, 112, 115–16
Military Commissions Act of 2009,
    120–21, 135, 272
military necessity, 129–30
    deference to in times of war, 132–37
    fundamental values and, 134–35
military tribunals, 19–22, 25, 79–80,
    111, 114, 135, 279
    appellate review and, 81
    establishment of, 155
    procedural deficiencies of, 89
    *See also* military commissions
minimalism, xvii, 56, 69–102
    dangers of, 69–70, 76–77
    democracy and, 70, 90–91
    dilemma of each individual justice,
        94–98
    *Hamdan v. Rumsfeld* and, 82–83, 86
    as a judicial strategy, 94–95, 96
Mobbs, Michael, 16–19, 22, 23, 29, 30,
    47
Mohammed, Khalid Sheikh, 101, 120,
    232
    trial of, 156–57, 158–59, 232, 259
Mukasey, Michael B., 22–24, 176–77,
    193, 198
Mumbai, India, terrorist attacks in, 104

National Security Agency (NSA), xv,
    101, 109, 200–202, 221–22, 227,
    232, 273
    warrantless wiretapping and,
        112–13
*New York Times*, 33, 198, 227, 229, 260
*New York Times Co. v. Sullivan*, 208
*New York Times v. United States*, 197
Nixon, Richard, 177, 236

noncitizens, 63
vs. citizens, 273
constitutional rights of, 22, 53–68,
74–75, 78–89, 107, 112, 115–16,
180, 182, 272–73
due process and, 3, 13, 40, 53–68
as enemy combatants, 112
FISA and, 240–41
in Guantánamo prison, 13–14
habeas corpus and, 12–15, 40, 53–68,
70–71, 78–89, 88, 107, 122, 165–66
imprisonment without trial and,
163–64
legal status of, 3, 13
military commissions and, 112, 121
principle of freedom and, 165
USA PATRIOT Act and, 12
warrantless wiretapping and, 273
Non-Detention Act of 1971, 44–46,
164–65
Northern Alliance, 7, 13, 15, 16, 17
*North Jersey Media Group, Inc. v.
Ashcroft*, 29–30
Northwest Airlines, attempted bombing
of, 119

Obama, Barack, 99
avoidance of phrase "War on
Terror," 153
banning of torture, 157
decision against truth commissions,
118, 194–95
decision not to criminally prosecute
previous administration, 118,
194–95
decision not to prosecute CIA
agents, 194–95
executive order banning torture, 118
executive orders confining CIA to
interrogation based on Army
Field Manual, 193
executive order to close
Guantánamo, 156, 193
Guantánamo detainees' hunger strike
of 2013 and, 143, 144–45

national security agenda of, 221–22
policies on torture, 193–95
policy on imprisonment without
trial, 156, 159–67
policy toward the Taliban, 150–51
promise to change counterterrorism
policies of Bush Administration,
117–18
promise to close Guantánamo prison,
xiii, 99, 117, 121–22, 143, 259
promise to develop system of
"judicial and congressional
oversight," 159–60
on proportionality rule, 270–71
reasons for continuing Bush
administration policies, 123
speech at National Archives 2009,
99–100, 150–52, 156, 159, 163, 165
speech at National Defense
University, 270–71, 277
stated opposition to torture, 193
statement distinguishing between
imprisonment policy on citizens
vs. noncitizens, 163–64
targeted killing and, 260
vote against FISA Amendments Act
of 2008, 122–23
*See also* Obama administration
Obama administration, 101–2
Arar case and, 181, 194
AUMF and, 159–60
blocking of judicial inquiries into
extraordinary rendition, 118–19
*Boumediene v. Bush* and, 121–22
continuation of Bush-era policies, x,
xiii, xiv, 100–103, 117–24, 143–44,
150–51, 156–57, 159–67, 202, 219,
223–24, 259, 272–73, 285
detention policy and, 161–67, 272–
73, 310–11n8
electronic surveillance program of,
222–58
extraordinary rendition and, 193–94
FISA Amendments Act of 2008 and,
231–33

Obama administration (*cont.*)
    Khalid Sheikh Mohammed trial and, 120
    military commissions and, 119–21
    oversight system for imprisonment without trial, 159–61
    principle of freedom and, 147, 161–67
    targeted killing of citizens and, 273–74
    Terrorist Surveillance Program and, 231–33
    torture and, 118–19, 123, 193–95
    warrantless wiretapping and, 122–23, 231–33
    war with al-Qaeda and, 117–24, 219, 268
    *See also* Obama, Barack
Occupied Territories, 129, 131, 133, 138, 310n7
O'Connor, Sandra Day, 4–5, 34
    *Boumediene v. Bush* and, 311n11
    *Hamdi v. Rumsfeld* and, 46–48, 49–52, 79–80, 113–14, 135, 164–65, 278–79, 290n14, 290n20
    as minimalist, 69
    *Rasul v. Bush* and, 95
    *United States v. Verdugo-Urquidez* and, 64
Office of the Director of National Intelligence, 160, 242
*Olmstead v. United States*, 234, 254
Omnibus Crime Control and Safe Streets Act, 235–36
*One Case at a Time* (Sunstein), 70, 93
overbreadth doctrine, 256–57, 310n89

Padilla, Jose, 22–24, 35–36, 38–45, 67, 158, 164
    downgrading of charges against, 43–44
    habeas corpus and, 41–44
    sentencing and resentencing of, 36
    transfer to civilian custody, 289n7
    See also *Rumsfeld v. Padilla*

Palestinians, 131–32, 138
    *See also* Occupied Territories
Panetta, Leon, 193–94
Pentagon Papers case, 197
Persian Gulf War, 10
"personal" injury, 126
Philippines, 183
plea agreements, 25–26
political advocacy
    coordinated versus independent, 218
    criminalization of, xiv–xv, 200–220
    democracy and, 218
    First Amendment and, 207–15
political question doctrine, 282–83
Powell, Lewis, 236, 237
presidential power. *See* executive branch
principle of distinction, 270
principle of freedom, xiv, 39–40, 70, 81, 146–67, 289n12
    adjustments in War on Terror, 154–55
    bifurcated exclusionary rule and, 144, 157
    citizens and, 165
    exceptions for war, 105–6, 119, 144, 147–48, 154–56, 167
    imprisonment without trial and, 163
    noncitizens and, 165
    Obama administration and, 161–67
    procedural protections provided by, 147
    U.S. Constitution and, 37–38, 42–45, 52, 77, 147
prisoners, 12–15
    *See also* Bagram Air Field detainees; Guantánamo detainees; prisoners of war
prisoners of war, 12–13, 22, 67, 288n22
    Third Geneva Convention and, 175–76
privacy
    protections of, xvii, 108–10
    reasonable expectation of, 253–54

right to privacy, xvii
  warrants and, 235
probable cause, 201
  FISA and, 244, 307n52
  warrantless wiretapping and, 244–50
  warrants and, 238–39
proportionality, 137–38
  proportionality rule, 270–71, 274–75
  proportionality test, 135–36
Protect America Act of 2007, 113, 122

qualified immunity doctrine, 185–86,
  195

*Rasul v. Bush*, 34–35, 38, 52–68, 78–79,
  80, 81, 86, 88–90, 95, 96
  Breyer and, 95
  Ginsburg and, 95, 96–97
  Kennedy and, 66–67, 95
  O'Connor and, 95
  Souter and, 95
  Stevens and, 53–68, 66, 69–70, 78–79,
  95
Rehnquist, William, 42, 95
  *Hamdi v. Rumsfeld* and, 46–48, 279
  *Rumsfeld v. Padilla* and, 114
  *United States v. Verdugo-Urquidez*
  and, 58–60, 62–66, 74–75, 78,
  96–97, 246–48
Rehnquist Court, xii, 170, 226
rendition. *See* extraordinary rendition,
  definition of
Ridge, Tom, 198
right of access, 30, 80, 85
right of presence, 85
right of self-defense, preemptive strikes
  and, 266
right to counsel, 47–48, 80
right to privacy, xvii
Roberts, John, x, 95–96
  confirmation hearing of, 208
  *Holder v. Humanitarian Law Project*
  and, 198, 204–7, 209–16, 217–18,
  219
  military commissions and, 95–96

Roberts Court, warrantless wiretapping
  and, 226
*Rochin v. California*, 169
rules of evidence, 79–80, 84, 120
Rumsfeld, Donald, 175–76
*Rumsfeld v. Padilla*, 30–31, 34–36, 38,
  40–45, 114–15

Saudi Arabia, 264, 290n27
Scalia, Antonin
  *Hamdan v. Rumsfeld* and, 96
  *Hamdi v. Rumsfeld* and, 46, 278–79
  *Olmstead v. United States* and, 254
  principle of freedom and, 289n12
  on probable cause, 307–8n53
  *United States v. Jones* and, 254
  *United States v. Verdugo-Urquidez*
  and, 64
searches and seizures, xv, 58–60, 65, 74,
  132, 196, 234, 250–51, 253–56
secretary of state, designation and
  regulation of foreign terrorist
  organizations, 203–4
secret evidence, disclosure of,
  157–58
separation of powers, 110, 111, 116,
  135, 166, 257–58, 268–69
Shahzad, Faisal, 163
Sixth Amendment, 39, 41, 48, 183
Snowden, Edward, xv, 221–23
Sotomayor, Sonia, 216
Souter, David
  *Hamdan v. Rumsfeld* and, 96–97
  *Hamdi v. Rumsfeld* and, 46, 48, 49,
  80, 278
  as minimalist, 69
  *Rasul v. Bush* and, 95, 96–97
sovereignty
  territorial, 265–66, 272
  U.S. exercise of, 14–15
Spanish-American War, 183
"special needs" exception, 250–53
speech, criminalization of, 197–99
Sri Lanka, 198, 202, 203, 204–5, 212,
  213, 214

state secrets doctrine, 188–92, 194, 195,
    280–81
Stevens, John Paul, 66
    *Hamdan v. Rumsfeld* and, xiii, 82–89,
        96
    *Hamdi v. Rumsfeld* and, 46, 278–79
    *Holder v. Humanitarian Law Project*
        and, 215–16
    minimalism and, 75–76
    as minimalist, 69–70
    principle of freedom and, 289n12
    *Rasul v. Bush* and, 53–68, 69–70,
        78–79, 95
    retirement of, 215
    *United States v. Verdugo-Urquidez*
        and, 64
Stewart, Potter, 236
Stotzky, Irwin, 6
structural injunction, paring back of,
    170
substantive rationality, 137–38
Sunstein, Cass, *One Case at a Time*,
    69–70
surveillance, xv, 228–56, 273, 307n51,
    309n74
    *See also* intelligence gathering;
        wiretapping
Suspension Clause, 166
Syria, 105, 129, 180–83, 185, 188

Taft, William Howard, 234, 254
Taliban, 7–8, 13, 15–16, 19–20, 39, 47,
    77, 104, 107, 111, 113–14, 227, 266
    citizens as, 164
    as enemy combatants, 21–22, 27–29,
        149–50, 153
    Geneva Conventions and, 148–53
    in Guantánamo prison, 155
    imprisonment without trial and,
        148–53, 162
    Lindh and, 24–25, 26–28
    Taliban army, 27–29
    war with, 118, 119
Tamil Tigers, 202, 204–5, 212–13, 214,
    219–20

targeted killing, xv, 101, 133, 136, 260,
    262–85
    of citizens, 272–74
    civilian deaths as a result of, 271–72,
        274–75, 280, 310n7
    claims for damages as a result of,
        280–81
    congressional oversight of, 276–77
    due process and, 267–70, 273–75, 280
    of enemy combatants, 262–85
    judicial review of, 275–85
    legal standards for, 265–85, 276
    Obama administration and, 273–74
    oversight of, 276–82
    procedures for assessing compliance,
        276–82
    prospective vs. retroactive inquiry
        into, 281–82
telephone communications
    as evidence, 238–39
    surveillance of, 222, 227–58
    transcripts of, 238–39
terrorism, 21–22, 103–4, 202, 217–18
    Barak's rulings on, 133
    civilians affected by, 136–37
    constitutional rights and, 129
    in Israel, 128–39
    rule of law and, 128–39
    threat of, 266
    *See also* War on Terror; *specific acts*
terrorist organizations
    criminalization of political advocacy
        on behalf of, 201–20
    peaceful/humanitarian vs. violent
        support for, 204–5
    regulation and designation of,
        202–4
    *See also specific organizations*
terrorists, alleged
    imprisonment of without trial,
        146–67
    targeted killing of, 262–85
    torture and extraordinary rendition
        of, 172–95
    warrantless wiretapping of, 225–58

Terrorist Surveillance Program,
227–33, 241, 256–58
Third Geneva Convention, 19–21,
22–29, 67, 148–49
prisoners of war and, 175–76
Thomas, Clarence
*Hamdan v. Rumsfeld* and, 96
*Hamdi v. Rumsfeld* and, 46, 278
*United States v. Verdugo-Urquidez*
and, 64
Times Square, attempted bombing in,
119
torture, xiii, xiv, 101, 105, 108, 110, 116,
118, 157, 168–70, 172, 229
Bush administration policies, 174–79
constitutional prohibition of, 178,
179–80, 186, 188
definitions of, 105, 174, 176–77, 178
Detainee Treatment Act of 2005 and,
110–11
exclusionary rule and, 157
extraterritorial, 169–70 (*see also*
extraordinary rendition)
international law and, 169, 172
interrogation and, 174–76
Israel's prohibition of, 131–32
memoranda defining guidelines for,
174–75
Military Commissions Act of 2006
and, 112
Obama and, 118, 157, 193–95
outsourcing of, 105, 178–80
prohibition of, x, 105, 131–32,
168–69, 172, 186, 188, 291n34
suits for damages after, 280–81
used by CIA, 171
truth commissions, 118, 194
Turkey, 198, 202, 203, 204–5, 213, 214

UN Convention against Torture (1984),
172, 186, 291n34
Uniform Code of Military Justice
(UCMJ), 85
Article 21, 83, 86, 87
Article 36, 84, 86

United Nations, 217
Charter of, 7–8, 9, 265–67, 270, 272
Convention against Torture (1984),
172, 186, 291n34
PKK and, 213, 214
Security Council, 8, 10, 11, 266
*United States v. Jones*, 253–55
*United States v. O'Brien*, 216
*United States v. Verdugo-Urquidez*, xvi,
58–60, 66, 74, 246–48, 250
Brennan and, xvi, 60–61, 62, 64–66
Fourth Amendment and, 63–66
Kennedy and, 64–67, 246–47, 250
Rehnquist and, 62–66, 78, 96–97,
246–48
unlawful enemy combatants, 22–23,
136–37
citizens as, 164
concept of, 35
constitutional rights of, 23–24, 33,
35, 120–21
Guantánamo detainees as, 175–76
habeas corpus and, 115–17, 122
imprisonment of, 33–34, 115–17,
158–59, 175–76
legal status of, 24–26, 33–34
*See also* enemy combatants
UN Security Council, 8, 10, 11
USA PATRIOT Act, 12, 239
and Foreign Intelligence Surveillance
Act (FISA), 240
U.S. citizens, 3, 273
as members of al-Qaeda, 22, 164
constitutional rights of, 15–16,
22–24, 33–35, 80, 106–7, 180,
272–73, 279–80 (*see also specific
constitutional rights*)
due process and, 3, 15–16, 23–24,
39–40, 80, 113–14
as enemy combatants, 80, 106, 164,
262–85
evidentiary hearings and, 106–7
FISA and, 240
habeas corpus and, 15–16, 39–40,
41–44, 106–7, 113–14, 163–64

U.S. citizens (cont.)
  imprisonment without trial and,
    163–64
  as members of the Taliban, 164
  principle of freedom and, 165
  targeted killing of, 261, 272–74
  warrantless wiretapping and, 273
U.S. Congress, 61–62, 76, 90–91, 101,
    123–24, 156–57, 218, 242
  adoption of FISA, 227–28
  approval of Bush administration's
    counterterrorism policies, 113
  Authorization for the Use of Military
    Force (AUMF), 159–60
  complicity in Bush's War on Terror,
    104–17, 258
  criminalization of political advocacy
    by, 201–20
  designation and regulation of foreign
    terrorist organizations, 202–4
  Detainee Treatment Act of 2005
    and, 80–81, 82, 110–11, 113, 115,
    184–85
  FISA Amendments Act of 2008 and,
    113, 122–23, 234, 242–43
  Foreign Intelligence Surveillance Act
    (FISA), 109
  habeas corpus and, 247
  Holder v. Humanitarian Law Project
    and, 205–6, 217
  Katz v. United States and, 235–36
  Keith case and, 236
  Military Commissions Act of 2006
    and, 70, 87–88, 112, 113, 115–16
  military commissions and, 70, 85,
    87–88, 112–13, 115–16
  Obama's first address to joint session
    of, 193
  Omnibus Crime Control and Safe
    Streets Act and, 235–37
  oversight of executive branch's
    counterterrorism activities,
    276–82
  passage of USA PATRIOT Act, 12
  as a political institution, 184–85

power of, 228–30, 267–68 (see also
    separation of powers)
  Protect America Act of 2007 and,
    113, 122
  resolution authorizing military force
    against al-Qaeda, 267–68
  response to Hamdan v. Rumsfeld,
    87–88
  Senate Select Committee on
    Intelligence report on CIA's
    interrogation and detention
    program, 171
  warrantless wiretapping and, 109,
    112–13, 122–23, 234, 242–43
U.S. Constitution, 20, 87, 90–91, 130,
    255, 282
  Article I, 38, 77–78, 177–78, 230
  Article II, 145, 228–30
  Article III, 144, 186–87, 188, 259,
    284–85
  Article IV, 62
  ban on "Cruel and Unusual
    Punishments," 168–69
  complicity of other branches in
    violating, 202
  cosmopolitan view of, 60–63
  declaration of war and, 267–68
  doctrine of enumerated powers,
    61–62
  due process and, 274–75, 276
  extraterritorial reach of, 170, 180, 183
  federal judiciary's responsibility to
    safeguard, xi–xii, xv–xvi, 12–17,
    19, 29–30, 50, 68, 71, 76–77, 89–94,
    98, 100, 113, 137, 170–71, 178, 192,
    223–24, 257–58, 261, 275–76
  habeas statute, 53–56 (see also habeas
    corpus)
  Preamble to, 218
  principle of freedom and, 37–38,
    42–45, 52, 77, 147
  prohibition of torture in, 172–73,
    178–80, 182–83, 186, 188, 195,
    291n34
  state secrets doctrine and, 190

Supreme Court as guardian of the, 89–94

torture as violation of, 105

treaties and, 266–67

See also Bill of Rights; separation of powers; specific amendments

U.S. Court of Appeals for the District of Columbia Circuit, 12–15, 17, 57, 81, 82, 88, 111, 115, 166, 203–4

U.S. Court of Appeals for the Second Circuit, 23–24, 41, 44, 45, 119, 181, 183–85, 186–89, 233, 263–85

U.S. Court of Appeals for the Third Circuit, 29–30

U.S. Court of Appeals for the Fourth Circuit, 4, 15–19, 43–44, 114, 189-90

U.S. Court of Appeals for the Sixth Circuit, 5, 30

U.S. Court of Appeals for the Ninth Circuit, 31, 119, 191, 194

U.S. Court of Appeals for the Eleventh Circuit, 36

U.S. Department of Defense, 16–17, 22, 41, 47, 114, 152, 160, 311n11

affidavits filed to avoid evidentiary hearings, 106–7

establishment of military tribunals by, 155

leak of internal memoranda on torture, 174–78

military commissions and, 108

U.S. Department of Homeland Security, 160

U.S. Department of Justice, 160

FISA Amendments Act of 2008 and, 242–43

leak of internal memoranda on torture, 174, 176–77

Office of Legal Counsel, 174, 177

U.S. Department of State, designation and regulation of foreign terrorist organizations, 203–4

U.S. District Court for the Eastern District of Virginia, 24

U.S. District Court for the Southern District of New York, 44, 45, 101, 120, 162

U.S. House of Representatives, 230

See also U.S. Congress

U.S. Senate, 158, 230

adoption of FISA, 227–28

authorization of Iraq War, 4

FISA Amendments Act of 2008 and, 242–43

Judiciary Committee, 230–31

passage of USA PATRIOT Act, 4

response to Hamdan v. Rumsfeld, 87–88

Select Committee on Intelligence, 171

See also U.S. Congress

U.S. Supreme Court, 3, 30–33, 130, 173

Al Odah v. United States and, 30–31

Berger v. New York and, 310n89

Bivens decision and, 184–85

Boumediene v. Bush and, xii, 4–5, 70–71, 116–17, 121–22, 165–67, 278–79, 283, 311n11

Brandenburg v. Ohio and, 208, 209, 217

Brown v. Mississippi and, 169

Bush administration and, xiii, 33–36, 37, 104–17

congressional enactments and, 89–94

cosmopolitanism and, 74

Ex Parte Milligan and, 125

Ex Parte Quirin and, 125

FISA and, 122–23, 135, 233, 234, 238–39

freedom of speech and, 197–99, 269

function of, 76–77, 89–94

fundamental values and, 35, 137

as guardian of the Constitution, 89–94, 98, 100, 113, 137, 223–24, 257–58

Hamdan v. Rumsfeld and, xii, xiii, 81–90, 93, 95, 97–98

U.S. Supreme Court (*cont.*)
  *Hamdi v. Rumsfeld* and, xii, x, 4–5,
    30–31, 33–35, 38, 70–71, 79–80,
    98, 113–14, 135, 164–65, 277–79,
    283–84, 290n14, 290n20, 290n27
  *Holder v. Humanitarian Law Project*
    and, xiv–xv, 207–15, 215–22
  *Katz v. United States* and, 234–35,
    237–39, 245, 249–51
  *Keith* case and, 236–39, 245, 249–50
  *Korematsu* case, 137
  *New York Times Co. v. Sullivan* and,
    208
  *Olmstead v. United States* and, 254
  overbreadth doctrine and, 256–57
  policy of avoidance, 110–17
  political question doctrine and, 283
  proportionality and, 137–38
  *Rasul v. Bush* and, 34–35, 38, 52–68,
    78–79, 86, 89–90, 95–96
  *In Re Yamashita* and, 125
  *Rumsfeld v. Padilla* and, 30–31,
    34–36, 38, 40–45, 114–15,
    289n7
  state secrets doctrine and, 189
  substantive rationality and,
    137–38
  *United States v. Jones* and, 253–54
  *United States v. Verdugo-Urquidez*
    and, xvi, 58–60, 246–48, 250
  warrantless wiretapping and, 109,
    226

Verdugo-Urquidez, René Martín, 59–60
Vietnam War, 197, 216, 236
Vinson, Roger, 222–23
Volokh, Eugene, 198

War on Drugs, 58–59
War on Terror, x, xiii, xv–xvii, 3, 12, 24,
    29–31, 33–35, 37, 76, 104–17, 118,
    125, 262–63
  declaration of, 227
  rule of law and, 37–68
  torture and, 172
  warrantless wiretapping, xv, 112–13,
    200–201, 222, 226, 250–53, 273
  Burger Court and, 226
  Bush administration and, 122,
    227–31
  citizens and, 273
  congressional authorization of, 201
  Fourth Amendment and, 243–58
  noncitizens and, 273
  Obama administration and, 122–23,
    231–33
  *See also* FISA Amendments Act
    of 2008; Foreign Intelligence
    Surveillance Act (FISA)
warrants, x, xv, 235–39, 241–42, 250–51,
    253–57, 307–8n53, 307n51, 310n89
Warren Court, 61, 74, 108, 234–35,
    236
Warsame, Ahmed Abdulkadir, 162
waterboarding, 105, 118, 171, 175, 176,
    194
*Whitney v. California*, 98
Wilkinson, J. Harvie, 17, 19–20
wiretapping, 101, 109, 238–39, 309n74
  *See also* warrantless wiretapping
World War I, 197, 207
World War II, 108, 218, 219

Yemen, 260–61, 263, 264–65, 272, 285
Yoo, John, 174, 176, 177–78

Owen Fiss is Sterling Professor Emeritus of Law at Yale University. He clerked for Thurgood Marshall when Marshall was a Court of Appeals judge and later for William J. Brennan Jr. on the U.S. Supreme Court. He is the author of many articles and books, including *Troubled Beginnings of the Modern State*, *Liberalism Divided*, and *The Irony of Free Speech*. He lives in Connecticut in the New Haven area.

Trevor Sutton is a graduate of Stanford, Oxford, and Yale Law School. He served as a law clerk on the U.S. Court of Appeals for the District of Columbia Circuit and as a fellow in the Office of the Secretary of Defense. He now lives in New York City and works on anticorruption matters for a global consulting firm.

# Publishing in the Public Interest

Thank you for reading this book published by The New Press. The New Press is a nonprofit, public interest publisher. New Press books and authors play a crucial role in sparking conversations about the key political and social issues of our day.

We hope you enjoyed this book and that you will stay in touch with The New Press. Here are a few ways to stay up to date with our books, events, and the issues we cover:

- Sign up at www.thenewpress.com/subscribe to receive updates on New Press authors and issues and to be notified about local events
- Like us on Facebook: www.facebook.com/newpressbooks
- Follow us on Twitter: www.twitter.com/thenewpress

Please consider buying New Press books for yourself; for friends and family; or to donate to schools, libraries, community centers, prison libraries, and other organizations involved with the issues our authors write about.

The New Press is a 501(c)(3) nonprofit organization. You can also support our work with a tax-deductible gift by visiting www.thenewpress.com/donate.